Successful Catering

BERNARD R. SPLAVER

Jule Wilkinson, Editor

CAHNERS BOOKS
A Division of Cahners Publishing Company, Inc.
89 Franklin St., Boston, Massachusetts 02110
Publishers of Institutions/VF Magazine

Library of Congress Cataloging in Publication Data

Splaver, Bernard R
  Successful catering.

  Includes bibliographical references and index.
  1. Caterers and catering. 2. Cookery for institutions, etc. I. Title.
TX911.S64   642'.47   75-30645
ISBN 0-8436-2061-7

ISBN 0-8436-2061-7

*Cover illustration courtesy of Kitchens of Sara Lee
and Bloomfield Industries, Inc. Photograph by Ma-
selli Studios under direction of Antonios Pronoitis,
Director of Art Department, Audrey Garvey, Creative Projects Director, Judy Whitt, Staff Artist,
Institutions/VF Magazine.*

Printed in the United States of America

This book is dedicated to my dear
wife, Thelma, and I borrow my
sentiments from Proverbs, 31 ——
*"Many daughters have done
worthily*
But thou excellest them all."

Acknowledgements

THIS BOOK WAS completed with the assistance of many people whose efforts will always be remembered gratefully and to whom acknowledgement should certainly be made:

To Jacob Rosenthal, President-Emeritus of the Culinary Institute of America, who initially urged that the lessons learned by the author, during his many years as owner of a successful catering business, be converted to teaching material to be used in a course at the Culinary Institute, and who then encouraged the compilation of those teaching materials for publication.

To fellow faculty members at the Culinary Institute of America who helped in the refinement of ideas, and with constructive criticism; and also to the many students in the catering courses who have helped in numerous ways, including preparation of foods for photography, as well as taking many of the photographs that serve as the basis for the drawings that appear throughout the book. Finally, to Ms. Lila Jones, special appreciation for her exhaustive efforts in checking facts and organizing and preparing all of the materials for final publication in this book.

BERNARD R. SPLAVER

Contents

ABOUT THE AUTHOR

BERNARD R. SPLAVER, currently a visiting lecturer at Cornell University's School of Hotel Administration, has also served in this capacity at the University of New Haven in Connecticut and at the Culinary Institute of America in Hyde Park, New York. Early in a foodservice career that spans some 40 years, Mr. Splaver served as manager of Ye Old Tavern Restaurants in New Haven and the Hotel Brunswick in Lakewood, New Jersey. Later he became owner of Wetherby's Restaurant, in Derby, Connecticut, operating this business for ten years.

In 1946 he opened the firm of Splaver's Caterers, which grew to become one of the largest social caterers in New England. After 22 years in the catering business, Mr. Splaver retired to become an instructor at the Culinary Institute of America in Hyde Park in 1968. He served as Dean of Faculty there for five years, "retiring" for the second time in 1973 for the life of a visiting lecturer. The author is a member of the International Wine and Food Society, the American Culinary Federation, and the Food Service Executives Association.

Preface

THE TERMS *Social Catering* and *Social Caterer* are heard frequently today. But what precisely do they mean?

In a simplistically brief description, *Social Catering* can be defined as the business of supplying food, goods, and organized services for public and private social functions of all types. The *Social Caterer*, on the other hand, is the person who performs these activities.

The field of Social Catering is a rapidly expanding one. And the services of a qualified, competent, and creative Social Caterer are in great demand. These services are highly sought after by individuals, families, and organizations who recognize that they are not only a convenience, but often a necessity, in fast-paced, contemporary living.

The reasons for this situation are many. They include: movement from large homes to apartments and/or smaller houses; increased numbers of women in the working population; more leisure time; greater use of food, parties, and entertainment functions as business and fundraising tools; and the desire of hosts and hostesses to spend more time socializing with their guests, less time in the production of the party.

As a result, large-scale entertaining, which calls for the services of a Social Caterer, has increased and, more often than not, is done outside the home in hotels, restaurants, and banquet halls. Even persons with ample space and proper facilities in their homes are using the services of a Social Caterer due to the difficulty in finding competent domestic help.

For the Social Caterer, this is where hard work and know-how become vitally important. In operating a business and performing a service, the Social Caterer must see to it that customers are fully satisfied; if they are not, the business will be short-lived. And a successful operation requires considerable time, much hard work, and an extensive knowledge of food and beverages and how to serve them properly. It also takes a sizable financial investment for the necessary equipment and rolling stock.

Equally important, however, is the fact that it takes a special type of individual, one who is both business person and artisan, to operate such an organization. The Social Caterer must: provide gracious but not ostentatious service; be respectful to, yet not overawed by, clients; and, perhaps of greatest importance, instill in co-workers and/or employees pride in accomplishment and the desire to give customers proper and courteous service.

Therefore, the purpose of this book is twofold: to show those who wish to become caterers how to get started and to help those who are already established in the field to improve their business.

But a word of caution, based on Sir Winston Churchill's famous phrase. . . "blood, sweat, and tears," which is often used to describe the efforts, frustrations, and disappointments faced by individuals who strive to attain desired goals.

Hopefully, this book will reduce, if not eliminate, the "blood and tears" by making the soon-to-be caterer aware of the many, many pitfalls he or she may face. However, those already practicing the profession will no doubt agree that the Social Caterer can *never* eliminate the "SWEAT."

Getting Started/1

GOING INTO BUSINESS for yourself is not a move ever to be taken lightly. Further, the highly specialized skills and professionalism needed in the business of catering, particularly Social Catering, are unlike those required in a retail business. For example, in a retail establishment, factors of location, traffic count, parking, and competitive outlets are vital considerations. Effective merchandising displays, advertising, reasonable prices, and good service also must be evaluated to attract customers and keep them coming back.

In Social Catering, many of these considerations—location, for example—are of relatively minor importance. *Exposure* is the primary goal in Social Catering and the way to get and keep business. Potential clients want to know who you are, what you can do, and how well you do it.

Furthermore, you have to know your territory. It would be foolhardy to incur the expense of establishing a commissary (a place where food is prepared, stored, and shipped) only to discover that your equipment is either inadequate or unnecessary or, on the other hand, that your fine china and silverware are unusable because the nature of your business calls for disposables.

There is a way to avoid such a frustrating, disheartening, and expensive experience. The answer is time, together with preliminary groundwork. *Take time!* Take time to: (a) evaluate your own qualifications; and (b) survey the catering potential in your community.

EVALUATING YOUR QUALIFICATIONS

To assist you in this effort, take the following quiz. A self-evaluation, it should enable you to determine if you are qualified and if you are sufficiently prepared to meet the heavy demands of the catering business.

Do you have a basic knowledge of food and beverages?

Knowledge of food is, of course, a prime requisite. However, a knowledge of wines and other beverages and the types of food with which they should be served is a real plus. This is especially true today. Wine consumption has increased considerably, and people are much more knowledgeable as to its origin, care, and presentation.

Are you familiar with various types of foodservice?

Are you capable of preparing an elaborate classical buffet? Can you effectively and efficiently serve a banquet for many people under improvised conditions? How conversant and adept are you with American, French, and Russian service? Do you know how to make flaming spectaculars? Can you put on a clambake, barbecue, or picnic for a large number of people?

Can you personally make the foods you wish to feature?

If your response is negative, would you be able to engage the services of specialists skilled in this work? How good a cook, garde manger, or baker are you?

What aesthetic abilities do you possess?

Do you have the "feel" for artistically arranging and draping tables, fruits, and flowers? Can you do tallow or ice carvings?

Do you have a basic understanding of mathematics?

Remember, you must know how to check invoices, figure discounts, determine recipe costs, and compute weight losses in production. You must also be able to figure wages, sales, and inventories and to reconcile bank statements. Other needed skills include estimating the amount and type of help needed, based on anticipated number of guests or on dollar volume. Finally, you must be able to set dollar and cent controls for areas where outlay costs are excessive.

Will you be able to establish and maintain good working relationships with your employees and, at the same time, maintain authority and control?

It is important not to become emotionally or socially involved with employees. Also, do not grant special favors or share privileged knowledge. Do not "play favorites" or show partiality to any one employee or group of employees.

A caterer *must*, at all times, be above reproach. Aloofness is not necessary, but a sense of dignity founded on respect for your abilities and propriety in conducting business is.

Are you familiar with foodservice equipment and its proper maintenance and care?

If minor equipment malfunctions occur, can you make temporary repairs? Can you replace compressor belts, worn washers in faucets, unplug a clogged drain, or make firm electrical connections in a socket or plug? Do you know the proper safety precautions for electric, gas, and electronic equipment?

Are you a good mixer and comfortable with others?

In this profession, you are "thrown in" with people from all walks of life. You must be comfortable with people, with crowds. You must also be gracious and sincere in providing service.

Are you familiar with prevailing rules of etiquette and social protocol?

The caterer is viewed as an authority on functions such as weddings, confirmations, and showers, to name just a few. Thus, to complement your own knowledge, you should have on hand a good book or two on etiquette, as well as popular periodicals focusing on bridal functions, gourmet foods, and entertaining in general.

Are you by nature a "cool" individual?

In a crisis situation, can you take command and not lose control? Can you handle emergencies—sudden illnesses, guest misbehavior, collapsing tables, hot food spills, fire? If someone were choking, would you know what to do? Would you know how to go about getting and using an inhalator?

Are you physically able to cope with the demands of catering?

In the foodservice field, a great deal of physical ability and energy is required in arranging tables and chairs, pushing dollies, moving furniture, carrying dishes, tableware, pots and pans of food, and for cleaning up. Do you have the stamina for such hard work, as well as for long hours? Do you recover quickly from fatigue?

Do you have the money?

Not only will you need money to set up a commissary, but you will need it to purchase supplies, pay for basic installations, and to cover current rent, utility, and insurance bills. Your cash reserve must be sufficient to enable you and your family to live comfortably and to pay personal/home expenses until your business starts showing a profitable return. This is extremely important. Based on U. S. Chamber of Commerce statistics, one of the greatest causes of business failure is *undercapitalization.* Be forewarned. Do not become a statistic!

ANALYZING CATERING POTENTIAL IN YOUR COMMUNITY

After carefully evaluating your personal qualifications, your next step is to survey the catering potential within your community. Be thoroughly familiar with the area and be able to determine if and, indeed, how you might provide a service.

Check the Bureau of Vital Statistics for figures on marriages, births, deaths. This last item, *deaths,* is an important one because many religious/ethnic groups use caterers for wakes or after-funeral dinners.

Visit the office of every church, temple, or synagogue in your area to learn about the number and types of social gatherings held in their facilities. Many of these institutions rent their social halls to the public for various functions.

Find out which fraternal and social organizations have club rooms or halls with kitchen facilities that they not only use, but which they rent to others. Such groups would include The Grange, American Legion, Veterans of Foreign Wars, Knights of Columbus, Knights of Pythias, Masonic Lodge, Moose, Elks, and the Odd Fellows. (A special note: Some religious, social, and civic organizations frequently have very lovely social halls but forbid the use of alcoholic beverages on the premises, which thus limits their usability.)

DECIDING SERVICE(S) TO BE OFFERED

After appraising both personal qualifications and the catering potential within the community, the next step is to determine the type(s) of service you may be able to offer. Although a well-established caterer may eventually become involved in all three major categories of Social Catering—On-Premise, Off-Premise, and Accommodator (In-Home Cooking and Serving)—the beginner usually starts out in one area and then expands to the others.

On-Premise Catering

For this type of business, the caterer has his/her own banquet hall with attached kitchen and commissary, thus enabling the operator to offer catering services which are similar to those offered by a hotel or restaurant.

On-premise catering requires an initial outlay of a substantial sum of money to build or rent a building and then to equip it properly. Therefore, the beginner should pursue the possibility of installing a catering operation in a hotel, restaurant, or local club that has the facilities but does not offer the service.

Off-Premise Catering

Here, the caterer has the kitchen and commissary but not the facilities for serving food. As a result, the operator always goes to the customer. Thus off-premise catering is highly personalized and provides services for affairs such as private dinner parties, banquets, wedding receptions, and bar mitzvahs, which may be held anywhere from private homes to public beaches and picnic grounds.

The off-premise caterer may provide "take-out" or "special delivery" food business or may also specialize in one or more services: in-home cooking and serving, barbecues, and clambakes, etc.

Another area that could be quite profitable is specialized catering to ethnic or religious groups, especially if they make up a large part of your community's population.

In order to specialize, however, you must be thoroughly familiar with the particular group's traditional dishes, as well as its social and religious customs. Even then, it would be wise to seek the guidance and cooperation of the group leader to learn about possible differences from the norm. You may also wish to bear in mind that your customers, who will be members of this religious/ethnic group, may have expertise in this area equal to your own. Therefore, you should be quite certain about your own abilities.

Accommodator (In-Home Cooking and Serving)

Accommodators, whose services represent an important and profitable branch of catering, are individuals or groups of individuals with particular skills in cooking, baking, and/or serving. Because they contact their clients by phone and operate directly from their own homes, they are often called "free-lance" foodservice specialists.

The services of the accommodator are engaged either by individuals or by organizations to assist with or to take over completely the preparation of food and service for special functions held on the host's premises. Thus, an accommodator is an employee rather than an employer.

While a great deal of in-home cooking and serving is done on a part-time basis to augment regular income, it can also be developed into a full-time activity. In fact, many Social Caterers who now have their own premises initially started out as accommodators.

CREATING A MARKET, SELLING A SERVICE

All too frequently, beginners are impatient. Anxious to get started and into "full swing," they neither allow themselves sufficient time to become established in the community nor to accumulate the necessary cash reserves.

In Social Catering, which is based primarily on personal service and personal abilities, this can be disastrous. The community *must* be fully acquainted with the caterer, his/her capabilities and talents. In fact, the better known, the more distinctive the service, the more frequently will the community seek him or her out.

An excellent way to establish a reputation *initially* is to approach organizations in the community and offer your services for upcoming events. . .free (for the first time) or at a nominal rate.

If your offer is accepted, your skill and professionalism (or lack of it) will soon be apparent. Because most committee members and groups with whom you will be dealing are amateurs, your superior techniques and abilities will stand out. Your ability will be recognized if you present a better-cooked, better-tasting meal; arrange a professional-looking buffet or offer quicker, more efficient and effective table service.

You, as the individual responsible for this impressive performance, will be remembered and sought after for future affairs. People attending the function will be impressed and want to know your name, address, phone number, and other pertinent information for future reference.

In this manner, you are building your reputation for ability, integrity, and dependability—three vital attributes for any successful catering business. Later, after you are more firmly established, you may wish to try other avenues such as advertising.

ADVERTISING

One of the most effective ways to seek clients is to advertise. If possible, seek assistance from a small advertising agency in the community; by having one of your "neighbors" do this, you will receive:

1. Expert ideas as to the marketability of your services
2. Local opinion regarding the status of your establishment
3. Advice on the use of rural or suburban newspapers to obtain greater coverage from your advertising budget
4. Information on the potential of radio and TV advertising for your business
5. Good will from the agency, as well as the potential business it can generate

If it is not possible for you to engage the services of an advertising agency to promote your business, do it yourself.

Newspaper Advertising

Newspaper ads can be elaborate or simple. (See samples, pp. 11-14.) They should be inviting, give just enough information to whet a potential customer's interest, and appear frequently enough to keep the caterer's name established with the public.

Direct Mail

Direct mailings—flyers, throwaways, brochures, and letters—can be extremely effective but they are expensive. They must be expertly designed and executed to arouse curiosity and interest or else they will be discarded without being read.

OTHER SOURCES

There are several other sources that lead to new business.

Cooperative Business Leads

Contact local business persons who provide services related to social functions—bridal shops, florists, photographers—who may be willing to supply leads for prospective customers. This, of course, is a two-way street. In turn, you must be prepared to reciprocate by also providing leads or suggesting these businesses to your clients.

Local Newspapers

Read the society pages of newspapers for engagement announcements. Then call or write a note of best wishes and congratulations to the young lady. At the same time, describe your facilities and offer your expert help with her future plans. Stress, of course, the fact that there is no obligation if she consults you about her plans. Be sincere with your offer of help and, regardless of whether or not it is accepted, you will have gained immeasurable good will.

Also from the newspapers, you may learn about upcoming plans for testimonials, special luncheons, reunions, bowling banquets, fraternity get-togethers, or fund-raising affairs. Since many of these items deal with future events, plans have not been finalized and, therefore, the options are wide open. It could be advantageous to contact personally the person mentioned in the news item and promote your services.

Community Involvement

Social affiliations, participation in civic affairs, working on committees, and involvement in popular causes/political activities can be very valuable and can generate reciprocal benefits. They may help to increase your business and will certainly keep your name favorably projected to the public.

SPECIAL EFFORTS

A good response may also be created by such activities as these:

Employ a professional sign painter to create a distinctive outdoor or window sign to help sell your services to passersby. Be sure the sign reflects the image that you desire to project to the community.

Offer special price breaks for quantity take-out orders.

Utilize talented employees to produce beautiful party platters or hors d'oeuvre, canapes, and pastries, or special seafood, meat and poultry dishes to sell at reasonable prices at your place of business.

Use the telephone directory. A spread in the yellow pages, as well as a telephone listing should be considered as an essential budgeted expense.

SUGGESTED ADVERTISING

Jewish-style In-home cooking and serving. Tasty Jewish dishes prepared in our own home and served graciously. Call Mrs. J. H. . .574-628

Continental chef available weekends and holidays only. For large home parties and complete charge of organization dinners. Henri. . .654 Middle Ave. . .816-4324

House Party Helpers—Will assist with cooking and serving and clean up. Call Anne or Marie. . .768-0987

Maitre d' available evenings only. Will organize your home party and serve with "a little bit of class." Francois 567-8907

Carnivale Italianno—Serve a gala Italian dinner party at home! Will prepare food in your home or in mine. Can furnish carnival "props." Call for details. Rico. . .764-0758

Bartender and/or Butler for home parties. Have portable bar and glasses, if desired. References. Ask for Joe. . 987-432

Setting Up a
Commissary/Kitchen/2

IF AFTER OBJECTIVE study and careful analysis you find that you wish to take full advantage of the additional opportunities that exist in the market you have created, you may then be ready to establish a commissary/kitchen.

In setting up such a business, be prepared for a shakedown period during which operations, cost patterns, and systems for performing functions will gradually evolve.

This period can be chaotic and frustrating. Emerging business patterns may differ markedly from what you had anticipated and for which you had so carefully planned. Not only that but this particular period can also be very costly. So you, the expanding caterer, must be adequately prepared and financially able to cope with many unforeseen difficulties.

While careful planning is essential, no scientific formula exists to assure a hand-in-glove fit. But do not be discouraged. In time—with considerable attention and objective evaluation of all factors—your business should eventually become a very smooth-running operation.

SEEKING PROFESSIONAL HELP

Although an expert in the food business and knowledgeable about the mechanical and physical necessities for a commissary/kitchen, you can hardly be expected to know all the legal requirements—local, state, and federal—with which you must comply. Therefore, you *must* hire a lawyer.

While retaining a lawyer is an essential operating expense, it is also a valuable business service and one of which you should take full advantage. Seek your attorney's advice on all matters, such as drawing up a lease or making arrangements for construction of a building.

In fact, *before signing* legal documents of any type, *consult your lawyer.* Do this under all circumstances, regardless of how simple the transaction seems or how well you understand it. This action could ultimately save you time and money, as well as involvement in lengthy legal proceedings.

It is also essential to engage the services of an accountant. In addition to obtaining your state sales tax and Internal Revenue identification numbers, the accountant will also set up, organize, and properly maintain your financial records, making certain that they are in full compliance with all governmental regulations and laws and are able to pass regular and unannounced inspections by local, state, or federal auditors.

Although the services of a professional accountant are usually not inexpensive, they are a wise investment. The accountant, who is an expert in business/financial matters, will see to it that you take advantage of all tax and business deductions to which you are entitled. You will, as a result, save financial resources because you will not pay out unnecessary monies for taxes.

An additional point of which your accountant will inform you is the fact that both accounting and attorney fees are tax deductible.

ZONING

Your physical plant—where you house equipment, store supplies, and from which you prepare and deliver foods—is subject to proper clearance from the local Zoning Board. Since requirements differ from place to place, as do the classifications assigned to catering establishments, it would be wise to have your attorney look into these ordinances.

Local ordinances may impose restrictions on where you can locate your business. They may also require provisions for employee parking but prohibit truck storage and/or parking. This would be a serious disadvantage; the nature of Social Catering is such that your trucks must be readily available for deliveries at any time of the day or night.

In addition to restrictions on the size/type of trucks, ordinances may ban them from operating on Sundays and holidays or during certain times, such as between the hours of 11 p.m. and 7 a.m., for example.

Garbage collection may be another area covered by local ordinances. For example, if outside garbage collection areas are prohibited, you will have to develop an alternate plan, perhaps refrigeration of your garbage.

While these ordinances may seem unimportant, they should not be taken lightly. Pressure from environmental and civic groups has often caused municipal authorities to enforce existing regulations rigidly, particularly those relating to food and its service. Caterers who ignore zoning ordinances, or who operate without the proper licenses, risk having "the book thrown at them." Therefore, you and your attorney should know thoroughly, understand completely, and comply fully with all zoning ordinances. Failure to do so could jeopardize your business and lead to expensive litigation.

LICENSES

After meeting Zoning Board specifications, you must then secure the necessary licenses. Of utmost importance is the license from your local Board of Health.

Remember, a Board of Health license is *mandatory*. Without it, you *will not* be permitted to operate, to offer your services to the public. Local boards will vary as to how they may classify a catering business. Your establishment might be considered a commissary, a restaurant, or even a food-processing plant.

However, determining the proper type of license for which to apply should be a carefully considered decision and one made with an eye toward the future. Select a license that will permit flexibility, allow for business growth and provide broader privileges. The small additional fee incurred at the outset could be well worth the expense because it may eliminate the time-consuming red tape and even greater cost of applying for a different license at a later date.

During this same period, you will also be contacting other municipal officials to make certain that you meet additional requirements. Consequently, fire, building, plumbing, and electrical inspectors will visit your premises to check required safety precautions in each of these areas.

INSURANCE

The advice of both your attorney and accountant will be invaluable in selecting the type(s) of insurance you must and should carry—workmen's compensation, accident/liability, general business insurance, etc.

Unless you specifically request otherwise, all your trucks and cars will have insurance coverage for *personal purposes only.* Thus, if you use your personal car for a business trip and it is involved in an accident during that period, the damages may not be covered by your policy. The company could refuse to honor your claim on the grounds that your personal car is *not officially and specifically covered.*

Therefore, if at all possible, purchase an insurance policy with a *comprehensive coverage clause.* It will cost a few cents more, but it is well worth the price. Regular insurance covers the probabilities, while comprehensive coverage gives protection from the improbabilities. Since the uniqueness of the Social Catering business frequently puts you in direct contact with the improbabilities, protect yourself.

One of the least-known categories of insurance is *product insurance,* which no foodservice operation should be without. Basically, product insurance provides protection in the event that foreign objects are found in your food or that contamination of foods processed by you causes illness.

If, on the other hand, a foreign object is found in foods processed by someone else but served by you, you could still find yourself in the middle of a law suit. However, if covered by product insurance, your insurance carrier will first come to your aid with protection and, then, may take action against the manufacturer of the product.

GENERAL FACILITIES PLANNING

While careful attention must be given to budgetary considerations, equal attention should also be given to equipment costs. From an economic standpoint, the purchase of high-quality equipment is a sound move. In addition to giving superior performance, it will, no doubt, lessen the possibility of breakdowns and high repair costs.

GOOD KITCHEN VENTILATION IS A MUST!

Most local building codes and fire prevention associations require that kitchens be ventilated. Some are specific in their requirements, while others outline objectives rather than design details. A good exhaust system must be engineered, and to comply with the various codes requires professional knowledge. The inadequacy of poorly designed systems can create many problems, as well as cause excessive operating costs. So, do not try to plan your own system; get professional help.

In planning your operation, allow adequate space for shipping and receiving areas. This includes space for a 4-ft. by 8-ft. table, which will be most helpful for assembling items to be packed and transported to jobs.

The production area should be physically separated from other areas and have as little cross-traffic and interference as possible. Dishwashing facilities should be close to the glass, silver, and china storage areas. Linens and miscellaneous dry foods must be stored in a well-ventilated place and away from pipes. *Never put anything directly on the floor.* Use standard or improvised pallets to keep all merchandise at least 8-in. off the floor. Flour, sugar, rice, potatoes, and onions should be stored in covered containers. Before refilling these containers, make certain that each is spotlessly clean.

A CHECKLIST FOR FACILITY REQUIREMENTS

1. Check all floors, walls, and ceilings for cracks, holes, and peeling paint. *(Do not use lead-based paint in any area.)*

2. Check for possible fly and/or insect infestation. Have all doors and windows properly screened.

3. Have adequate lighting. With fluorescent lighting, cool white bulbs should be used because other shades tend to give food an unattractive appearance. Lighting fixtures should be easy to reach and to clean.

4. Check natural ventilation. In planning your kitchen, carefully consider placement of ovens, ranges, steam kettles, etc., so that the mechanical exhaust units above them will be able to operate at peak efficiency and not have too long a "drag area."

5. When planning exhaust hoods above cooking areas, be certain they include automatic fire-fighting equipment.

6. Carefully plan the placement of all equipment you will be using. Allow sufficient aisle space so that refrigerators, freezers, and ovens may open to their full swing and to allow room for food trucks and dollies. (A comparatively easy way to plan this is to make a scale floor plan using graph paper. Cut out templates—patterns of paper—scaled to the size of your equipment—measurements are available in company catalogues—and arrange the pattern in the most effective way. [See Illustrations pp. 20 to 27.] Blueprint and architectural supply stores may have preprinted templates of kitchen equipment.)

7. Be certain that the lavatory space is sufficient to meet the local ordinances.

8. If possible, arrange to have one sink for exclusive use by the chef,

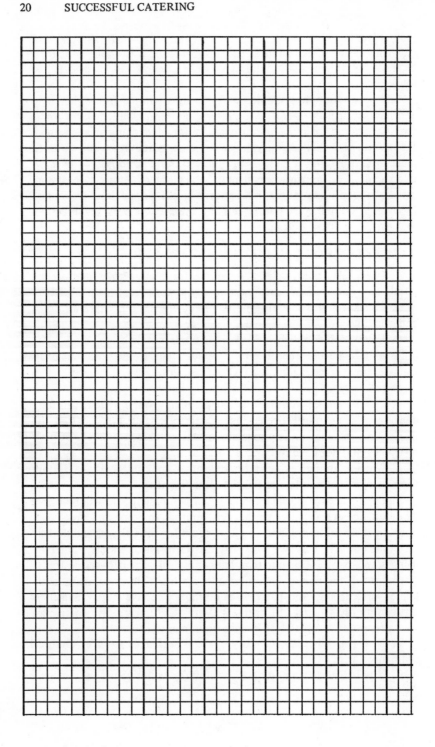

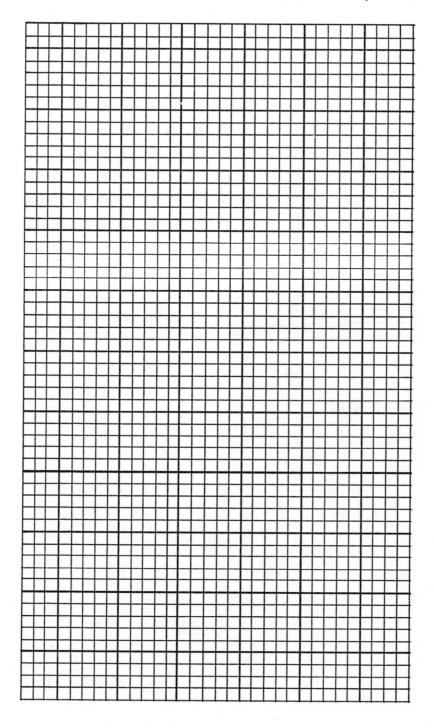

TEMPLATES FOR KITCHEN EQUIPMENT
1/8 INCH = 1 FOOT

These and the templates on the following pages are drawn to scale for use with the paper on the preceding pages to work out the plan for a specific kitchen.

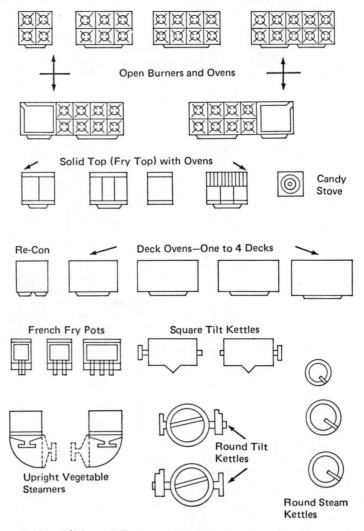

Open Burners and Ovens

Solid Top (Fry Top) with Ovens

Candy Stove

Re-Con   Deck Ovens—One to 4 Decks

French Fry Pots   Square Tilt Kettles

Round Tilt Kettles

Upright Vegetable Steamers

Round Steam Kettles

Scale: 1/8 in. = 1 Foot

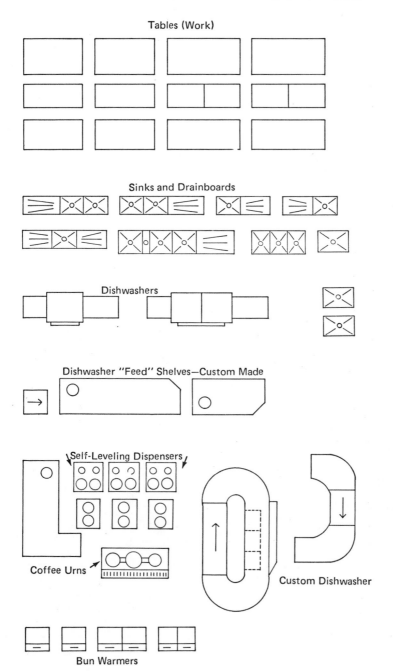

Tables (Work)

Sinks and Drainboards

Dishwashers

Dishwasher "Feed" Shelves—Custom Made

Self-Leveling Dispensers

Coffee Urns

Custom Dishwasher

Bun Warmers

Sinks—1/8 inch = 1 Foot

and Drainboards =

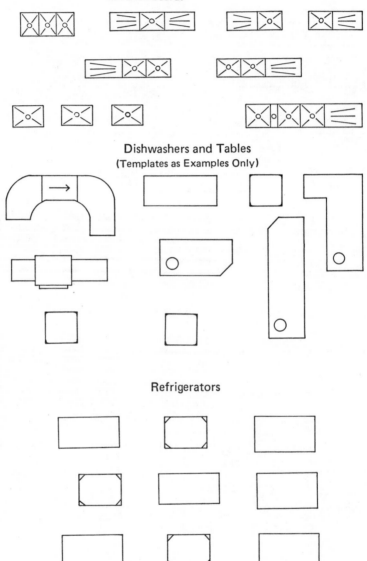

Dishwashers and Tables
(Templates as Examples Only)

Refrigerators

WORK TABLES–KITCHEN, 1/8 INCH = 1 FOOT

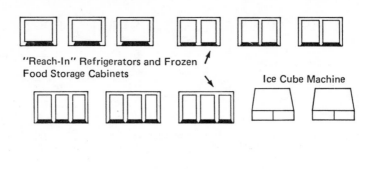

"Reach-In" Refrigerators and Frozen
Food Storage Cabinets

Ice Cube Machine

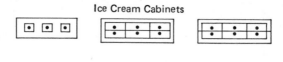

Ice Cream Cabinets

Walk-In Reefers—Freezers (with shelves)

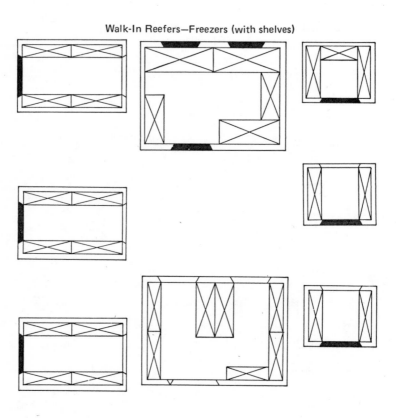

Stoves—Ranges

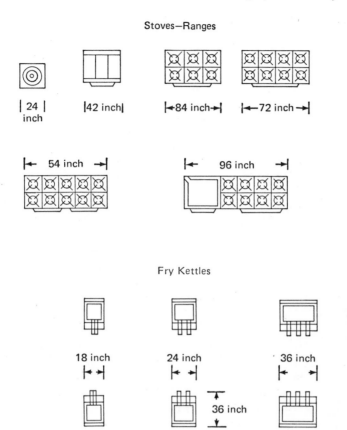

| 24 |
inch

|42 inch|

|←84 inch→|

|←72 inch→|

|← 54 inch →|

|← 96 inch →|

Fry Kettles

18 inch
|← →|

24 inch
|← →|

36 inch
|← →|

36 inch

Steam Kettles

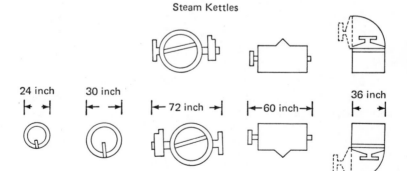

24 inch
|← →|

30 inch
|← →|

|← 72 inch →|

|←60 inch→|

36 inch
|← →|

another for utility work, and a third for pots. Your local Board of Health may also require installation of a special hand sink in the kitchen.

9. Dishwashing, receiving and storage, and packing areas should, if at all possible, be separated from, but within easy access to, the kitchen.

10. Allow sufficient parking space for your employees.

NOTE: It is unwise to establish a commissary in the building where you must use an elevator either to enter the commissary or to go from one department to another.

PLAN FOR DELIVERIES

In planning facilities, all factors involved in the delivery of food and equipment to off-premise jobs are important. Keep in mind that certain streets may be restricted to truck traffic during certain hours and that trucks may be prohibited in residential areas. Therefore, you will have to use other routes.

You may also have to adjust your pattern for school bus routes and in locations where schools, factories, office buildings, stadiums, and other recreational/amusement areas will be closing and cause traffic jams.

Be aware of road construction and detours. If uncertain, check with State Police or the local automobile club. Also listen to local radio reports; many give traffic information that could be important, particularly in bad weather.

Always allow plenty of time for deliveries. Give your driver sufficient traveling money for emergencies, additional gas, or tolls. He should also have enough money to pay for minor repairs and be supplied with the names of reputable service stations with towing facilities in the areas where he works. *He should always know where* YOU *will be and how he can get in touch with you.*

It might be advantageous to install a mobile phone in your trucks, as well as in your lead car. Short-wave communications may also be of value.

Put a "Hide-a-Key," in a place known only to you, on each vehicle that you own. Keys can get lost or misplaced; so, it is a good idea to know where one set is at all times.

Catering Personnel/3

THE TYPE OF PERSONNEL you employ can often spell the difference between success and failure. Therefore, it is essential that you find suitable employees and place them in the appropriate jobs.

To do this, you must know what work is to be done, how it should be accomplished, and what skills are required for each job. Armed with this information, you will then be able to determine the kind of individual who can best perform the job, the training needed, and a fair wage.

The number and type of employees needed depend on the type of service offered and the size of the facility.

An on-premise caterer's staff would probably consist of a chef, cook, assistant cook, garde manger or cold meat/salad man, kitchen man, waiter(s)/waitress(es), busboy(s), bartender, secretary, and maintenance crew.

The off-premise caterer would require a similar staff, as well as a driver(s) for vehicles used to transport food and equipment.

You, the *caterer*, are responsible to the client and are required to provide everything agreed upon in the contract. You book the job, write the contract, work out the menu, arrange and supervise all details of the affair, and assume responsibility for your employees and their on-the-job activities.

The *chef* or chief cook prepares all food and oversees the entire kitchen operation. The person who holds this position must have a thorough knowledge of food preparation and service.

The *assistant cook* helps the chef and cooks with the food preparation and service.

The *garde manger* prepares and decorates appetizers, hors d'oeuvre, cold meat/salad plates and trays, salad dressings, cold sauces, and all cold foods for buffet service.

The *kitchen man,* who may have dishwashers under his direction, is responsible for the cleanliness of all dishes, pots, pans, and service ware. He may also help serve food and move food/equipment to and from storage areas.

Waiters and/or Waitresses have the responsibility for properly serving food to guests. They must be well trained in the various methods of serving food. The job also includes the setting up and clearing of tables after the meal. For buffet service they should see that the food trays are replenished as needed.

Busboys do not serve food directly to guests but may pass rolls, serve coffee, and keep water glasses filled. They also help set up the room for service and clear tables when the meal is over.

The Bartender is responsible for serving liquor and wines as required. He must be familiar with the recipes for popular mixed drinks and which glasses to use. For off-premise jobs he may also be required to set up the portable bar and clean up afterward.

A *Secretary/Office Worker* will be needed by the moderate-sized or high-volume catering operation to handle paper work and office records.

The Maintenance Crew needed will depend on the size and type of the catering business.

SOURCES OF EXTRA HELP

The menu and type of service to be used for a function will determine the personnel required. But sufficient personnel must be provided to set up, serve, and clear tables within a reasonable period of time. While your basic crew will be able to handle most affairs, there will be times when additional workers will be needed.

Undoubtedly, many sources of part-time skilled kitchen help are available in your area. Approach chefs/cooks in local hospitals, nursing and retirement homes, as well as the public and private schools about their interest in and availability for part-time work. Many chefs in these facilities work a five-day week and would welcome an opportunity to make extra money.

For the less skilled help—drivers, packers, prep and "on-the-line men/women"—you may require, the Post Office is an excellent source of dependable part-time workers. These civil servants are honest, intelligent, dependable, and accustomed to working in all kinds of weather and conditions; many are also skilled drivers.

To "break into" this source, talk to your mailman who, in all likelihood, will be glad to help. He may advise you to ask the postmaster for permission to post a notice on the bulletin board or, if permitted, may do it for you.

Teachers may also be a good source of extra personnel. However, teaching is now more lucrative than it once was, so it may be difficult to meet or compete with the pay scale.

Remember that you, the caterer, are responsible for the actions of your employees, whether they are full-time, part-time, or temporary. Thus, select the right people for the job and be sure the employee knows what the job is and how you want it performed.

UNIFORMS

Clean, crisp, attractive uniforms will make a good impression on clients and staff members as well. Uniforms must be spotless; so, provide your kitchen staff with extra sets of whites when they are to serve "off-premises."

Chefs, cooks, and kitchen men should also be in whites—white shirts, coats, and aprons. (Gray denim work pants are acceptable in some areas.) Hats are a "MUST" for all kitchen workers.

Busboys should wear white or colored jackets.

Waiters' uniforms are available in traditional and contemporary colored models.

The uniform for the waitress has traditionally been a black or gray dress with white apron, collar, and headband. However, colored uniforms are seen more and more frequently today, especially for informal affairs.

Linen rental houses stock a wide variety of uniform accessories. Such service is not unduly expensive and assures a clean and uniform staff appearance—a help in creating a good impression.

Equipment for Kitchen /4

WHAT EQUIPMENT will I need? Is it economical? How well and how fast will it cook? Will it be easy to clean and operate? How well does it meet my present and anticipated needs? These are typical questions which every caterer has in mind when contemplating the purchase of equipment.

Information about the selection, use, and care of equipment is of primary importance if you want to get the most from your investment. Many sources of information are available—technical data from equipment designers, manufacturers and suppliers; articles on field use in trade periodicals; and books/other publications on foodservice equipment such as *The Complete Book of Cooking Equipment*.[1]

Before making equipment selection and purchasing decisions, you should take full advantage of these resources. In addition, you should consult with your chef—the one who will be using the equipment.

---

1. Jule Wilkinson, *The Complete Book of Cooking Equipment*, Rev. (Boston: Cahners Books, 1975).

You, the caterer, would be well advised to select not domestic but rather commercial-type equipment which meets standards set by the National Sanitation Foundation, American Gas Association, and Underwriters Laboratories.

Commercial equipment is more expensive but its heavier construction and larger capacity can make it a wise long-term investment. Since it is a specialized line, commercial equipment is handled by hotel/restaurant equipment supply companies who usually offer planning, designing, and servicing assistance as well. As a beginning caterer with limited funds, you may wish to check with some of these supply houses. They sometimes have good second-hand equipment at reasonable prices.

However, do not purchase second-hand equipment just because it seems like a bargain. If it does not fit your needs and fit them exactly, *do not buy.* If and when you do decide to buy second-hand equipment, make certain that: (1) it meets National Sanitation Foundation, American Gas Association, and/or Underwriters Laboratory standards; (2) it is a standard make; (3) replacement parts are available; and (4) all parts/areas function properly.

TYPES OF EQUIPMENT

Scales

The importance of having and *using* accurate scales cannot be over-emphasized.

Every item purchased by weight *should be weighed upon receipt* and compared with the weight stated on the original invoice. Therefore, your receiving department *must have* either a platform scale or a spring scale with a large round dial for easy reading. (See illustration, p. 34.)

A portion scale should also be an integral part of your kitchen equipment; and you should insist that it be used. This practice will assure portion control and, properly portioned foods when served, will create customer satisfaction because of their uniformity.

Food Storage

DRY—The dry-storage stockroom should be dry, well ventilated, out of direct sunlight, and maintained at a temperature of 55°F. to 65°F. Since too low (freezing) or too warm temperatures can damage canned goods, a good wall thermometer should be placed in a prominent place, and checked regularly to prevent wide temperature fluctuations.

Dry-storage shelves ought to be at least eight (8) inches off the floor and made of metal. They should be arranged to: (1) provide "first-in, first-out" distribution; (2) allow maximum circulation of air; and (3) avoid high stacking of items such as cereal, flour, and sugar.

SCALES—THE BACK
DOOR CASH REGISTER

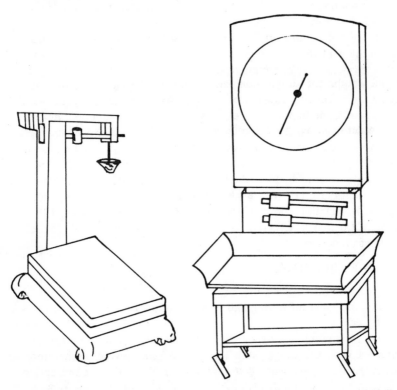

PORTABLE BEAM SCALE—
to 1000 lb.

RECEIVING SCALES—to 250 lb.
(can be larger and heavier capacity)

REFRIGERATED—Perishable foods require storage at 38°F. to 40°F. in refrigerated cabinets. In selecting refrigeration units (refrigerators or frozen food cabinets), give first and prime consideration to the interior.

No matter what the type—reach-in, roll-in, or walk-in—each unit should be evaluated by how well it meets basic requirements for:

1. *Good air circulation.* Does the unit have multiple cold air outlets to cool quickly and uniformly under maximum loading? Does it have adequate space and can you easily reach most inside areas? These are important questions because improper or inadequate air circulation can cause freezing and/or food spoilage.

2. *Humidity.* Relative humidity, which is an important consider-

ation, should be maintained at 80 to 85 per cent to keep food from dry-ing out.

3. *Temperature.* The refrigeration system components and how they are assembled affect efficiency and economy.

a. The compressor or pump which circulates the refrigerant at a determined pressure is controlled by the temperature needs of the cabinet interior. There are two types of compressors—standard and high torque. To utilize optimum capacity and to meet sudden high-power demands, it is preferable to have high-torque compressors.

The following popular "reach-in" refrigerators, for example, *should not* have compressors with a horsepower rating *less than* that stated:

Cabinet Size	Horsepower Rating
19.7 cu. ft.	1/4
36.5 cu. ft.	1/3
45.5 cu. ft.	1/3
71.8 cu. ft.	1/2
96.5 cu. ft.	3/4

b. The condenser, which cools the refrigerant, should be loca-ted in an easily cleanable place, and one where it will be exposed to air. Ease of access will encourage regular cleaning which is necessary. Dust and dirt accumulations prevent proper air circulation; this can cause overloading of the compressor and lead to a breakdown.

c. Fiberglass and polyurethane are both good insulating mater-ials but today most manufacturers use polyurethane because it can re-sult in a much stronger construction when properly done. The effect of proper insulation, however, can be diminished due to air leakage through seams and door gaskets.

d. While most commercial units are equipped with thermome-ters, readings refer to the air within the cabinet and not the product. To get a more accurate reading of the unit's efficiency, insert thermome-ters into glasses of water or into vegetables or fruits placed in different areas of the cabinet.

For further protection, install a battery-operated alarm system with visual or audible signaling devices for either or both high and/or low temperature warnings.

4. *Sanitation.* A cabinet that is difficult to clean is a potential health hazard.

a. Reach-in cabinets should have few interior seams and *pref-erably* none. Interior construction must be coved all around.

b. Shelves should be zinc-covered, anodized aluminum, stain-less steel, or chromed, as well as adjustable and removable. They should have a minimum of corners, extrusions, and few crossings in shelves, shelf standards, clips, trays, or pan slides because they collect spillage which, if not adequately cleaned, can lead to bacteria growth and mold.

c. Walk-ins should have tight and durable junctures to reduce the possibility of food spillage, and debris forming under and between panels.

5. *Adaptability.* Refrigeration equipment must be evaluated not only on its food preservation function, but also for its contribution to other kitchen operations. For instance, tray slides are designed for 18- by 26-in. baking pans or 14- by 18-in. cafeteria trays. Thus, salads, desserts, and other pre-portioned foods can be prepared in advance, put in a pan or tray, and stored in the refrigerator. The items are more accessible, and the capacity of the unit is more fully utilized.

However, be sure the refrigerator door has safety grip handles rather than the latch type to eliminate the chance of clothing catching on the latches.

What is popularly called a freezer is really a *frozen food storage cabinet.* Its basic use is to store at $0^\circ F$. those foods that are already frozen. Although foods can freeze at $0^\circ F$., the use of these cabinets for freezing foods in quantity for future use results in unsatisfactory quality, and is potentially dangerous.

There are some combination units available that store refrigerated foods on one side and frozen foods on the other. But this type of unit is generally not practical for the catering kitchen. A frozen food storage cabinet should be a separate unit having easy-to-open doors.

Self-defrosting units are slightly more expensive to operate but because they operate without temperature fluctuations, they offer more product protection. Also, this unit does not need frequent shutdown for removal of ice build-up. Although exterior and interior features of frozen food cabinets are similar to refrigerators, their compressors are at least twice as large.

True (air blast) freezers are not essential unless you produce in large quantities for long-term storage, or operate a frozen food carryout business. When used properly and by following proper technical procedures, a blast freezer will produce professionally frozen products. However, compressors on blast freezers are 10 times larger than those of refrigerators, and, consequently, are more costly to operate.

PREPARATION EQUIPMENT

A large and varied group of items are designed to prepare food for service or for further processing. Since these items are built to last, they are generally expensive.

You should evaluate each piece of equipment as to the type and size needed for your operation, reliability of the manufacturer, availability of parts and service, ease of cleaning and operating, safety features, flexibility, and durability. As a beginner faced with many expenses, you may want to consider purchasing second-hand equipment from a reliable supply house.

Electric Mixer

A mixer is an essential working tool. The most popular and convenient is the 30-qt. size with supplementary 10-qt. bowls and suitable paddles, whips, and fingers. Meat-grinding attachments can eliminate the need for a separate meat grinder. Furthermore, you can mount the mixer on a dolly and move it from one area to another as needed.

Meat Grinder/Chopper

Many caterers find that a separate, heavy-duty meat grinder/chopper is a valuable piece of equipment. Available in a variety of sizes to meet many needs, they also come with fine, medium, and coarse cutting plates.

Food Cutter or Buffalo Chopper

One of the most versatile machines in any kitchen, it chops ingredients for salads, and dices, cubes, or minces vegetables. It makes bread crumbs and, with attachments, can become a dicer, vegetable or fruit slicer, shredder, grater, french fry cutter, a juice extractor, and even a tool sharpener!

Extremely durable, the food cutter is easy to clean and comparatively simple to operate—especially when placed on a wheeled table. It is available in different sizes and finishes. As an indication of its value, the food cutter is probably the most difficult piece of equipment to pick up second-hand.

Slicer

Because considerable savings can be realized by machine slicing rather than slicing by hand, the slicer is probably one of the first pieces of equipment most caterers buy. Select either a semi-automatic (hand-driven) or variable speed, automatic machine (most practical where large quantities of foods must be sliced).

Be sure the model selected is easy to clean; has a large blade; will not slide when used; has adequate safety guards; an easy-to-read control handle, and safety on-and-off switch. For ease and flexibility of operation, place the slicer on a wheeled dolly. Have a "box" made to cover the machine so it can be moved by truck to off-premise jobs.

COOKING EQUIPMENT

Ranges

An electric or gas range, containing four to six stove-top burners and an oven below, is the basic unit for the catering kitchen. This unit will handle preparation requirements for up to 100 meals.

In selecting a range, give careful consideration to:

1. *Production capacity*

    a. Type of burner tops

Are they interchangeable, giving flexibility for hot top, oven top, and griddle burner sections?

Are "open-top" grates properly tempered so they will not snap when heavy pots are placed on them?

Are heating units properly placed for even heat distribution under "flat tops"?

    b. Oven size and capacity

Is the oven large enough to take oversize roaster pans?

Are shelves adjustable? If fixed, are they set at the half mark rather than the two-thirds mark? (The two-thirds mark is less desirable because of heat intensity).

2. *Temperature controls*

Are they reliable?

Are thermostats accurately calibrated?

3. *Ease of cleaning*

Insist on telescopic legs, which will put the unit at least six (6) inches off the floor, making it easier to clean underneath.

Are corners coved and oven linings easy to clean and maintain in proper condition?

4. *Ease of dismantling and reassembly*

Steam Cookers

Steam-jacketed kettles and cookers can offer versatility plus savings in labor, food value, and operating costs for both small-batch and large-quantity cooking.

The most common steam cookers today are: (1) the large compartment steamer with six 2-1/2-in. or four 4-in. pans that cooks at five (5) lb. pressure (225°F.), and comes in semi- and fully automatic models; and (2) the high-pressure steamer which is smaller but cooks more quickly at 15 PSI (250°F.). It will take three 12- by 20- by 2-1/2-in. or two 12- by 20- by 4-in. pans or combinations. One type has a perforated plate for use in defrosting, as well as heating frozen foods quickly. Another is designed to prepare small batches (2 1/2 to 22 lb.) of frozen vegetables and other foods in continuous supply.

Steam kettles are available in a wide variety of sizes from 10- to 20-qt. table models, 5-gal. stationary, trunnion and fast-chill models, to 60-gal. and larger styles. Model differences cover such things as: kettle depth; steam jacketing (full or two-thirds jackets); mounting-pedestal, wall or legs; tilting or stationary; and steam-supply method (direct or self-generating).

Before selecting and purchasing steam-cooking equipment, consult with the manufacturer and/or local foodservice equipment supply houses because many factors must be considered. They include:

- installation costs
- source and character of steam supply
- availability and cost of gas and electric power
- availability of adequate water connections
- adequate floor space for uncrowded operation
- drainage facilities
- proper ventilation in the area
- ease of operation for personnel
- menu requirements
- ease of cleaning and maintenance
- adequate safety devices
- accurate pressure gauges and timers
- shelves and shelf supports removable without the use of tools

Although it offers great flexibility, steam-cooking equipment is expensive to buy and to install. A beginning caterer, in particular, should not undertake such a large investment until a definite business demand pattern has been established.

Ovens

Many types and styles of ovens are available to today's foodservice operator. Selecting the correct type for the job requires an understanding of what each type can do. Other factors that must be considered are:

- available floor space
- installation and operating costs
- all welded structural steel construction for durable, rigid frames
- ease of cleaning and maintenance—ceramic material, if used, must be non-absorbent and able to withstand abrasion
- concealed wiring
- outside bodies of 16- to 18-gauge metal attached to solid frame support
- inner linings of 18-gauge rustproof sheet metal reinforced to prevent buckling

- sturdy doors, counterbalanced for easy opening and closing; heavy-duty hinges
  - fronts with complete one-piece construction
  - durable heating units
  - outside indicating thermometers, timers; signal lights to indicate when oven is on
    - precisely calibrated thermostats
    - properly vented chambers
    - the capacity to heat quickly plus good heat recovery ability
    - adequate insulation of oven, doors, and door handles

Most caterers will find that conventional ovens provided with commercial ranges or as separate units are adequate for their needs. However, as the business expands, other types to consider are:

DECK OR PEEL OVENS—Constructed in sections, these ovens have special baking (7-in.) or roasting (12-in.) decks which can be combined in any desired arrangement. Decks may be supplied with hearth tile for special baking purposes. Each oven has an individual temperature control, and added value is obtained if each of the decks has removable shelves.

CONVECTION OVENS—Where large numbers of meals must be prepared in a short period of time, convection ovens have proved to be very successful. They operate on the principle of forced air convection—blowing hot air over the food to cook it faster. Baking time is figured in minutes rather than hours. And production capacity is increased because food is cooked on multiple racks instead of on a deck.

Convection ovens are invaluable for the volume caterer and professionals who do their own baking. They are expensive, however, and definitely not for the beginner.

RE-CON OVENS—A small re-con oven is a most versatile piece of equipment and of great value to the off-premise caterer because of its speed. Hors d'oeuvres can be heated and processed in the unit. Creamed chicken, turkey dishes, seafood Newburg, and pasta products, such as lasagna or macaroni/cheese, can be reconstituted from their frozen state to serving temperatures in a very few minutes.

The effectiveness of this machine is further measured by the fact that:

1. No special wiring is required; it operates on 110 volts using regular plugs.

2. It is not too bulky—varying from 23- to 35-in. in height and width, and legs can be obtained with lock-wheel dollies, or it can be placed on a counter or table that has wheels to make the oven easy to place where needed most at each point in the production schedule.

3. It is not too heavy, it weighs between 125 and 267 pounds.

4. It is simple to operate: insert the food; close the door; push a button, and the food will cook to the pre-set time; at this point the unit will shut off automatically.

Broilers

A broiler should be an essential piece of equipment. Although off-premise caterers do not "finish" broiled items in their commissary/ kitchens, the broiler can be used to "mark" steaks, chicken, and so on. It can also be used to glaze and/or top-brown casseroles and items such as escalloped potatoes, macaroni and cheese, and seafood au gratin which gain special appeal from crusty toppings.

HEAVY-DUTY BROILERS—These broilers are generally of the same width as range sections and can be bought with overhead ovens heated by the broiler. They have powerful gas or electric burners and ceramic radiants which supply intense and uniform heat. They are designed primarily for large-volume production.

THE SALAMANDER—The salamander or elevated broiler is a miniature broiler mounted above a heavy-duty range. It also has ceramic radiants but, of course, smaller grid space. Its chief advantage, however, is that it requires no floor space.

In selecting a broiler, you, the caterer, must first determine the quantity and kind of broiled food you expect to serve, as well as the available floor space.

Deep Fryers

Essential for frying breaded items, a deep fryer is also a "must" for blanching and/or finishing deep fried seafood, turnovers, certain types of hors d'oeuvres, french fried potatoes, and other vegetables.

When making a purchase, consider overall capacity, as well as ease of cleaning and maintenance. Should your requirements be greater than the standard 14 by 14 unit with a capacity of 30 lb., you would be wise to consult a food facilities engineer. The heat generated may require a complete fireproof ambiance, variable speed exhausts, and special filters to trap the high fat vapors.

Heat/Exhaust Fans

These fans should be placed or hung over all heat-producing areas. Since many variables (fan-speed required and proper type of filters) determine the most effective fans for a particular installation, you would be wise to seek the advice of a professional food facilities engineer. Also, some municipalities insist that firefighting equipment be an integral part of the hood construction.

Coffee Makers

Providing good coffee is as important for the Social Caterer as it is for the restaurateur. It requires the use of a suitable coffee maker.

There are many types—urns, glass coffee makers, pressure coffee brewers, and automatic percolators, plus a variety of sizes from which to choose. Select the size(s) and type(s) best suited to your needs.

Probably the secret of good coffee lies more in keeping the coffee maker clean and in good working order than in the type of maker used. So, when purchasing, consider ease of cleaning along with design and service requirements.

Work Tables

A variety (4-, 5-, 6- and 8-ft.) of stainless steel work tables with metal legs, shelves, and/or drawers are necessary for food production areas, as well as for receiving and packing areas.

All tables should be constructed for ease of cleaning, safety, and durability. Also, you may wish to consider having one or two tables without shelves or drawers so dollies or carts may be stored underneath.

Sinks

Two- or three-section preparation sinks, and at the least one two-section pot-washing sink, with heavy-duty faucets, splashboards, over-hangs and drain shelves, are minimum requirements. They should be placed at proper heights for employee use, as well as be easily cleaned and maintained. Some municipalities may also require separate hand-washing sinks.

DISHWASHING EQUIPMENT

Dishwashers

To select an appropriate dishwasher requires serious analysis. How large a machine should be purchased? (The size of the machine must be based upon the volume of business anticipated.) How quickly must dishes be returned to the point of service? Also, *how much space* is available?

DOOR-TYPE DISHWASHER—This unit takes one rack of dishes at a time. As soon as the door is closed, the washing and rinsing cycle is usually triggered automatically, although it may be necessary to push a button to activate the mechanism.

Usually 25-in. square, this machine can handle up to 50 trays per hour. These units are available in straight through models or as corner models

SINGLE TANK RACK CONVEYING MODEL—This unit is a more productive machine in that a rack of soiled dishes is pushed into the opening and a mechanical arm locks in to the rack, pushing it through a washing and rinsing cycle, and then discharging it at the other end. On this type of single-tank machine, there is an automatic interruption between the end of the wash cycle and the start of the rinsing cycle. This machine can take 100 or more racks per hour.

The above mentioned model is recommended where limited space and limited volume will not permit installation of a two- or three-tank rack-conveying model. Needless to say, however, the machines with two tanks (wash and rinse) and with three tanks (pre-wash, wash, and rinse) have a direct rack entrance from the wash to the rinse cycle without shutdown time, thus permitting a greater number of dishes to be washed during a given period.

The machine has the capability of washing 130 racks per hour and its speed can be adjusted. It, as well as the flight type machine (a discussion of which follows), comes in two sizes—the standard 25-in.-wide model and the extra wide 30-in. model. The extra wide model should be considered, because it can handle serving trays, sheet pans, and even some pots and pans.

FLIGHT TYPE MACHINES—This unit is similar to the rack conveyer but *rack-filling is completely eliminated.* Instead, dishes are placed on an endless belt containing rubber, plastic, or composition "fingers" which hold dishes in place as they pass through the pre-rinse, rinse, and wash cycles. Upon completion, dishes are removed and placed directly onto dish trucks or storage shelves, which is very economical and effective for large operations.

Structurally, there are so many options available that you can virtually design your own dishwasher. (See illustrations, pp. 44, 45.)

Water Heaters

An adequate hot-water supply is absolutely essential for proper dishwashing. While hot water may be available from the primary system, it must be boosted in temperature to the minimum 180°F. required for sanitizing.

If feasible, a booster heater should be installed under the dishwasher or placed not more than five (5) feet away. This unit, which can be either the instantaneous or automatic-storage type, guarantees that the proper temperature of the water will always be available on demand.

Racks and Tables

Dishracks normally are not supplied with dishwashing machines, because needs vary since different-sized dishes, cups, glasses, and supremes

DISHMACHINES

RACK CONVEYOR TYPES

Can fit in areas 28 in. or wider   Can fit in areas 44 in. or wider

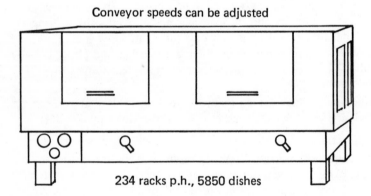

Straight
or Corner

50 racks p.h.   194 racks p.h.

Conveyor speeds can be adjusted

234 racks p.h., 5850 dishes

FLIGHT TYPE—ENDLESS BELTS

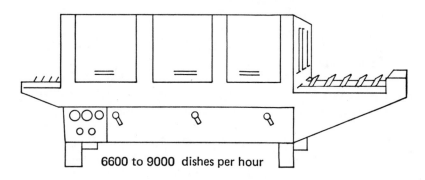

6600 to 9000 dishes per hour

STANDARD WIDTHS—25 in.; EXTRA WIDE—30 in.

**ALL CAN BE BUILT TO INDIVIDUAL SPECIFICATIONS—
MAKING COMBINATIONS ENDLESS**

may be used in each operation. For example, if you want the racks to be stored with the dishes, cups, or glasses in them, different structural designs may be required.

Dish tables for entrance or exit areas of the machine must also be purchased separately. They should be large enough to allow for proper rack loading and for clean stacking and packing.

The tables should be made of heavy gauge stainless steel or fiber glass. Make certain *they are tightly fitted into the machine at entrance and exit areas.* Improper fit will result in dangerous, wet, and slippery floors.

Slanted overhead shelves for holding cups, glass racks, and other odds and ends should be on either side of the dish tables. A small drain should also be at one end or the other of the shelves.

If space permits, provide two soaking sinks—one for silver; the other for dishes. These will be particularly useful to the off-premise caterer, since many affairs are held at areas where no dishwashing facilities are available, and food will be dried on the dishes upon their return to the commissary. If space does not permit fixed sinks, then two (2) large, heavy-duty plastic tubs will be adequate.

Waste Disposers

A garbage disposer is usually part of the dishwashing layout because it can be a valuable time and labor saver.

Depending upon the complexity of the dishwashing system, the disposer can be inserted under the pre-rinse sink, or in a special trough with running water.

Before investing in a disposer, though, consider the following:

If adequate scraping is done before dishes come to the dishroom, will a disposer really be needed?

Is the disposer's design rugged enough to take all scraps, or will it be necessary to hand-feed certain waste materials into the machine?

Does a local code prohibit the use of disposers?

Will the electrical supply be adequate or will fuses blow as soon as both it and the dishwasher are turned on?

Does it have a reversing switch? This is very handy when the disposer gets jammed or clogged.

Since it will be used with and around water, are electrical controls properly safeguarded so that no danger exists for the operator?

Last, but by no means least, who is responsible for service and warranty on the unit?

A disposer can be useful in the preparation area, too. However, in considering "need," determine the type of food products to be used, that is, fresh or processed. If the former, then obviously there will be a lot of peelings and other waste which can be conveniently thrown into the disposer.

Dish/Utensil Storage

Whatever means are used to store dishes and utensils, do not overlook the cleaning and sanitizing performed in the washing operation. Generally, the most desirable system is one that requires the least amount of handling between the time utensils are washed and their next use, and provides maximum protection for cleanliness. For this reason, storage of *uncovered* utensils in a cupboard is not recommended.

If possible, portable carts should be used in the dishwashing area so that sanitized and dried items can be stored quickly. The items can be protected by a sanitary cover until needed, at which time the cart can be wheeled to the proper place and uncovered.

Portable carts are available in various sizes/types to meet any requirement. However, selection should also be based on ease of maintaining sanitation for both the utensils and the cart; durability of material used; size in relation to portability; type of casters and whether they have locking devices, and design.

In regard to the latter, a word of caution. There are many types of carts, varying from the simple or general utility to those designed for a particular size of dish or tray, each with a corresponding increase in cost. *Do not buy what you do not need!*

CLEANING EQUIPMENT

Vacuum Cleaners

A heavy-duty, tank-type vacuum cleaner with a 10- to 12-ft. flexible hose is an invaluable tool. It can be used for hard-to-reach areas behind ranges and other pieces of equipment.

The vacuum cleaner should be used frequently to keep refrigerator coils from plugging up with dust, which can reduce the unit's efficiency. It is an effective tool, too, for the superficial cleaning of filters.

There are also tank-type, liquid absorption vacuum machines which do an excellent job in cleaning quarry and asphalt tile, concrete and similar surfaces.

SMALL TOOLS/UTENSILS

The exact type of small tools and pots/pans that you will require is impossible to forecast. But as business develops, your needs will become more evident.

However, all kitchen utensils should be regular *institution ware* of either standard or heavy-duty gauge construction. While the initial cost is high, the ultimate cost will be less because this ware is more durable than the lighter-weight housewares. Porcelain or enamelled ware should be avoided because this ware can chip and stain easily.

Today, many utensils having "non stick" coating are on the market. They resist abrasion of metal spatulas and spoons and, so, are virtually scratchproof, and easier to clean. However, for certain types of cooking, especially those requiring the "crusts" of cooked particles to make a tasty sauce or gravy, this type of cookware will be ineffective.

One of the most versatile and valuable utensils to have is "the squarehead," a heavy-duty aluminum roaster, approximately 18- by 20- by 7-in. You should purchase the roaster with heavy-duty flat covers that can also be used as heavy-duty grills. Besides holding substantial quantities of foods (approx. 42-qt.) to be heated on the range or in the oven, "squareheads" stack beautifully in refrigerators and trucks.

Vacuum pots, airtight transfer containers—call them what you will—these 3- to 10-gal. capacity containers are useful for storing and transporting foods. By virtue of their construction, they can effectively retain heat or cold for 24 hours or more.

Attractive in appearance, they can, on many occasions, be used on the buffet table as coffee, tea, and/or punch dispensers or for transporting and dispensing ice cubes. Moreover, when kept clean and shined, these metal units will be more pleasing to the eye than those made from synthetic materials.

CHECK LIST FOR SMALL TOOLS/UTENSILS
(Not Including Knives)

BRAZIERS—5- to 24-qt.

CAN OPENERS—heavy-duty manual or heavy-duty electric (with additional gears and cutters for replacement)

CAST IRON SKILLET—to 14-in.

CHINA CAPS—fine or coarse

CLEAN UP EQUIPMENT—brooms, brushes, mops, squeegies, buckets, pails

COLANDERS—from 1- to 16-qt.

COMMERCIAL DUTY BLENDERS—for pureeing, vegetables, etc.

DISH OR SALAD PANS—from 14- to 40-qt.

DOUBLE BOILERS—(can be improvised by using available pots, etc.)

DREDGES—for sprinkling sugar, cinnamon, etc.

FOOD STORAGE CONTAINERS—round and square from 1-qt. up, made of metal or plastic

FOODMILL—grinder/foodmill

FRY PANS—from 6- to 14-in.; treated with non stick coating, from 8- to 14-in.

FUNNELS—from 3/8-in. opening to 1 1/2-in. or higher

GARBAGE CONTAINERS

HEAVY DUTY FOIL

HOT FOOD SERVICE PANS—approximate size: 13- by 2- by 2 1/2-in.

ICE CREAM SCOOPS—assorted sizes and shapes

MALLET—of solid aluminum, used to break down fibers or flatten meat

MEASURES—from 1 cup to 4-qt., aluminum, stainless steel, or plastic but *not glass*

MEAT SAW/CLEAVER—for flattening purposes; *do not chop bones with cleaver*

MIXING BOWLS—1 1/2- to 12-qt.

PIANO WIRE WHIPS—assorted sizes

PORTION SCALES—from 32- to 50-oz. to achieve uniform individual portions

RECEIVING SCALE—absolutely a must and *to be used constantly*

ROAST AND BAKE PANS—(Squareheads) with a heavy-duty cover that can also be used as a grill; approximate size: 17- by 21- by 7-in. high

ROASTING PANS—standard weight and heavy-duty from approx. 12- by 20-in. to 17- by 26-in. (Check your ovens for largest size they will hold.) Purchase some half-size roasters also.

RUBBER COMPOSITION CUTTING BOARDS—to be used whenever necessary

PLASTIC SELF-SEALING WRAP

SAUCE PANS—1 1/2- to 10-qt.

SAUCEPOTS—4- to 24-qt. (Larger sizes are available but they are too awkward and difficult to handle.)

SCOOPS—for bulk flour, sugar, rice, etc.

SHARPENING STONES—to keep knives constantly sharp

SHEET PANS—approx. size: 18- by 26-in. (Mobile racks to store these will be helpful.)

SKIMMER—6 1/2-in.

SOUP LADLES—from 2- to 10-oz.

SPOONS—wood; solid, slotted, and perforated

STOCKPOTS—with or without faucets and from 24- to 40-qt.

STRAINERS—to 5-qt.

THERMOMETER—one for roast beef; another for candy, jelly, or frostings

TONGS—from 7- to 10-in.

UTILITY PANS—from 2- to 10-qt.

WAX PAPER

Guest Service Equipment/5

SERVICE WARE INCLUDES all equipment used by you in serving guests—china, flatware, buffet service, linens, disposables, portable equipment, and other special items.

CHINA

The first rule to remember in buying china is *not to buy close outs or discontinued patterns.* Because of their low price, it may seem an irresistible temptation but it is very poor economy. The reason is obvious: when it is necessary to replace broken dishes or to increase your stock due to expansion of your business, the original pattern may not be available. You then, will be compelled to purchase an entirely new set of dishes. If you do not, the use of assorted shapes, sizes, and patterns of dishes may well discourage a client who is considering your services. Also, standardization in dish weight, design, and shape lead to greater efficiency in washing, handling, stacking, and storing.

The function of china should be considered from the following standpoints of: (1) serviceability; (2) durability; and (3) beauty.

The heaviness or thickness of china is quite often assumed to be the only criterion for its serviceability. This is not always so since employees are prone to be less careful in handling heavy dishes.

The weight of the dishes, when stacked one on top of another, tends to rub off the glazed surface with which they come in contact. Also, when the dishes are stacked atop each other, the weight, in transport, can cause shock waves, and may result in a greater number of cracked and broken dishes. (When packing for transport or storage, *never* stack more than 20 to 24 dishes high.)

Cautiously consider the purchase of any dishes with raised patterns. Raised surfaces chip more easily, and can also be dust and dirt traps that require more attention in cleaning.

Medium-weight dishes are much more practical, and generally considered more aesthetic. Dishes of this weight when packed in transporting racks add up to less weight per rack. Rolled-edge dishes are definitely a plus because the rounded edges act as "bumpers," reducing chipping and breakage.

There is an almost endless choice of decorative patterns and many are individualized to personal specifications. All dishes are "vitrified" or glazed for total resistance to penetration. The pattern is applied prior to the final coat or "overglaze"; china is then baked by special type fires at comparatively low temperatures. Patterns applied by this method are fairly durable; however, chemicals used in dish machine compounds sometimes attack these areas and, in time, deterioration may become obvious.

Social Caterers work in variously furnished and decorated areas. Some rooms may be extremely gay and colorful, while others may be subdued to the point of drabness. Tablecloths may be bright and flashy, pastel-colored, or white. After a catering business has become established, it may be economically feasible to have dishes to match the colors of the tablecloths available, or the predominating color of the room. In starting out, however, it is wise to choose simple and delicate patterns in pastels, or with metallic decorations. Metallic decorations, such as gold or silver (platinum), are aesthetically the safest as far as fitting into a large number of color schemes, but they are not as serviceable as colors.

If you wish to have your personal logo or monogram a part of the china pattern, it should be incorporated as part of a pleasing decoration, and not appear as an obvious bit of advertising.

In selecting dinner plates, consider the 10-3/4-in. (brim-to-brim) size. An adequate "show plate" to use as a base for starter courses at banquets, and a satisfactory meal-presentation plate, it is large enough to present the food course without crowding, giving a desirable impression of spaciousness. For "oversize" beef cuts or pasta presentations, you may use the 12-3/4-in. steak platter.

Coffee cups come in various shapes and sizes—low cups, high cups, tea cups, and mugs. Many mugs are footed which not only makes them graceful in appearance, but allows them to be used without saucers. Cup sizes range from 4-1/2 ounces (the after-dinner or demitasse size) to 7-, 7-1/4-, 7-1/2-, 7-3/4-, and 8-3/4-ounce capacity.

Coffee and bouillon cup handles are not molded with the cup, but are applied separately during the manufacturing process. Check these handles very thoroughly. Will they be able to withstand the abuse that comes in packing and delivery? (When packing cups, do not nest them. Cups should be packed as a single layer in individual racks.) Give thought to purchasing bouillon cups *without handles* rather than the standard two-handled bouillon cup. When one handle of a bouillon cup is broken, you might just as well discard the cup.

Do cup bases have separately attached rings, or are the bases an integrally molded part of the cup? Is the base of the ring fully glazed, or is it rough? A rough ring can become a magnet for dirt, and this will make cleaning very difficult.

GUIDE TO PURCHASING DISHES

Ideas vary as to the type and quantity of dishes needed, depending on mode and scope of service, dishwashing facilities, availability of dishes for re-ordering, reserve inventory that is feasible, and the funds that are available. However, the following suggested list of basic quantities required for serving 100 guests may be helpful:

Basic Dish Requirements For 100 Guests

Dinner plates	250
Underliners or salad plates	300-400
Bread and butter plates	300-400
Platters (optional)	50-100
Cups and saucers	300-400
Bouillon cups	200-250
Fruit dishes	250-300
Grapefruit dishes	200-250
Soup bowls	100-200
Sugars and creamers	50 sets

STAINLESS STEEL FLATWARE, CHAFING DISHES, TRAYS, ETC.

Stainless steel equipment is acceptable in most establishments today. However, this should be quality stainless, a metal that has "good feel, substance, and body," with pattern details articulated and finished off, instead of just being "punched out" as is sometimes the case.

Reputable silver manufacturers have lines of stainless ware comparable in price to their silver line. The advantage of stainless ware over silver is, of course, the upkeep. Polishing and burnishing are practically eliminated. As the stainless ware is harder than silver, it will show fewer signs of abuse.

Basic Flatware Requirements Per 100 Guests

100 Dinner Knives	100 Fish Forks
100 Luncheon Knives	100 Dessert Forks
100 Butter Knives	100 Round Bowl Soup Spoons
100 Cocktail Forks	100 Bouillon Spoons
100 Dinner Forks	200 Teaspoons
100 Luncheon Forks	100 Iced Teaspoons
100 Salad Forks	100 Dessert Spoons

You may, on occasion, resort to cheap stainless ware and you will be justified in using it—for example, to serve a large outdoor party where flatware may be carried off, or inadvertently discarded. Of course, in such instances, *heavy-duty* disposable plasticware could be used; remember, however, that plasticware tends to break. Plasticware or other disposables *should not be used without the full knowledge and consent of your client.*

Serving Pieces

The type of service offered will determine what you need. However, for general service, you must have a good supply of the following:

Large Serving Spoons
Cold Meat Forks
Salad Tongs/Large Salad Forks and Spoons
Cake Knife/Servers

Chafing Dishes

You will want to have in stock an assortment of chafing dishes in different shapes and sizes for various buffet needs. Available in round, oval, and oblong shapes, in sizes ranging from two (2) quarts to eight (8) quarts, and larger; and in a variety of metals (silver, stainless steel, and combinations of copper, brass, and aluminum), they add a decorative note to your buffet.

Trays

For use by waiters, cooks, and bartenders, select heavy-duty metal, plastic, or fiber glass utility trays. For serving hors d'oeuvre and for the buffet, there should be more elaborate round, oval, and oblong trays to complement the food.

Tea/Coffee Service

To cater "teas" and "coffees," you will need: (1) a silver or stainless tea service (tea server, hot water pot with warming unit, creamer, sugar bowl, and matching tray); (2) a silver or stainless coffee serving urn with a self-contained heating unit, matching creamer, sugar bowl, and tray to add a touch of elegance to the tea/coffee table.

Polished silver pitchers have long been used in foodservice operations for serving coffee and tea to seated guests. However, although decorative, they are heavy to handle and are not insulated. You may prefer lighter-weight insulated pitchers with heat-resistant handles.

Candelabras

Candelabras add an elegant touch as the focal point of a buffet or head table. They are available in assorted sizes and styles. The quantities, sizes, and styles you will need will be determined by the type of service you are offering.

GLASSWARE

A Social Caterer requires a large supply of glassware, in assorted sizes and of various types, to meet the demands of the variety of service to be offered, as well as for replacements for breakage. The type and number of glasses required will depend on the service offered. However, the following list may be helpful as a basic guide:

Types Of Glassware Required
3- to 5-oz. juice glasses
8- to 10-oz. water tumblers or goblets
12-oz. iced tea glasses
Supreme glasses/liners
Relish trays
Parfait glasses
Compotes for candy, nuts, petit fours
Creamers and sugars
Sherbet glasses
Champagne glasses
Wine glasses
Ash trays

LINENS, NAPERY, ETC.

As a beginning caterer, you will probably find it best to rent linens, which means that you do not have to make an immediate cash outlay for cloths. Of course, the disadvantage is that you are always at the mercy of the laundry service.

As a result, you may be forced to compromise on quality, and, on occasion, have to accept patched, mold-stained, torn, or improperly folded and ironed cloths and napkins. Also, by renting linens, your offerings will be the same as other caterers who use the same service; thus, you will not have that "linen edge."

Owning your own linens has certain advantages. You can choose your own colors, quality, and sizes. (Example: Most laundries supply 72-in. by 72-in. cloths as standard for 54- and 60-in. round tables. The drop this size cloth permits on a 54-in. table is adequate, but the drop (i.e., amount of cloth that hangs down from the table) on a 60-in. table is skimpy. You may have to use skimpy cloths because they are the only size available from your laundry.

Rental laundries use the 72-in. by 72-in. size because bolts of table-cloth material generally come in standard 72-in. widths. If you wish to order cloths made up in larger sizes, it will cost more but the aesthetic value may be well worth the extra charge. The generous cloth could also provide an added feature that your catering service offers and one that your competitor cannot match.

The synthetic fabrics used today by many companies making table-cloths and napkins are of such fine quality that they can be used at the most elegant affairs. Many are spot and stain resistant and, if handled as directed, require no ironing, which is a tremendous boon to many foodservice operators. Furthermore, servicing or laundering these synthetics may not require commercial laundry service; neighborhood laundromat owners might well be interested in "taking on" this additional business.

In selecting tablecloths, it will help to know the cloth sizes that will fit various sized tables.

Fitting Cloths to Tables

CLOTH SIZE	TABLE SIZE
44-in. by 44-in.	Bridge table or cocktail tables
54-in. square	44-in. to 50-in. Bridge or Round
64-in. square	48-in. to 54-in. Round or Square
72-in. square	60-in. Round
81-in. by 81-in.	72-in. Round
90-in. by 90-in.	84-in. Round

54-in. by 72-in.	5-ft. Oblong
54-in. by 84-in.	6-ft. Oblong
54-in. by 120-in.	8-ft. Oblong

Napkins are basically of two (2) sizes:

| 18-in. by 18-in. | **or** | 20-in. by 20-in. |

Kitchen Linens

Be sure to maintain an adequate supply of pot holders, dish towels, hand towels, bar towels, and cleanup cloths for your employees to use in the kitchen and "on location." Many commercial laundries may supply these on a rental basis along with the chef coats, pants, aprons, bar coats, waiter and waitress uniforms you require. They may even "emblemize" uniforms or furnish certain colors to meet your specifications, provided long-term contracts are negotiated with them.

DISPOSABLES

Modern technology has produced papercloths and napkins of extremely fine quality and serviceability. They so closely approximate cloth texture that it is often very difficult to tell the difference. If this type of covering can be used, then by all means do so!

There are excellent absorbent paper towels available for kitchen use, as well as some synthetic combinations that can be washed and re-used. They should never be substituted for hot pot pads, however.

Food Transporting
Equipment/6

AS AN OFF-PREMISE caterer providing foodservice in a variety of locations, your menus and service ware must be sufficiently flexible to fit in with the varied facilities each location offers. It is essential, therefore, that careful consideration be given to the types of food transporting equipment that will be required for the wide variety of equipment and ware needed to meet all demands.

VEHICLES FOR TRANSPORTING PEOPLE, FOOD, EQUIPMENT

Station Wagons

A station wagon probably has more aesthetic than utilitarian value, at least from the standpoint of equipment-carrying ability. A six-passenger wagon allows some deck space, but after checking the interior height from the deck floor to roof, you will find that this space rarely exceeds 36 in. If it is a nine-passenger wagon, deck-carrying capacity is reduced to nearly zero. This lack of space should be carefully considered before you purchase a station wagon.

Van

Unquestionably, the most practical vehicle for catering purposes is the van, which can carry nine passengers or more, and still have ample room for equipment. In addition to rear doors, many vans have side doors that slide or fold open to more than half the vehicle length; this permits easier loading for large and bulky pieces of equipment. Most vans also have side windows, and this is definitely an asset.

Requirements

A FEW WORDS OF CAUTION ON WAGONS AND VANS: Instead of number of passengers or cubic-feet capacity, you should be interested in *how much weight can be carried.* Remember, dishes are heavy; silverware is heavy; and equipment is heavy; in addition, you must also consider the weight of any passengers.

Get a heavy-duty motor capable of carrying more than the rated capacity at a sustained speed for any distance, without breaking down or burning up.

Find out if additional leaves can be added to springs in order to distribute weight over a greater area, and also use oversize tires. Although heavy-duty springs and oversize tires cause a rougher ride when the vehicle is empty, they assure a safer, surer ride when it is fully loaded.

TRUCKS—PURCHASE, LEASE, OR RENT

Purchase

Purchasing a truck requires a substantial cash down payment as well as monthly payments over a period of several years. Before making this investment, consult your accountant to determine whether your liquid cash is sufficient to meet this obligation, and to learn the appropriate dollar depreciation and other tax advantages of such an acquisition.

Owning your own truck has many obvious advantages, but you must be prepared to accept the responsibility for proper maintenance. Trucks must be mechanically sound, and kept in top-notch condition— immaculately clean and always "at the ready."

Do you have a dependable garage man to whom these responsibilities can be delegated? Does he have a towing service that can be used in the event of a late-night or early morning breakdown? If catering services are offered at distances more than 25 miles from your commissary, a list of garages in those areas that can be called upon for towing and for service should be available to drivers.

Leasing

Leasing is beneficial because of the small down payment required, leaving additional cash on hand for other purposes, and reduced maintenance problems.   There are also tax advantages to leasing, but they vary according to the profitability of each business.

There are two basic types of leases—open-end and closed-end. An open-end lease calls for small payments each month, but, at the end of the lease, which is usually three years, the "balloon payment" for the remaining value of the car or truck is due *all at once.* Also, a maximum mileage stipulation may be part of the lease and if this is exceeded, there is a mileage penalty which runs from 3 to 5 cents per mile, at the very least.

Most leasing companies will not contract for less than a two-year period.   Termination of this contract can be expensive because repainting, removing dents, and other work must be paid for by you at the *submitted price of the lessor.* Remember, leasing is a purchased service, and the rental concern is in business to make money, too.

A closed-end lease requires larger monthly payments but no balloon payment at the end of the contract.   The car is returned to the leasing agency which then disposes of it—*probably selling it back to you at a price.* . ."caveat emptor," let the buyer beware.

Renting

If there is a reputable truck rental agency in your area, one that has trucks available on demand, renting trucks as you need them might be a very wise move.   In fact, it may be exactly and only what you need. If you do rent, check costs every few months to determine, from a cost point, whether you should continue to rent, whether you should lease, or whether to buy your own vehicle.

There is one very important fact you should always keep in mind. *Trucks rented or leased for food transportation must be refrigerated and used only for the transporting of food.* It is illegal, as well as hazardous, to transport food in a rented truck previously used to move household goods or other merchandise.

If using a rented truck, spray its interior with a non-toxic (to humans) insect spray after the completion of each job, but prior to your return. This spray will work while you are in transit to your commissary, and greatly reduce the possibility of transferring roaches and other insects to your facility. Upon return, all the equipment you used and carried in the truck should be thoroughly washed and sterilized, before being covered and placed in the storage area.

PORTABLE EQUIPMENT

Dish Carriers

One of your greatest problems will be dish and equipment carriers. Many are not rugged enough, and not easily adaptable for off-premise use. You may have to improvise and adapt on-premise equipment to make it serviceable for your off-premise needs.

For example, glass and cup racks have protrusions, either on the diagonal sides of each top corner or on all of the four top corners, to allow racks to be stacked on top of each other, and locked in position. This is perfectly acceptable for stacked racks that are stationary, but not for those that must be transported. If racks that are transported are not properly wedged in by other equipment, they may slide or topple over while the truck is moving, if it makes a sudden stop, or hits a pot hole. To prevent this, it is necessary to: (1) order racks with larger lock-guiding devices (which could be expensive); (2) tie racks in place with washable nylon rope; or (3) place 2-in. by 3-in. wooden uprights with eye hooks on the outside center of the stack and tie them in.

Dish holders, carrying boxes, and baskets are constructed of heavy wire, coated with layers of rubber or pliant plastic. The heavier the layers, the more jar-and-bump resistant the carrier will be, thus reducing possible damage to the contents.

When replacing carriers, purchase them from the original manufacturer. In this way, they will be the same size, and have the same corner-locking devices.

Plastic tote boxes are available in various sizes, and come with swing-in metal handles that can be used as a base for storing other tote boxes. *Never Stack More Boxes Than The Manufacturer Suggests* because handles may snap and/or boxes may split.

Corrugated cardboard boxes should be used only in emergencies, and *Should Never Be Stored Or Packed On The Floor Of The Truck.* If the truck floor is wet, the bottom of the boxes may fall out when they are lifted, which could cause a loss of merchandise, and take extra time for clean-up and repacking. Furthermore, the glued areas of corrugated cardboard boxes can also be a haven for roaches.

There are also disadvantages to wooden tote or carrying boxes. They retain moisture; have a tendency to mold; are difficult to clean, and may have slivers that can cause injuries to the handler.

Foot lockers, the type available in Army-Navy stores, are excellent carriers of silver trays, and other valuable pieces of equipment, because they have reinforced corners, and are sheet-steel jacketed or vinyl-covered. However, it would be wise to install a hasp so the locker can be padlocked with your own lock and key.

Your operation will often be judged by the type of equipment you carry. In view of this, as well as sanitation hazards, and your desire to have food arrive at its destination in the best possible condition, you should use the best possible food-carrying equipment.

Many excellent, insulated metal, food-carrying cabinets are on the market today. Some can be hand carried and have drop handles. Larger ones may require either two men to carry them, or they may be mounted on neoprene wheels; companion dollies can be used for moving and stacking. These square and solidly constructed containers pack beautifully in the delivery truck. Because they are covered on all sides, food is well protected from the intrusion of foreign contamination. They will also hold standard sheet and hotel pans securely, assuring that food arriving at the point of service is in good condition.

These carriers have several more factors in their favor. For example: (1) dry ice, if needed to chill food, can be kept in them; (2) portable heating units can be placed inside to heat food; and (3) inside and outside cleaning can be done very easily.

Portable Coffee Urns

Although some locations at which you will be catering will have coffee urns in their kitchens, you cannot always count on their being adequate for your needs. Therefore, you should plan to have enough portable urns in inventory to provide two (2) cups of coffee for the total number of guests you anticipate serving at any affair.

There are many new, portable coffee urns available today. They not only make good coffee, but are decorative, easy to clean and handle. For catering in private homes, a 30 to 50 cup coffee maker will generally be adequate.

All carrying containers as well as other equipment should have your name or some identification conspicuously painted, burned, engraved, or indelibly marked on them.

There is a limited number of manufacturers of institutional utensils and equipment, and the possibility always exists that duplicate ware may be in the facility where you are catering. Therefore, it is *imperative* to properly identify your equipment as soon as you buy it. A good engraving tool is an inexpensive investment. Its use will save you embarrassment and will help your employees identify your equipment when out on a job.

When purchasing equipment that may be transported to a job, consider the following:

1. How easy is it to store?
2. Can it be disassembled and stacked without marring?
3. Is it lightweight but rugged? Will it show abuse?
4. Do vulnerable parts protrude in a hazardous manner?
5. Are locking devices easy to use?
6. Are parts that rest on the floor self-leveling; do they have abrasive surfaces?
7. Are some of these interchangeable and can they be converted or adjusted to different levels?
8. Are companion dollies available to facilitate handling?

Portable Bars

Before purchasing a portable bar, examine it thoroughly. See how long it takes to disassemble and how quickly it can be assembled on the job. How much space will it take up in the truck? (To be practical, a bar should not be wider than 12 in. when folded.) Can it be carried without scratching or damage? Can you improvise a container into which you can slip the bar to prevent damage in transit?

Is the shelf for bottles strong enough to support anticipated weights? Check the hinges. Are they fragile looking and fastened to the surface with wood screws? Or, a better way, are the hinges bolted on? Hinges of the "piano type" (long, reinforced, and of brass), indicates the bar has been well constructed.

It is a matter of personal choice as to whether you want a padded bar covered with plastic or leather, or a smooth formica-type facing. It is more important that the bar be practical, conservative in color to blend with any decor or surrounding, and that it have an alcohol- and stain-proof counter top.

There are also small, portable, modular bars. These built-in units can be connected to make a larger bar—even connected at right angles— depending on your need. Instead of one large bar, several small bars used in different areas of the same room will help divert traffic and prevent congestion.

Rolling Bars

In making a purchasing decision, scrutinize a rolling bar as carefully as you would a portable bar. How well constructed is it? Does it have ample capacity? Are the legs strong enough and properly anchored? Is the bar transportable? Does it have large wheels? Since most dining areas are carpeted, this is important because carpets make it very difficult to push a bar unless the wheels are large.

Sanitation/7

IT IS BOTH your moral and legal obligation to set up and maintain high standards of sanitation for your place of business.

If you are an off-premise caterer, you must be even more acutely aware of these responsibilities because you work in many different locations. Not only must your commissary and kitchen conform to rigid standards set by the U. S. Public Health Service Code, National Sanitation Foundation, local Boards of Health, and other regulatory bodies, but your transporting facilities (packaging, equipment, vehicles) and food serving areas must also meet these same stringent standards.

As an off-premise caterer, you are constantly exposed to a great many potentially unsatisfactory conditions. For example, if serving an affair in an infrequently used facility, you must have the area thoroughly and meticulously cleaned before bringing in equipment and/or food. Also, you must carefully and vigorously check the location for insect or rodent infestation.

Moreover, as a *professional,* you must have the courage to refuse to serve for any affair which is to be held in an area where there is a possible health hazard, or from which there is a danger of carrying insect/rodent contamination back to your own premises.

PERSONNEL

Personal and personnel cleanliness cannot be overemphasized. Most municipalities require that food workers be examined by health authorities, and carry a health card attesting to the fact that that individual is "licensed" as a food handler. It is for your protection, and in your best interest, that you enforce this regulation.

Also, remember that the individual who is in charge of the dishwashing operation, and to whom responsibility for proper sterilization is entrusted, is one of the most important people in your entire organization. Thus, it is a prime responsibility to select for this position a person *who knows and accepts this responsibility and is conscientious in fulfilling it.*

Since improperly and inadequately washed dishes, glassware, and silverware can be a source of infection with often serious consequences, this person's value to your organization must never be minimized. Furthermore, his/her responsibility should entail not only sanitation of eating ware, but also machine maintenance, and proper storage of all equipment once it has been properly sanitized.

Thus, selection of a responsible individual to head such a department would be a wise and excellent investment. But to guarantee yourself a dependable, conscientious, and competent employee, be sure to offer this person a salary that is commensurate with the responsibility.

CLEANING

Definite cleaning schedules must be established for: floors, counters, cabinets, sinks, stoves, ovens, broilers, steam jackets, refrigerators, freezers, walls, and windows.

Containers used for transporting food must be easily cleanable metal or plastic, so they can be cleaned and *sterilized* after each service. They should also have tight-fitting covers. If such covers are not available, heavy aluminum foil is an effective substitute. Original plastic bags *should never be reused* for carrying or covering foodstuffs.

Boil or steam out all gas burners at least once each week. Drip pans should be lined with heavy foil to catch overflows and to make cleaning easier.

Steam cleaning is fast and much more effective than other conventional methods. But if permanent steam lines are not available, investigate the possibility of buying one of the small, "fixed," portable steam generators currently on the market.

A heavy duty, tank-type vacuum cleaner with a 10- by 12-ft. flexible hose is an invaluable tool for use for both sanitation and cleaning tasks. Not only can it be used for hard-to-get-at areas, but also frequently and effectively on refrigerator coils to keep them from plugging up with dust, as well as for the superficial cleaning of filters. Additionally, tank-type liquid absorption, vacuum machines are most effective for use on asphalt and quarry tile concrete, and other such surfaces.

PROPER SANITATION IS BENEFICIAL

Since careless operations and lack of cleanliness can lead to damage claims against your business, you should place as much emphasis on sanitation standards as you do on food quality and cost control. Moreover, proper sanitation: (1) saves money; (2) saves time; (3) aids safety; (4) improves food quality and service, and (5) projects a favorable public image for both management and personnel.

A Money Saver

Properly maintained and used utensils/equipment last longer.

Foods stored, refrigerated, prepared, and served according to sanitary rules prevent waste, enhance quality, improve appearance, and increase customer acceptability.

The danger of food poisoning, with its consequent cost to management, is minimized.

A Time Saver

The sanitary way is the *right* way and experience has shown the right way is both the best and the quickest way.

Consistent practice in proper sanitary methods has proved this.

An Aid to Safety

Regular mopping times and proper methods reduce the possibility of falls caused by wet, slippery floors.

Similarly, when floors are kept clean, employees avoid the risk of slipping on dropped and spilled pieces of food.

Correct methods of handling sharp knives, dishes, glassware, and silverware reduce the danger of cuts and subsequent infection.

Strict adherence to sanitary procedures also prevents transmission of illnesses commonly associated with foodservice.

A Way to Improve Food Quality and Service

In addition to preventing the serving of contaminated food, safe food and clean equipment/utensils ensure a truly appetizing food flavor.

Sanitary service is *correct* service. Make sure your employees realize this, as it will aid them in developing the confidence, poise, and pride inherent in quality service.

And, remember, high quality food and service are the basis for building a successful catering business.

A Way of Projecting a Favorable Public Image

A clean, sanitary establishment always creates a favorable atmosphere. Your customers are certain to notice appearance and the use of correct serving methods by trained foodservice workers.

The goal of a good sanitation program is to prevent food-borne illnesses, food poisonings, and food infections.

The following edited list of food protection suggestions, taken from Treva Richardson's book, *Sanitation for Foodservice Workers,*[1] will be helpful in eliminating food contamination and spoilage.

1. All food purchases should be made from sources approved by local, state, and/or federal health authorities and protected from contamination/spoilage during handling, packaging, storage, and while in transit.

2. Shellfish, meat and meat products, poultry and poultry meat products should be purchased from properly inspected sources and so stamped or tagged.

3. Use and serve pasteurized fluid milk and fluid milk products only. Dry milk products may be reconstituted if used solely in and for cooking purposes. Serve milk and fluid milk products for drinking purposes in the individual containers in which they were packaged at the milk processing plant.

Serve cream, whipped cream, or half-and-half either in original containers or from an approved dispenser.

PREVENTING CONTAMINATION OF FOOD

1. Wash and scrub all vegetables carefully, but especially those to be used in salads or eaten raw because they may contain residuals from chemical sprays.

2. Examine canned food for bulges, dents, leakage, and other distortions prior to use. Open cans having either an odd odor or an unusual appearance should be inspected immediately by you or some other responsible person.

3. Custard- or cream-filled pastries must be refrigerated *imme-*

---

1. Treva M. Richardson, *Sanitation for Foodservice Workers* (Boston: Cahners Books, 1974), pp. 38-42, 128-29.

diately or, if time is short, quick-chilled in a freezer first before serving. But, whenever practicable, test with a thermometer to make certain center is cooled. According to health authorities, when only temporary refrigeration is possible, custard-filled pastries should be rebaked for 30 minutes at 375°F. before being served.

4. Refrigerate sandwiches containing potentially hazardous food, such as egg, ham, poultry salads, and similar fillings.

5. Cook pork until well done (150°F. or above in center of mass). Test with meat thermometer.

6. Thoroughly cook all foods, stirring and mixing frequently to assure that heat is uniform throughout.

7. After preparation, do not allow food to remain at room temperature for any length of time before serving. Temporary holding periods are 45°F. or below, or 140°F. or above.

8. Test the temperature of food on steam tables to be certain it is not below 140°F.

9. Heat leftovers thoroughly; do not merely warm. Keep leftovers for one day only and *never* mix them with fresh food to "extend" supply. Remember that ground, minced foods are especially easy to contaminate because much of the food is exposed during the grinding process.

10. Correct washing and sanitizing of dishes, eating utensils, and all equipment or surfaces that come in contact with food are absolutely essential for proper protection.

11. Use small, shallow pans to refrigerate food rather than one large, deep container. For storage purposes, pans three or four inches in depth are suggested.

12. Chemicals, sanitizers, and other cleaning materials should not be kept in food preparation areas. All cleaning materials and tools should be stored in a cabinet used especially for that purpose. Also, do not wash scrub mops in dishwashing or pot sinks.

13. Hands and arms should be washed thoroughly before beginning work, after coughs or sneezes, after handling soiled dishes and utensils, or after cleaning/handling poultry or raw meat.

14. While food is in the kitchen, protect it from droplet infection, flies, dust, etc., by keeping it covered.

15. Never put a spoon used for tasting back into the food.

16. Keep fingers away from mouth, lips, face, and soiled surfaces.

Do not handle foods that can be picked up with tongs, scoops, forks, or spoons. Avoid mixing salads and ground meat with the hands, and never work with food if you have a sore, boil, or infected cut on your hands or arms.

In some areas, foodservice workers wear disposable plastic gloves while preparing or dispensing foods such as cooked meats used in sandwiches, hamburger patties, wieners, bread, buns, cookies, vegetable sticks, and fresh fruit.

However, merely wearing gloves does not guarantee a sanitary situation; hence management and employees should not get a false sense of security or relax their alertness on required sanitation procedures.

When making sandwiches, a disposable plastic glove can be worn on the hand which touches cooked meat, but should *not* be worn on the hand holding a knife or operating a slicer. Furthermore, workers must understand and follow carefully the safety rules for using the slicer guard and picking up the cooked meat.

If sandwich making is temporarily interrupted, the plastic glove should be discarded and a new one put on when work is resumed.

If worn for a long period, plastic gloves—like hands—can become contaminated. For example, hands can brush against the hair, rub the eyes, scratch the nose, or be wiped on soiled towels.

It is suggested that disposable plastic gloves be discarded when they become cut, punctured, or obviously soiled. In fact, it would be safest to change them frequently when continuously preparing or dispensing foods. Similarly, plastic gloves should be changed after the worker has handled raw poultry or meat, and before he/she handles other foods.

17. Store food above the floor.

18. Do not smoke while preparing food.

19. Refrigerate milk and milk products at all times.

20. Milk containers, bottled drinks, and fruit juices kept cold in ice should never be covered by melting ice water. The reason is simple; if ice water penetrates the containers, the contents could become contaminated.

21. Preparation and work tables should be cleaned frequently with a germicidal detergent solution.

SEWAGE CONTAMINATION

1. Overhead drainage pipes should not be located over work tables, refrigerators, or places where unprotected food is stored. If they are, sheet metal drip pans should be suspended below them to catch condensation and sewage drippings, particularly at joints. Unprotected food should never rest on the floor where it would be subject to contamination from overflow or flooding.

2. A refrigerator should drain through a trap to the open and then into the sewer. There *must not* be a direct connection to the

sewer. This blocking off any connection to the sewer is done to prevent a backflow of sewage due to any stoppage and to prevent cockroaches, rats, or sewer gases from entering from the sewer.

3. Drinking water can become contaminated, especially if other floors are above your establishment. Therefore, local inspectors from the City Sanitary Engineer's office will inspect piping arrangements to be sure that no sewage or contaminated water can be siphoned off into your drinking water supply.

PROTECTING FOOD AGAINST RODENTS AND INSECTS

1. All outside openings must be sealed to prevent the entrance of rodents.
2. Remove rodent nesting places.
3. Protect food by keeping it in covered containers.
4. Use only approved insecticides.
5. Inspect all produce in bags and crates for roaches; other pests.
6. Seal pipe openings, cracks, and crevices.
7. Eliminate insect breeding places.
8. Put garbage in closed metal containers with tight-fitting lids.
9. If possible, use a trash compactor.
10. *Practice Good Housekeeping and Be Eternally Vigilant!*

SUCCESSFUL ATTITUDES

The success of any sanitation program, however, depends to a large extent on the attitudes and actions of the catering staff as a whole. Management must instill in employees the realization that good sanitation practices are not only essential to their health, but also to the people who avail themselves of the services they provide. Plant sanitation and personal cleanliness are an integral part of good food production and service, and both require constant vigilance by employer and employee.

In planning and implementing your sanitation program, provide for good supervision and employee training. Many excellent sources of information are available to aid in the development of such a program. Local health department sanitarians can be of great help, as can your State Health Department. Its library will be able to provide listings of movies and other materials offered by the various governmental health agencies.

Another excellent source of information and advice is the Center for Disease Control, U. S. Dept. of Health, Education and Welfare, Public Health Service, Training Program, Community Services Training Section, Atlanta, Ga. 30333.

Several well-known manufacturers of foodservice industry equipment and supplies have produced films and film strips on sanitation routines for their products. These clear, practical depictions of correct procedures are well worth viewing by both management and personnel. Ask your dishmachine and detergent field technicians for information.

Write the Environmental Health Committee, Single Service Institute, 250 Park Avenue, New York, N. Y. 10017 for copies of its posters, handbook, and other printed material.

You may also contact: The International Sanitary Supply Assn., 5330 N. Elston Avenue, Chicago, Ill. 60630. A variety of worthwhile sanitation material is available to customers of member firms.

The National Restaurant Assn., Educational Materials Center, 1 IBM Plaza, Suite 2600, Chicago, Ill. 60611 has available a list of food sanitation material developed by its organization.

The National Sanitation Foundation, P. O. Box 1468, Ann Arbor, Mich. 48106 has published *A Reference Manual of Food Service Sanitation Educational and Training Materials* that any owner or manager would find very helpful. It is available at a moderate cost.

Contracting for Catered Services/8

BECAUSE OF THE varied circumstances under which off-premise catering is performed, many factors must be considered in setting your price for an affair. They include:

1. Condition and location of the dining/service areas
2. Required equipment
3. Distance from your commissary and food
4. Labor and overhead costs

DETERMINING CHARGES

Use the following suggestions as a guide but modify them to suit the requirements of your own operation:

Get a minimum number guarantee for guests

This is a major factor. If guests are few in number, your charges must, of necessity, be much greater. If there are too few guests anticipated, it may not even pay you to book the party.

Take, as an example, a Sunday dinner at a private home for 20 persons. If there is a $12.50 per person charge for food and service, your gross receipts would be $250 (20 x $12.50). Deducting 33 percent for food costs and 38 percent for payroll costs (a total of $177.50) would leave you with $72.50 to cover costs for transportation, laundry, china, equipment, rent, light, heat, insurance, and other related items. As a result, you might well feel that you had wasted a day and worked for practically nothing. Consider, too, the time spent negotiating for the party, plus the fact that you may have also made a few costly phone calls for additional details.

Thus, judge each party on both its gross and net profit. In Social Catering, do not count on large parties carrying smaller ones. Each affair must be treated separately and each must be profitable.

What will food costs be?

At the time of this writing (1973-74), accountants specializing in foodservice estimate that a realistic food cost figure for off-premise caterers should not be more than 35 percent. Although restaurants, hotels, and other eating places may safely spend up to 42 percent, the profit spread for Social Caterers must be greater.

A catering business is sporadic; moreover, the work is much more physically demanding than work in fixed eating areas. Unlike many other foodservice operators, a caterer cannot reuse leftovers for next day luncheon or dinner menus.

Determining your labor charges

Since you are emphasizing service as well as food, you must analyze the personnel requirements of each function. How many employees and how much time will be needed for food preparation? How much time is required for travel? Service? Set up and break down?* With all these points to consider, a 38 percent payroll cost is realistic.

Think in terms of distance

How far is the party location from your commissary? How long will the round trip take?

If using your cars/trucks for transporting food and equipment, incorporate their per-mile cost into your total charges. To determine a fair charge, check with local car and truck rental agencies for their rates.

Compute charges for your personal services

Too many caterers forget to charge for their personal services, which can be a costly omission. Skill and ability must be rewarded, and the

---

*Some union contracts stipulate a lower rate for set-up and breakdown time and a higher rate for actual service time. When in effect, this contract works on a rotating basis so that all employees have an opportunity to put in extra time on set up and breakdown.

value of your personal services should be double that of your highest paid employee.

Since *you are the leader* and must organize each part of the event to produce successful results, your true worth would become immediately obvious if you were unable to handle a scheduled affair due to illness or an emergency. Someone else would have to replace you and this person would, of course, have to be paid. However, if your estimate did not include a charge for your services, then your profit would be reduced substantially.

Set a use charge for dishes, glasses, and other equipment

Check your packing list for the quantity of dishes, glasses, and other units required for the job and charge for their use. You cannot afford to ignore the costs involved in packing, transporting, washing, storing, and replacing damaged equipment. To figure equipment-use charges, contact local rental agencies listed in the yellow pages of the phone book. Compare quality and cost, and if your dishes/other equipment are of a higher quality, your charges should be greater.

Review factors in delivery

This factor is often overlooked in computing charges. Consider such labor- and time-consuming factors as: a location inconvenient for loading or unloading; inability to use the driveway, or not being able to "dolly" equipment and, instead, having to carry or tote it up and down steps. Since it costs *you* more to set up and break down, these costs must be passed along to your client. (Incidentally dollies, if used, should be rubber-tired to reduce noise and to prevent surface marring.)

Is there an elevator?

If the party is to be held in an area accessible only by elevator, allow extra time for equipment delivery and return. Elevator space is limited, and only so much goods can be moved at one time. If the elevator must be shared with tenants or other freight, the wait between loads can be agonizing and expensive.

When an elevator must be used, notify the building superintendent beforehand to be sure it will be available when you need it. (To express appreciation and thanks for assistance, you may wish to give a gratuity to the superintendent.) To prevent scratching the elevator or damages to your equipment, insist that the elevator be "padded." (Padding simply means that buffer blankets are hung from hooks screwed into the walls near the ceiling of the elevator.)

What is to be the duration of the party?

When guests insist on "hanging around" after a party is over, it generally indicates that the affair was successful. However, these guests can prevent you from cleaning up, and removing equipment as per contract or understanding, which can cut sharply into your profits.

Therefore, prior to the affair, make it clear to the host, either orally or in writing, that you will serve only a specified number of hours. If the host subsequently asks you to remain longer, you must be paid for that time.

A home cocktail party usually lasts from three to four hours. A formal dinner should not last more than four hours, including speeches and entertainment. Considering set-up and breakdown time, as well as commissary return time, you and your employees will spend more than one-third of a day at a party.

In summary, to estimate the cost of a catered meal, it is necessary to determine the costs of the following:

1. Total amount of raw food to be used
2. Personnel required for food preparation service, set-up and breakdown, transporting, and clean up
3. Equipment usage
4. Overhead—utilities, rents, insurance, etc.
5. Party service time—mileage, delivery, service
6. Expected profit

To obtain the per-person, per-meal charge, divide this total figure by the number of guests to be served. (See Figure 1 on facing page.)

CONTRACTS AND DEPOSITS

Practically every business activity involves a contract—a *binding agreement* between two or more parties. This is also defined as "an agreement creating an obligation."

In other words, the caterer is obligated to supply the food and service implied or detailed. The client, on the other hand, is obligated to pay for food, and the specific/implied services *if satisfactory!* If either party fails to fulfill its obligation, then the other party may have the right to legal recourse.

Each and every "job," unless intended as a gift, *must have a contract,* even if it is to be done for a close friend or relative. You should not be embarrassed to require execution of a contract. You can explain that it is your firm business policy, and that you consider it inadvisable to digress from established procedure.

Furthermore, putting agreements in writing assures smooth and pleasant client relationships. A contract, written in even the faintest ink, is tangible, and more readily acceptable than the most indelible memory. (A contract can be simple—see Figure 2—or complete and minutely detailed—see Figures 3 and 4.)

FIGURE 1—FACTORS IN DETERMINING CHARGES

CATERING INCOME	100	percent
DIRECT COSTS		
Food and supplies	26	percent
Payroll	38	percent
Payroll taxes	—	
Purchased services	6.2	percent
TOTAL DIRECT COSTS	-70.2	percent
GROSS PROFIT	29.8	percent

OPERATING EXPENSES
Advertising and promotion
Auto and delivery expenses
Bank charges
Contributions
Depreciation: auto and trucks
Depreciation: furniture and fixtures
Freight and express
Gas
Water
Insurance
Laundry and cleaning
Light and heat
Maintenance and repairs
Permits, licenses, and fees
Professional services: accountant, lawyer
Refuse removal
Rent
Equipment rental
Replacement of china, silver, etc.
Stationery and office supplies
Taxes: property, state, and business
Telephone
Miscellaneous

TOTAL OPERATING EXPENSES	-15	percent
NET INCOME	14.8	percent

SUMMATION:

Catering income	100	percent
Minus direct costs	-70.2	percent
Gross profit	29.8	percent
Operating expenses	-15	percent
NET PROFIT	14.8	percent

FIGURE 2–SAMPLE CONTRACT
JOHN DOE CATERING COMPANY
45 Spring Street
Hyde Park, New York 12538
Phone: (914) 452-9600

CONTRACT

THIS AGREEMENT, made and entered into this _____ day of

_____ 19__, by and between JOHN DOE, doing business

as the JOHN DOE CATERING CO. (hereinafter called "Caterer"), and

_____ of _____ , _____
                                        city   state

(hereinafter called "Purchaser").

WITNESSETH

In consideration of this Agreement, the parties hereto agree as follows:

1) The Caterer agrees to cater an affair according to menus submitted and mutually agreed upon on the day and date of _____ 19__ at _____ commencing at _____ a.m. ____ p.m.
      place

2) The Purchaser agrees to pay the sum of $_____ per each guest guaranteed. Guarantee for number of guests to be confirmed in writing by the Purchaser at least five (5) days before the affair. (Caterer will not accept guarantees for less than 100 guests.)

3) The Caterer will be prepared to serve five percent (5%) more guests should the occasion warrant.

4) The Caterer acknowledges receipt of a deposit of $_____ and the Purchaser agrees to pay the balance upon presentation of bill, immediately upon the completion of service. Adjustments, if any, either by the Purchaser or the Caterer will be fully made by either party within 72 hours.

DATED AT _____ this day of ____ 19__

John Doe, for John Doe Catering Co. _____

Purchaser _____

Purchaser _____

FIGURE 3—SAMPLE CONTRACT

CONTRACT

JOHN DOE CATERING COMPANY

Poughkeepsie, New York 12538

Banquet or Party Function Contract

AGREEMENT between JOHN DOE CATERING CO., hereinafter called the <u>Caterer</u>, and _____ Date: _____, 19___

_____, hereinafter called <u>Patron</u>.

Full Name of Patron _____ Phone Number _____

_____

address   city   state   zip code

If club or organization, give name: _____

Principal address: _____

Club president's name _____ Club treasurer's name _____

_____

address   address

(Cont.)

FIGURE 3–SAMPLE CONTRACT (Cont.)

Committee representatives: Names/addresses

name _____ address _____

name _____ address _____

name _____ address _____

Guarantor: _____ Address: _____

Date of Function: _____ Hours: from _____ to _____

Area of Function _____

Minimum number of guests guaranteed _____ Price per guest _____

Extra charges as attached . . . . $ _____

Anticipated total bill . . . . $ _____

1.) IT IS FURTHER AGREED as a condition precedent of the agreement that the patron will pay 25 percent (25%) of anticipated total bill as computed above upon acceptance of this contract.

2.) All details of the Menu are set forth in letter dated _____ and attached extra charges which are made part hereof.

3.) Patron agrees to inform Caterer at least 48 hours in advance, in writing, as to definite number guaranteed. Caterer will be prepared to serve five percent (5%) increase above guarantee.

4.) This contract is subject to the terms and conditions printed on reverse side hereof and expressly made a part hereof.

Signature _____ Signature _____

Witness _____ Witness _____

REVERSE SIDE OF CONTRACT

1.) All federal, state and municipal taxes applicable to this function shall be paid for separately by the patron, in addition to prices herein agreed upon.

2.) The caterer will exercise all reasonable care in security of liquor supplied by patron and will furnish bartenders to dispense such liquor. However, the patron will not hold caterer liable if theft, breakage or vandalism should occur— or any other acts beyond reasonable care by caterer.

3.) Should affair be held in a facility with a liquor license held by the rentor, then all security and/or liquor service shall in no way involve the caterer.

4.) Patron agrees to begin function promptly at the scheduled time and to vacate premises at the closing hour indicated. The patron further agrees to reimburse the caterer for overtime wage payments or other expenses incurred by the caterer because of patron's failure to comply with these regulations.

5.) Patron assumes responsibility for any and all damages caused by any guest, invitee or other person attending the function.

6.) It is understood that patron will conduct function in an orderly manner and in full compliance with all applicable laws, ordinances and regulations (and any special requirements of rentor if set forth in contract).

7.) Patron agrees to reimburse the caterer for any extra meals requested for orchestra, entertainers, security, etc.

8.) Patron agrees to supply caterer with a tentative floor plan at least one week prior to the affair and a definite floor (and seating) plan no later than 48 hours before affair.

9.) In the event of breach of this agreement by patron, the caterer may keep the deposit and patron shall be obliged to reimburse caterer for any damage costs incurred by reason of breach thereof.

10.) This agreement is contingent upon the absence of strikes, labor disputes, accidents or any causes beyond control. The caterer also reserves the right to make reasonable substitutions if unable to secure specified items . . . but will make substitutions upon explanation and notification to patron.

11.) This agreement is not assignable.

FIGURE 4–ON-PREMISE CATERING CONTRACT

FUNCTION AGREEMENT FOR JOHN DOE CATERERS
Anystreet, Anywhere, U. S. A.
(This contract must be signed and accepted to guarantee function)

Name of Company or Function _____

Address _____ City _____ Phone _____

Individual guaranteeing payment _____

Address _____ City _____ Phone _____

Tentative number of guests guaranteed _____

Room or Facility or Area for Function _____

Day _____ Date _____ Time _____

Menu number _____

Extras, Specify and price for each _____

_____

_____

( ) Cash bar _____ ( ) Open bar _____ ( ) Bottle price _____

Time _____

Cake price $ _____   Orchestra $ _____   Flowers $ _____

To be paid by: _____ ( ) Check _____ ( ) Cash _____ ( ) Certified check _____

Accepted by: (For John Doe Caterers) _____

Customer's signature _____

TERMS AND CONDITIONS (Please read carefully)

1.) A minimum deposit of $1.00 per person must be made—for each person.
2.) Guaranteed number to be served must be submitted within three days of function. (CHARGE WILL BE MADE EVEN IF LESS ATTEND)
3.) ALL TAXES AND GRATUITIES MUST BE ADDED TO ALL PRICES QUOTED.
4.) Guaranteed number must be paid in full 3 days before affair.
5.) Contract must be signed and accepted to guarantee reservation. CREDIT CARDS ARE NOT ACCEPTABLE.
6.) Card-playing, gambling or showing of objectionable films PROHIBITED.
7.) Guests attending function but not eating will be charged $1.00 each.
8.) Function running beyond specified time will be charged extra $1.00 guest.
9.) In the event of prohibitive weather, occurring within 24 hours of affair, you have the choice of:
   a.) Holding the affair and paying only for the food and liquor consumed by attending guests plus the miscellaneous items on the guaranteed minimum. (Examples: Flowers, linens, gratuities, service fees, music, check room, cake, printing, etc.)
   b.) If you decide on a postponement with a confirmed date within thirty (30) days, no additional costs will be incurred by you.

Contracts are also valuable business documents: they can be used as collateral if you wish to borrow money for your business, and are also considered tangible assets in the sale of a business.

Under the terms of the contract, customer signing and acceptance requires (a) that the *host make a deposit*, which should be *no less than 25 percent of the anticipated bill*, and (b) that the balance of the bill must be paid upon completion of the affair. The reasons for this are sound. You, the caterer, incur considerable expense in properly completing your part of the contract. You must not only purchase, store, process, and deliver foods, but guarantee to perform a highly specialized service.

On-Premise Catering /9

ACCORDING TO ESTIMATES, customers spend two-thirds of their total foodservice expenditures in restaurant and hotel/motel dining rooms. The remaining one-third is spent in drive-ins and fast food establishments. Public eating places, individually and company-owned, represent the greatest number of U. S. retail outlets.

In vying for their share of the market, many restaurants and hotels use special promotions, which offer lower prices for certain foods on set days. Children's birthday parties, which are encouraged, include such special offers as birthday cakes, party favors, and menus that can be converted into carry-out toys (often displaying the restaurant's name in some conspicuous spot).

These promotions are nearly always aimed at *basic daily meal periods*—breakfast, lunch and/or dinner.

However, after peak periods, the average restaurant or hotel dining room is usually empty. Although they are attractive, comfortable, and air-conditioned eating places, they are nearly devoid of customers.

This presents a serious difficulty. The facility must be maintained, lighted, and heated. Furthermore, it is staffed with cooking and baking specialists who are not busy. With imagination and by greater utilization of working tools, these difficulties can be converted into assets by promoting on-premise catering.

Getting Your Operation Known

To start, you might attach clip-ons to regular daily menus explaining that your facilities are available for wedding breakfasts, bridge parties, sales meetings, service/fraternal club banquets, etc. Table tents at each table can elaborate on your on-premise catering or cite special prices. You can also have professionally lettered posters made up and posted in prominent positions. If you have to make space for them, often you have only to remove signs installed by cigarette and beverage salesmen and *PUT UP YOUR OWN SIGNS*, which *advertise your products and services.*

If you use floor stanchions to control traffic while guests wait to be seated, use part of them as a message board to display pictures of your buffet presentations, or a fully set guest table for a catered party. A handsomely decorated wedding or birthday cake (with dummy layers) placed in an appropriate location can be worth more than a thousand words.

Another possibility is to have a sign painter make an extra panel for your outdoor sign. The panel should contain, in addition to the word catering, a strong, positive adjective or a descriptive phrase, but not just a single word. Some examples include: Distinctive On-Premise Catering, Unexcelled Catering Facilities, Attractive Rates For Catering, Celebrate Your Next Happy Occasion With Us, or Ask About Special Rates.*

BANQUET HALL/ROOMS

Because of initial costs involved in building or renting and equipping a facility, most on-premise caterers were originally successful off-premise caterers before they expanded their services and moved into banquet hall/rooms operations.

A banquet-hall caterer can offer the same services as a restaurant/ hotel catering department. In addition to a commissary/kitchen, the caterer's facilities will include at least one large, tastefully decorated, air-conditioned room containing a stage or raised dais. He or she might also have several smaller rooms, which can be offered to small, informal groups for bridal showers, ladies' luncheons, business luncheons, and other such functions.

---

*For additional ideas, see "Creating A Market, Selling A Service" section in Chapter 1.

The banquet hall/rooms should be equipped with the following items:
    A public address system plus lecterns
    Enough tables and chairs for full-capacity seating
    Table coverings—cloths and napkins
    Dishes, glassware, and flatware
    Waiters' trays and tray stands
    Special foodservice items—chafing dishes, wine holders, and buffet service trays, etc.
    Screens and projectors for showing movies and slides
    Adequate lighting and spotlights
    Clean, accessible rest rooms
    Attractive dressing rooms for fashion show models and brides
    Checkrooms for coats
    Ample and accessible storage equipment space
    Adequate and convenient-for-use areas for food delivery, preparation, and service
    Ample parking facilities
    A competent janitorial crew
    Readily available electricians, plumbers, and carpenters

To attract customers, a banquet-hall caterer must make full use of the many and various forms of advertising.*

As soon as his services are retained by a client, the banquet-hall caterer, as well as any other Social Caterer, must then provide the agreed upon service with courtesy, efficiency, and "flair." Satisfied and well-pleased customers mean repeat business. Their "word-of-mouth" advertising is invaluable as it may well generate new business.

---

*For additional ideas, see "Creating A Market, Selling A Service" in Chapter 1.

Accommodator Service (In-Home Cooking and Serving)/10

THIS TYPE OF business, as stated earlier, has often been the starting point for many successful caterers. (The accommodator is not to be confused with *In-Home Catering*, which is detailed in another chapter.)

The client supplies the facilities, food, and equipment, while the caterer prepares and cooks *all* food *on* the client's premises.

Therefore, you need not equip a commissary; obtain Board of Health permits; register with the State Sales Tax Department; own trucks or other expensive rolling equipment; get involved in complex bookkeeping procedures, or have compensation and liability insurance.

The only investment required is a set of good working tools, baking necessities, two or three sets of working "whites" (uniforms), and a polyurethane cutting board.

FEES

Accommodator catering can be done on a part-time basis to provide you with a second income, or it can develop into a full-time occupation.

As an accommodator, you may charge a flat rate, or charge by the hour. If charging an hourly rate, your fee for consultation, preparation, and clean up should be less than the charge for time spent during the actual function.

EXAMPLE: Figures given are for this illustration only.

Consultation with host or committee		
for planning of function	2 hours @ $6.00	12.00
Preparation on day of function	4 hours @ $6.00	24.00
Time spent on service during the		
function	3 hours @ $9.00	27.00
Clean up	1½ hours @ $6.00	9.00
TOTAL FEE FOR FUNCTION		$72.00

The host/client pays the accommodator the full rate without deductions. You, the caterer, are then obligated to report this amount on your federal and/or state income tax returns.

RECOMMENDATIONS

The following recommendations will be of value, if you intend to specialize in In-Home Cooking and Serving:

1. Discuss the menu for the affair in the home of the host, or in the area where you will be doing the cooking. In this way, both you and your client will be aware of limitations in the service and production areas.

2. After deciding on the menu, determine the quantities of food you will need, and what additional dishes and equipment must be secured. Insist, if possible, that the host/client handle all rentals and purchases. Thus, you cannot be accused of "padding the bill," or of giving short weights. In addition, you will not have to use your car or spend your time on shopping. Time is money, and it is costly to operate a car. Therefore, if you must do the purchasing, be sure to charge for the time involved, as well as for the use of your car.

3. When your client purchases the food, it will be his/her responsibility to provide refrigeration and storage.

4. Any breakage or other loss that occurs from the time of purchase until the time of the actual event is also the responsibility of the host, if she/he makes the purchase.

5. Liability for injuries incurred on the client's premises is not the responsibility of the accommodator. It is generally covered by the host's homeowner's policy.

6. If you need extra help for the party, have the host hire workers

on a direct basis. In this way, the host assumes liability, and you are absolved from legal responsibility.

7. Do not transport additional help to the party location, and then charge them for transportation. If you do this, you could be in violation of local transportation ordinances. This could possibly lead to prosecution, or be in violation of your personal automobile coverage. Therefore, you would be wise to discuss this point with your attorney, the local public utility authority, and/or your insurance company.

8. *Remain until the party is over and assist with final clean up.* You should not only make certain that your own work area is left in immaculate condition, but also should assist the host with total clean up. This will gain you his/her appreciation, and could lead to repeat business in the future.

9. *A WORD OF CAUTION* is needed in regard to liquor. Liquor laws are strict in many communities, and you must exercise great caution. If there are to be alcoholic beverages at the function, have the host purchase and bring them to the place of service. Do not pick it up "on your way." There can also be a great deal of unpleasantness in the handling and dispensing of liquor. Thus, *never serve liquor to someone who is under the legal age, or to someone who obviously already has had too much.*

10. When arranging the menu, do not let yourself be talked in to preparing part or all of the food in *your own home.* If you prepare food in your home for eventual sale, you are breaking the law. Your home is strictly residential and is not zoned for business . . . no matter how small and insignificant the business. From a safety standpoint, preparing food in your home could create a potentially hazardous situation. Should you have a fire, your regular household insurance carrier will not honor your claim because of this technicality. (Look at your insurance policy. It specifically states that your premises are covered as *residential* property only.)

Also, should you be transporting home-prepared food to the job and become involved in an auto accident, your claim *may not be honored.* Your automobile insurance policy probably states that your car is specifically insured for pleasure purposes only and *not* for business purposes.

Off-Premise Catering / 11

THE MOST IMPORTANT primary step in off-premise catering is the preparation of a proper packing list. An itemized packing list (Figure 1, pp. 91-93) should be prepared for each off-premise job. Such a list can serve as a guide for assembling items to be used or packed for the upcoming event.

PACKING LISTS

When preparing the list, have the menu in front of you; then study each course to determine equipment needs. Inform your scheduler, or packer, as to the availability of dishwashing facilities, and whether you must take personnel to the job location to operate the machines.

If dishwashing facilities are available, then you will probably not need to pack as much equipment. As an example, if you are serving a 150-guest party, you will need highball glasses, which are normally packed 6 by 6, or 36 glasses to a rack. Where washing facilities are available, you could safely pack five (5) racks of glasses, giving you a total of 180 glasses, knowing that you can keep glasses clean as needed.

When dirty glasses are returned, accumulate them until you have enough for one rack, at which time they can be washed and returned to the bar. By the time they are ready to be used again, they will not only be clean, but cool enough so that beverages can be poured into them.

Without dishwashing facilities, on the other hand, you would have to pack at least 10 racks of glasses, which would take up more truck space and require additional time for packing.

This same principle applies to other items. For example, the under-liner used in the starter course can be used again, after washing, for the dessert course.

The packing list also serves as a record of where equipment was previously used. It pinpoints time and place and, if a particular piece of equipment is missing, can make the task of getting it back much easier.

Make notations on each packing list as to its accuracy, missing items, condition of equipment, and all other pertinent comments. *Do not destroy* the packing list but keep it with all other permanent records of that particular affair.

Miscellaneous Pointers

• In each truck, always have a broom, shovel, dust pan, mop, pail with squeegee, and a number of large heavy-duty plastic bags.

• Carry two pairs of work gloves for use in the event of mechanical breakdowns or for handling garbage cans and other such items.

• A good First Aid kit is a wise investment. It should be carried at all times, and include pamphlets explaining what to do in emergencies. These pamphlets are readily obtainable from all Red Cross offices.

• As an off-premise caterer, you may work in sparsely travelled areas or in unusual facilities (fairgrounds, isolated beach areas, picnic groves, party boats, and so on). Thus, a *portable oxygen inhalator* could prove to be a valuable addition for the first aid kit.

• Your catering tool box should be equipped with at least TWO can openers, which can be mounted or hook-fastened on a board or in a specific container. Remember, since electric power is not always available, include at least one manually operated opener together with the portable electric model. Nothing is more frustrating than trying to open a can and then learning you do not have a usable opener available.

• Many caterers find it advisable to carry several sturdy 30-in. square, folding tables. Those with 1-in. plywood tops are useful as extenders for regular 6- and 8-ft. tables. They are also useful for displaying wedding cakes and for use in preparation areas as extra work tables.

FIGURE 1—PACKING LIST

Job no. . . . . Supervisor . . . . Packed in truck no. . . . . .
To be packed by, day . . . . . , date . . . . . Scheduled by . . . .

JOHN DOE CATERING CO.		HYDE PARK, N. Y.	
PACK	**RET'D.**	**PACK**	**RET'D.**
Service plates		Lg. round silver trays	
Dinner plates		Lg. square silver trays	
7-in. plates		Lg. oval silver trays	
Bread and butters		Small ovals . . . Smaller	
Monkey dishes		Russian serving trays	
Coffee cups			
Saucers		Stainless bowls . . . size	
Bouillon cups		Stainless pans . . . lg.	
Relish dishes, china .		St. serving ladles small .	
Silver . .		Ice cream scoops, size .	
Casseroles, type . .			
Gravy boats, china .		Chef's tools (1. . .)(2 . . . . .)	
Silver . .		Bar tools	
Indiv. salad bowls		All-purpose tool box	
Demitasse combos		First aid kit	
Supremes		Stainless bar pitchers	

(Cont.)

FIGURE 1–PACKING LIST (Cont.)

PACK	RET'D.		PACK	RET'D.
		Rings for supremes		
		Insets, glass . . .		
		Silver . . .		
		Teaspoons	Gueridons	
		Bouillon spoons	Portable bars . . . 1 . . . 2 . . . 3 .	
		Salad forks	Stirrers	
		Dessert forks	Coasters	
		Oyster forks	Waste Baskets	
		Dinner knives	Garbage cans	
		Butter knives	Garbage liners	
		Demitasse spoons	Table numbers	
		Serving forks	Portable fry pots	
		Tongs	Silver chafing dishes, lg.. . small .	
			Marmite stands and insets	
		Water goblets	Rechaud burners	
		Hi-balls	Alcohol for burner fuel, lg. . . . small	
		Lo-balls	Electric extensions	
		All-purpose wines	Westinghouse ovens	
		Sherry glasses	Gas grills . . . . . Tank gas .	
		Manhattans	Skirts, color	
		Champagnes, saucer . .	Lace overlay	
		Tulip . . .	White cloths, size	
		Cordials	Colored cloths . . . size .	
			Silent cloths	
			Lace tablecloths	
			Chef coats	
			Aprons, bib . . . . half .	

Silver bread trays
Silver crumbers
Salt and peppers
Ash trays
Lg. mahogany salads
Small   ”
Silver water pitchers
Silver tea pitchers
Silver creamers
Silver sugar bowls
Silver dandy dishes
Silver coupes
Revere bowls, size
Silver ice bowls
Silver compotes
Silver coffee urns
Silver punch bowls
Silver candelabra
Silver ladles
Silver vegetable dishes

Frill picks
Plain picks
Ferns
Smilax
Flowers

Side towels
Bar jackets . . . . . Waiters
Corsage pins
Stapler
Candles . . . . . color
Cocktail napkins . . . color
Doilies . . . size . . . color
Place mats
Treated punch cups (cold)
Styrofoam cups
Folding table tops
Ice carving pans . . . tongs
Ice carving tools . . . .
Light wheel . . . Foil
Round tables . . . Long
Serpentine . . .

Ginger ale . . . . Club
Quinine . . . . Bitter lemon
Orange juice . . . Grenadine
Lemons . . . . Cherries

IN-HOME CATERING

In-home catering differs in size and scope from the in-home cooking and serving done by an accommodator. Unlike the services provided by the accommodator, an in-home catered party is usually larger, and requires more food, equipment, personnel, and services. Also, many foods are prepared in the caterer's kitchen and then transported to the "job" location for completion and service.

You can use standardized procedures for setting up in-home parties, but only as guides. Each house is built and laid out differently, and the needs, as well as the demands, of each client vary.

However, the following tips may be of benefit, especially if you are a novice in this particular area.

Traffic

If the party is large and many guests are expected to attend, street parking may be necessary. Should this be the case, tell the host to notify the Police Department and give both the beginning and ending times for the affair. This, no doubt, would be greatly appreciated by the police, neighbors, and guests by easing problems of traffic control.

For such a party, it may be necessary to have an officer direct the flow of traffic. If the police can "work-in" the traffic control as part of an officer's regular duty, then there may not be a charge. But if a special officer must be assigned to the task, a fee will, in all probability, be charged. In either case, be certain to provide the policeman on duty with food and beverage.

Bad Weather Procedures

In rainy weather, provide umbrellas for guests, and assign one of your employees the task of escorting them to and from their cars. If there is snow or slush, put a rubber or manila mat in front of the door leading to the house, as well as a carton at the protected entranceway for rubbers and boots. You should also provide a broom or a brush so that guests can remove snow from footwear.

Clothes Racks, Coat-Hanging Areas

You can provide serviceable folding clothes racks at a price that will cover their use, as well as your transportation and setting-up costs. However, with the permission of the client, you also can use a specific room where clothing apparel can be hung, or simply placed on a bed.

Guests should be responsible for their own apparel. If one of your employees takes the guest's coat to the "coatroom," then you, the caterer, have given *an implied assumption of responsibility*. When guests take care of their own coats, you cannot be held for any liability.

Food and Equipment Storage Area

This area should be located where it will not interfere with guest traffic. Store everything in an orderly, systematic manner—food in one stack, linens in another, china in yet another. By doing this, you will not have to search through all of your equipment to find what you need.

Food Preparation and Service Area

Generally, this is the kitchen of the home. The home range is smaller than commercial equipment, limited mainly to four surface burners, and its oven space is considerably narrower and shallower, which means it will not accommodate standard restaurant and hotel trays. Therefore, all pots, pans, and trays used in home-party service *must be smaller* than preparation pans used in your commissary.

Do not use heavy stock pots on the surface of home stoves. The amount of heat generated between the burner and the bottom of the pot resting on the grating may soften the range's porcelain finish, thereby causing it to buckle or crack, perhaps scorching the surface.

All personnel, but especially those who work in the kitchen, must wear impeccably clean uniforms, and keep their stations clean at all times. Plenty of clean side towels and extra uniforms should also be available.

A bag or other garbage receptacle should be in an *inconspicuous place.* Thus, if curious guests wander into the kitchen to see who you are, and how you manage to serve so much food from such a confined area, your operation will present a neat and orderly appearance.

It is *inadvisable* to use your client's garbage disposer. Most home units are not built to withstand heavy-duty use, and the extra strain you put on one of them could do serious damage to the unit.

Food Display Area

Advise your client to remove fragile crystalware, china, show plates, and other small valuable pieces from food-serving or other areas where guests gather. In such areas, crowding could conceivably result in an accident.

If these pieces cannot be completely removed, they should at least be pushed out of the way or displayed in an area less exposed to the hazards of guest traffic.

If you use your client's dining table, buffet credenza, or other pieces of furniture for food display or dispensing, place pads or buffers under trays and chafing dishes to prevent surface damage.

Avoid rearranging furniture as much as possible because (a) it will completely change the character of the room that your client has spent considerable time and effort in creating; and (b) furniture can be damaged when moved from one place to another.

Toilet Facilities

Remind your client to have additional reserves of toilet tissue and towels on hand.   Toilet facilities are usually taxed to capacity during a party, and much embarrassment can be avoided simply by having ample supplies of these necessities.

Bar Facilities

Since people tend to gather around the bar area and interfere with the smooth flow of traffic, bar or bars should be located at some distance from entrance doors.

Although the client provides the liquor, you should limit the variety of drinks offered, in order to facilitate the bartender's production. Drinks that require many ingredients and which take extra time to prepare, should be eliminated, or certainly discouraged.

Be sure to inventory the liquor at the beginning of the party and once again at its completion.   Also, provide your bartender with a sufficient supply of ice, mixes, and back-up glasses so that service will not be interrupted.   Remember, *a bar should never be left unattended.*

Help Assignments

Give each employee specific assignments and areas of responsibility. In addition to specific duties, they should be encouraged never to go to the kitchen empty-handed; they should pick up dirty dishes and glasses.

Make certain that at least one employee is responsible for keeping ashtrays clean.   Be sure to inform all personnel that they are to remain in the area(s) where they perform their duties. *They must not wander around the house to inspect rooms and furnishings.*

Following the party, thoroughly clean all areas.   Check all rooms for glasses, dishes, or any other property which belongs to you.   Even though an area may be provided by the host, *remove all garbage* so that the client will have sufficient space for his/her own garbage until the regular collection time.

Before leaving, inspect storage and service areas. In this way, any damage incurred during the party will be noticed immediately, thus reducing the possibility of a delayed claim or a dispute by either party at a later date.

CATERING IN RENTED FACILITIES

When catering in a hall or large dining room, which is an integral part of a club, church, temple, or fraternal organization, do not automatically assume that the kitchen or preparation area is of standard institutional construction and design or that furnishings are standard. You must make a personal inspection of the premises to see what facilities are available and what condition they are in.

Negotiations for the rental of facilities are generally taken care of by the client, who informs the superintendent or rental agent of the institution that the organization will bring in its own caterer. However, *the renting agent has the option of refusing to lease the premises* to any individual or organization using a catering firm with whom the lessor has had previous difficulties. Such a refusal is usually based on a caterer's previous disrespect and abuse of the facilities or because of late or non-payment of accrued fees.

Some facilities charge one fee for the use of the hall and the kitchen. Other facilities charge the client a rental fee for the hall and the caterer a separate fee, or per diem rate, for the use of kitchen/cooking facilities.

You may also have to pay for the use of the dishwashing machine and, perhaps, for the use of refrigerators, freezers, and for garbage removal. Some kitchens permit you—for a fee—to use their pots, pans, and other utensils. They may even allow you to use their dishes, glassware, and silverware. If you do use them, be certain they are returned to their proper place and are in perfect condition and clean. Should you inadvertently take any of these items back with you to your own premises, immediately notify the manager of the facility and then return them at the earliest possible moment. If breakage of facility items occurs, promptly report and assume responsibility for it.

Following these rules will assure your welcome for subsequent events at the facility and may even result in party referrals by the lessor. Expressing appreciation to the superintendent of the facility with a pre-affair gratuity will encourage cooperation and increase the possibility that all equipment will be available and functioning properly when needed.

Since some dining areas are rented without tables or chairs, your client will expect you to know where to obtain these items. If that happens, refer your client *directly to the proper agency.* Let the client make arrangements for rental and delivery of whatever is needed, as well as assume payment responsibility. Avoid, when possible, transporting tables and chairs; they are bulky, heavy, and take up much needed space in trucks. Furthermore, rental agencies have the special equipment for handling and delivery of these items.

Your client may ask you for a floor plan showing table placements and numbering so that some persons can be assigned to certain seats, or reserved areas. If the lessor cannot provide a floor plan, you will have to measure the area, and make scale templates to plan the table layout (see Chapter 2, "Setting Up A Commissary"). Keep a copy of that floor plan for your permanent records because you may again work in that facility. Also, make out a detailed work sheet for the use of your key people and the person(s) in charge of the affair (Figure 2, pp. 102-104), so that everyone will be aware of party details.

Liquor Arrangements

Some public halls may rent all facilities *except the bar*. The lessor may have a liquor license and not allow liquor to be brought in because it could jeopardize his/her license. If this is the case, the lessor would probably offer you one of the following options:

1. *Public or Pay Bar.* This would be open to all guests, who would then pay for liquor or drinks individually.

2. *Limited Bar.* The client would furnish tickets to guests, and they would have to present a ticket for each drink.

3. *Unlimited Bar.* Guests could order as many drinks as they wished. Payment would subsequently be made by the client, based on a predetermined charge per bottle.

If the facility in question does not have an on-premise licensed bar, then if liquor is to be served, you must furnish bartenders and portable bars, while the client supplies the liquor. This arrangement is similar to home-catering liquor dispensing, but since it is on a larger scale, the quarters may be roomier, and, therefore, you can serve a greater variety of drinks.

It is not uncommon for halls without a liquor license to raise the rental fee by offering the well-known "Bring Your Own Bottle" (B. Y. O. B.) option, with the lessor supplying ginger ale, ice, and glasses, and setting a "corkage charge" for each guest. Under this arrangement, no set-up bar or individual drinks will be available.

Organization Affairs

Since many organizations hold affairs on limited budgets, you may not make your deserved profit. Furthermore, if you assume these affairs will be of great advertising value, you could be wrong. *It could, in fact, have the opposite effect!*

To illustrate, in order to accommodate the organization's limited budget, you may set a lower rate for the party, which may necessitate "cutting corners." Such economical measures might include reducing portion sizes, eliminating a course, serving quality foods of lesser quality, using fewer serving personnel, or substituting paper for linens.

If any of these practices are deviations from your standards, your reputation will be harmed irreparably.   A guest is not concerned about whether or not you are making or losing money on an affair. He/she is concerned with enjoying the service, satisfying the "inner person," and gratifying a personal, aesthetic sense.

If you want to be a public-spirited citizen and serve these affairs, knowing full well that your profit will either be reduced or eliminated entirely, do so *WITHOUT COMPROMISING YOUR STANDARDS OF QUALITY OR SERVICE.*   You will gain greater respect for doing this, and it is also true that adhering to high standards will enhance your reputation.

TIPS FOR A SUCCESSFUL FUNCTION

In addition to good food and service, you should pay careful attention to the following items:

1. Coordinate the timing and service of the meal with the client's plans for speeches, entertainment, or ceremonies.   Determine in advance at what time, or place, or by what cue, service should cease or continue.

2. Do not serve a course while guests are dancing.   Food served before guests are ready for it will either cool, get warm, or wilt.

3. Caution waiters and other employees *not to move place settings from one table to another without permission from the client or committee chairperson.*

4. While the program is in progress, do not allow waiters to gather in groups in any part of the dining room.

5. Make sure water goblets are kept at the 7/8 level during the meal and are filled to this level prior to the departure of waiters for the start of the program.

6. Have all unused glasses, dishes, and unnecessary items removed from the tables as soon as possible.   It is not pleasant for guests to be forced to sit at a "cluttered table."

7. Keep ashtrays clean at all times.

8. Keep the client's or committee's original guest and seating lists accessible for ready reference.

RENTING OR LEASING A TENT

On some occasions, a client may want to hold the party in a tent. You should know which companies in your locality specialize in tent erections.   Awning makers generally are a good source for obtaining tents.

Once you have collected this information, pass it along to your client, who should then consult these companies to determine the feasibility of erecting a tent in the desired area.

For your purposes, the surface covered by the tent should be hard-topped or a *perfectly level* grass area. However, it may be necessary to place shims under table legs to keep the tables from rocking. Should the tables be inadvertently moved, it may be necessary to have them re-shimmed.

Comparisons should be made between the price of renting a tent and the tables, chairs, dance floors, and other necessary platforms, with the price of renting a fully enclosed, air-conditioned facility.

If a tent will be used, you, the caterer, will have many problems to resolve. For example, where should you set up your preparation or kitchen facilities? Can you get field cooking ranges? Will ample refrigerating facilities be available? What can you do about bugs, flies, mosquitoes, and how will you handle garbage disposal? Will your operating costs be increased considerably? And, finally, under such conditions, will you be able to maintain the standards for which you are known?

While the preceding are all negative factors, there are some positive ones:

1. Tent affairs can be gala and festive events.
2. A tent offers protection from the sun.
3. Generally, there is more "elbow room" for both the guests and the employees.

GENERAL CLEAN-UP

Clean-up following any party should be a systematic procedure. All glasses and dishes of the same type should be removed at one time from all tables. This speeds handling and packing in the dishwashing area and minimizes the number of packing cases needed at the exit end of the washing table.

Keep forks, knives, teaspoons, and other utensils in individual containers, each having a specified number of utensils, and then label each by contents and number.

When packing silverware, do not do so in a helter-skelter fashion. With forks, pack all tines in the first row close together and facing the same way; those in the second row should also all face the same way, but rest on the handles of those in the first row. Repeat this same procedure for the third and fourth rows and do the same thing with spoons.

When packing knives with hollow handles, place the flat side down, one row at a time. But remember to reverse the handles on every other row so that knife blades in one row will rest on knife handles in the row below.

Remove napkins separately and count before tying in a soiled but dry tablecloth. Leave tablecloths on two tables and, as the other cloths are removed, *shake them out onto one of the cloth-covered tables.* This has two purposes: (1) it keeps dirt off the floor; and (2) it enables you to discover quickly any valuables that have been inadvertently left behind.

After shaking the cloth, thoroughly examine remnants before discarding. Cloths already shaken out can then be thrown onto the second of the still clothed tables, counted, and tied.

Keep wet and damp cloths separate, and, after returning to your commissary, spread them out to dry. This will prevent mildewing, which may not wash out.

FIGURE 2--WORK PLAN

JOHN DOE CATERERS – HYDE PARK, NEW YORK

DETAILED WORKSHEET (SPECIMEN)
(To be issued to person in charge of affair)

NAME OF CLIENT: State Historical Association
ADDRESS: 149 Oregon Street, E. Chicago, Illinois
AREA OF PARTY: First Hungarian Church
ADDRESS: 1595 Sunrise Highway E. Chicago, Illinois
PERSON IN CHARGE: Mrs. D. R. Jones Mr. F. G. Hussen
DAY AND DATE: Saturday, January 18, 1983
TIME: Reception - 5:00 p. m. Dinner - 6:30 p. m.
NUMBER OF GUESTS: 250 persons
GUARANTEED NUMBER: 245 persons
SPECIAL ARRANGEMENTS: Use two church bars, but we supply two additional portable bars and supply four bartenders.
Association will provide all liquor, carbonated beverages, soft drinks, and ice. Our bartender will inventory all liquor at set-up; break-down. During dinner, our portable bars will be wheeled into the dining

(Cont.)

room, and each will be attended by one or more of our bartenders.

Association member in charge is Mr. F. G. Hussen.

RECEPTION:
(One of our persons in charge.)

In reception area, set up two 8-ft. tables (belonging to facility) with equal amounts of Wisconsin and New York cheese, celery sticks, carrot sticks, and cocktail rye slices (as packed) on each. (One waitress will be assigned to each table.)

Drape tables in blue and use 5-in. plates, service knives, and cocktail napkins.

PASS   BUTLER   STYLE—400 speared cocktail franks, 300 rondelles of lobster, and 300 cocktail meatballs (all as packed).

COAT ROOM:

Attendants to be supplied by church. (We feed.)

PARKING:

Handled by policemen provided by the organization. (We feed them and all other personnel.)

ORCHESTRA:

Provided by the organization. Band leader is Hy Williams; our coordinator is Bob White. (We supply sandwiches only; it is our treat.)

CENTERPIECES:

Floral centerpieces will be provided by the organization. (Guests will not be permitted to take centerpieces, which will be sent to Shriner's Hospital. Ork will announce.)

CIGARETTES:

Organization to supply—one package (in cups) each table, plus matches at each place setting.

LECTERN:

Tabletop, center head table, two mikes.

HOUSE COUNT:

Before soup course, check with organization's Mr. Hussen. Check program with Mrs. Jones of the organization.

HEAD TABLE:	12 guests, blue table top, gold lame front skirt, gold napkins, 2/3-tier candelabra, blue candles, and dagger ferns across front.
DINING ROOM:	According to floor plan submitted. Organization to set out table cards. (Retain master guest list.)
DINNER:	6:30 p. m. *sharp,* blue cloths, and gold napkins. (Edith and captain left side of dining room; Norman and captain right side of dining room)
MENU:	Fresh Fruit Cocktail, Supreme, Garniture of Strawberries (Silver coupes) In ice: Ripe and Green Olives, Radishes, Celery Hearts, Iced Butter Curls; bread and butter plates at each setting. From tureens: Potage Mongole Russian service: Chicken Kiev Escoffier of Vegetables Pre-plated: Wedge of Cheese Cake, pass warm Blueberry Sauce; 12 Petits Fours per table. Coffee, self-poured; one pitcher per table, on candle warmer. (Following coffee service—one dish mints and nuts per table.)
GENERAL DIRECTIONS:	Wash dishes and glasses as used, two church crew members and two of our regular crew members. (Pay church crew $3.00 per hour and tip at your discretion.) Following dessert service, one hour of dancing. All tables must be cleared, leaving only cloths and ashtrays. All dishes and glassware must be washed and truck-packed.

(Cont.)

DISPOSABLE GLASSES TO BE USED AT BAR DURING LAST HOUR OF SERVICE.

Broom-sweep dining room only, with brushes to be supplied by church.

Thoroughly wash   kitchen floor, clean work tables, stoves, and reefers (refrigerators).

Check garbage dumpster;   make certain no garbage on ground.

Check with church superintendent to make certain all areas meet with his/her complete satisfaction. Give superintendent gratuity check.

Kosher Catering/12

TRADITION AND HERITAGE play important roles in the food preferences of most groups, but this is especially true for Jewish people. Thus, if you decide to specialize in kosher and Jewish foods, many opportunities will be available.

First, you can be assured of a "ready-made" clientele who will automatically seek you out. Also, since American people are willing to try new and unusual foods, you have an additional opportunity for promoting these specialties among the non-Jewish population, and a never-ending way to increase volume.

To operate a kosher establishment, you must know and follow the dietary regulations of the Jewish people. These laws concerning the preparation, selection, and service of food—even though they were delivered to Moses more than 3000 years ago—are so deeply woven into Jewish religious and family life that they remain virtually unchanged today. They still also govern, to differing degrees, the eating habits of many Jewish patrons.

NECESSARY REQUIREMENTS

In order to operate a strictly kosher operation, you must have an authorized orthodox rabbi or his representative, a "Mashgiach," on your premises at all times. The "Mashgiach," who is normally assigned by the area rabbi, must be a man whose character is beyond reproach, and one thoroughly knowledgeable in all aspects of the dietary laws. In addition, you, the caterer, should also be fully familiar with Jewish dietary laws.

However, since only about one-half of the Jewish population is orthodox, requiring strict kosher food preparation, you might consider serving the Jewish patron who prefers Jewish-type foods, but does not require that they be in full compliance with all dietary laws. This has been the case in many operations featuring so-called kosher-style food, which is much less complicated in terms of preparation, although not purchasing.

PROCESSING AND PURCHASING

In serving Jewish patrons, considerable care and emphasis must be given to purchasing procedures. For example, laws governing the use of meat—the main commodity for many foodservice operations—prohibit the use of pork, and pork products, wild birds and game birds of prey, and seafood without scales and certain fins such as shellfish, lobster, crab, scallops, etc. Furthermore, the method of slaughtering them, as well as the procedure for preparing them, is subject to very rigid controls.

Hindquarters of meat may not be used unless blood-carrying veins are properly removed. This operation is not only very complex and expensive, but one which destroys the merchandising value of the meat, and, in most instances, makes it unfit for kosher use. Therefore, meat selection is generally limited to forequarters of cattle, sheep, goats, and deer, and the internal organs of the forequarter, while in the poultry classification, only the domestic variety of chicken, turkey, duck, geese, Cornish hens, and squash pigeons are permissible.

These limitations are further complicated by the fact that the foods must be ritually prepared, or koshered, within 72 hours of slaughter.

The "koshering" process is designed to remove all excess blood from the meat. After the various blood vessels are removed, the meat is put in cold water for a half hour. It is then removed, rinsed, sprinkled generously with coarse sodium chloride (salt), and placed on a slanted drain board for one hour. After that, the meat is again washed—by hose or faucet—in cold water to remove the surface salt. Only then is it ready to be cut up for cooking, aged, frozen, or eaten in a raw preparation, such as Steak Tartare, or to be cooked to the rarest degree of doneness.

Meat can remain in this form for three 72-hour periods (or nine days) from the time of slaughter. However, at the end of each 72-hour period, it must again be washed down. If it is not used by the end of the third period or ninth day, it is no longer kosher and, therefore, is unfit for eating.

This soaking and salting process, as well as the slaughter date, does not apply to liver, which is koshered only by *broiling*. Liver must be sliced, salted, and then broiled with the salt until it has turned color, or is edible. The salt is then washed off, and processed in any desirable manner. Liver may also be frozen for future use, without regard to the date of slaughter.

Kosher-prepared meat seems to have several strikes against it for the caterer. Unless your operation is large enough to hold meat in refrigeration for several weeks, it will have to be cooked too fresh. Also, during the koshering process, it will lose some of its water and salt-soluble ingredients. Lastly, the meats are limited to the less-tender, more rarely-available varieties.

However, if meat is soaked and salted within the 72-hour period, it is fit for kosher consumption, and may be stored frozen for an unlimited period, and/or shipped to any part of the country. But to have a really flavorful finished product, it is most important to purchase top quality meats, and to prepare them skillfully.

To be certain that all regulations have been followed, you should use the services of a certified kosher butcher, whose name can be supplied by an ordained, orthodox rabbi. Fortunately, once the butcher has been certified as kosher, you may make future purchases from him without concern or rechecking.

In addition to meats, poultry must also be bought from an approved kosher butcher. It can also be purchased from an out-of-town source, which has properly slaughtered it before freezing and shipping.

Purchase of other foodstuffs—salt, condiments, soup bases, cheeses, etc.—is not as critical as meat, but does require alertness if errors are to be avoided. Cheese is a good example. As a dairy food, there would seem to be no question as to its use on a kosher menu. However, since it may be prepared with rennin from a non-kosher animal, it must carry the rabbi's stamp of approval, certifying that is has been kosher prepared.

The rabbi's stamp does not make the product kosher. It merely testifies to the fact that it was prepared in strict adherence to kashruth regulations (Jewish dietary laws).

Fruits and vegetables, both the canned and frozen types, are not ordinarily covered by rules of the rabbinical council, and provide no special problems insofar as purchasing of these items is concerned.

PREPARATION AND MENU PLANNING

Preparation of foods for a strictly kosher operation must conform to another dietary law of the Jewish religion. Restrictions in preparation arise from the fact that Jewish laws list three classes of food (meat and meat by-products; milk and all dairy products; and neutral foods, which are purely chemical and vegetable in origin), and stipulate that food items from the first two classes (meat and milk) can never be prepared in the same dishes, or served at the same meal.

Obviously, with these restrictions, menu planning can be very limited, and quite a problem. If you are using meat as the main menu item, the rest of the meal is governed by a great many restrictions. Desserts, breads, and other items must all be prepared without the use of milk, butter, or cream. By the same token, meatless menus can be rather bland, unless you use considerable ingenuity.

These problems are obvious ones, but even deeper, more far-reaching ones are discovered when, for example, you prepare a dish such as creamed turkey. The sauce for the creamed turkey must be made with either chicken fat or vegetable shortening, flour, and turkey stock. The use of cream, milk, or butter would be prohibited. On the other hand, vegetable soup for a dairy meal cannot contain meat stock, but must rely on vegetable stock and seasoning for flavor.

To cover these criteria, most caterers and foodservice operators dealing in kosher foodservice have devised special recipes and/or rely on special commercial products. However, you can readily see that menu planning can and often does present many special and unique problems.

One menu planning aid not yet mentioned is neutral or parve foods—anything that grows on the land, or in the sea (and is edible), and all chemical-based foods or derivatives such as monosodium glutamate or meat tenderizers. These can be served at either dairy or meat meals, depending on their method of preparation. They include jams, cereals, fish, eggs, grains, sugars, syrups, fruits, vegetables, vegetable oils, and shortenings, seasonings, including the whole gamut of herbs, spices, and flavorings. . . .as long as no part of either a meat or dairy product is incorporated in their manufacture.

Therefore, while Jewish dietary laws exclude many foods, and combinations of foods, there is still much room for imagination and challenge in developing new uses for the approved foods, thus providing pleasing menus. The emergence of dairy, meat, and seafood substitutes on the food scene has also led to a whole new era in kosher food development. It is now an accepted and seldom questioned custom to serve coffee whiteners (of parve vegetable origin), whipped toppings, and "ersatz" ice cream. Of course, you must make certain that these substitutes do carry a symbol of kosher certification.

Reading the listing of ingredients on packages, and interpreting technical terms, can be time-consuming and frustrating. It can also cause you to reject a food product that meets all requirements, or, on the contrary, accept a product that might be "trefe," or forbidden. Therefore, many food manufacturers whose products meet dietary requirements, and who wish to take advantage of this captive and lucrative market, employ the services of the Union of Orthodox Rabbis.

This group will only give its endorsement if the entire production process is under its constant supervision, and if, of course, the product meets kashruth standards.

Products endorsed by the group carry the letter "U" enclosed in a circle, thusly Ⓤ. In many cases, there will also be information alongside the symbol as to whether the product is "milchig," "fleishig," or "parve."

The letter "K" enclosed in a circle, thusly Ⓚ, signifies that a product has been endorsed by another respected group, the O. K. Laboratories, which is composed of, and administered by, rabbis.

There is no hierarchy in the U. S. rabbinate. Rabbis may organize into groups or societies for religious or civic reasons, or for whatever reason(s) they wish. An ordained rabbi—with his own congregation—is the leader of his members only, and authority and parochial duties vary from synagogue to synagogue, and from city to city. For this reason, some processed kosher foods may show only the freestanding letter "K" alongside the brand name. This shows that the endorsement of kashruth has been given by only one individual rabbi.

Since Jewish dietary law prohibits dairy and meat foods from being prepared in the same dishes, many caterers plan and serve only one type of menu—meat, for example. However, caterers and foodservice operators serving three meals a day must, of course, prepare and serve both dairy and meat meals.

Under these circumstances, they must have two separate, completely equipped kitchens or, at least, one large kitchen with a double set of ranges, ovens, broilers, fryers, cookers, mixing bowls, etc., as well as two complete sets of china and silver.

MAINTENANCE

Two sets of utensils and dishes cause a problem—that of keeping meat dishes separate from dairy dishes. China is fairly easy since two distinct patterns can be used. However, utensils represent a great difficulty, and you must develop a system that works well for you. Some operations find that welding a plaque to the dairy utensils works well for them.

But other than keeping dishes separated, maintenance presents no really large problem for the kosher operation. Of course, as soaps and detergents are ordinarily made with animal fats, a special kosher soap must be used. Also strict adherence to kosher laws requires that articles of food preparation, and service, as well as the kitchen, be kept scrupulously clean.

PROFIT

As the owner of a kosher establishment, your profit range will be comparable to that of a non-kosher operation, providing all other factors are equal. For although the cost of food and preparation may be somewhat higher, the selling price is also correspondingly higher.

COMBINING KOSHER AND NON-KOSHER OPERATIONS

Up to this point, only the operation of a strictly kosher establishment has been discussed. If you desire to combine both kosher and non-kosher foodservice, you would probably find that a great deal more planning is required in order to meet Jewish laws.

Storage space would, of necessity, nearly double since preparation and serving of both types of food cannot be combined. While it is permissible in some instances for the same utensils to be used, the scouring process involved in clean-up must be so thorough that it is usually not practicable.

Although foodstuffs and items for dry storage can be stored with the non-kosher foods, meat must be held under separate refrigeration. With all these inconveniences, it would seem that operating a combination kosher/non-kosher establishment would be impracticable. However, actual experience belies this assumption.

Large operations, such as hotels serving a mixed clientele, report that catering to Jewish banquets and special celebrations has proved to be very profitable, and that the added initial cost and extra storage space really is a minor consideration.

Hotel, motel, and club managers with attractive dining facilities often make them available for kosher affairs. Since the caterer prepares and serves the affair, using all of his/her own kosher dishes, equipment, and experienced personnel, the facilities' operator need not be knowledgeable in the area, or have the specialized personnel. He or she is reimbursed by a percentage of the gross, a per guest charge, or a separate kitchen and dining area charge—any arrangement equitable to both parties. As a result, the facilities' operator not only retains his/her own bar operation, clothes checking, and parking facilities, but gets added revenue, since most kosher affairs are held on Saturday or Sunday nights, when dining room counts are down or nonexistent in many areas.

TRADITIONAL MEALS

Sabbath

The Fourth Commandment admonishes man to remember and keep holy the Sabbath. Thus, to the observant Jew, Sabbath is a day of special holiness, and one devoted to the soul. It is also a day of complete rest for both man and animals. All weekday cares and work must be completed before nightfall on Friday.

Since the home is considered a temple, and the table an altar, special preparations are made for the Sabbath meal. Twists of fine white bread, called chellahs, are baked, and meals are planned so that "warming or reheating" of food will not reduce its good taste. Typical of these dishes are gefilte fish, chicken, chicken soup, brisket of beef, tzimmes, cholents, noodle pudding, and sponge and honey cakes.

The Sabbath meal is a leisurely one, and includes many courses. Songs of peace, and of tribute to the ideal housewife (Ayshes Chail), are chanted. In addition, discussions of a spiritual nature and intellectual content are integral parts of this observance.

Passover

Passover, an eight-day holiday, is usually celebrated about the same time as the Christian observance of Easter. It celebrates the Israelites' release from bondage, which took place in Egypt more than 3000 years ago.

During Passover, rigid food regulations and restrictions are in effect. Forbidden are all cereals and their derivatives, leavening agents of any kind, and bread, biscuits, coffee substances derived from cereals, wheat, barley, oats, rice, dried peas, and dried beans.

Grain liquids, such as beer, and grain alcohol derivatives, such as rye, vodka, scotch, bourbon, and gin, are prohibited. Wine and fruit-based cordials must be produced under rabbinical supervision, and carry a special Passover seal to be accepted beverages.

All fresh and frozen vegetables—except peas, corn, and beans—are permitted, as are all fresh and frozen fruits. These must be packaged in natural syrup. If they are sweetened with corn syrup, for example, they would be unsuitable. Special labeling is not required on sealed packages of bean coffee, sugar, salt, tea, and spices.

Matzohs, flat wafers made of a specific type of wheat mixed with water, and apple cider are sometimes used. Matzohs, baked immediately after forming, are used as a bread substitute.

Olive, peanut, and cottonseed oils are the only non-animal, neutral fats used. Milk, cream, cheese, and butter must be produced under special supervision.

Pots and pans, as well as the silverware and dishes used during the rest of the year, are put away. Special dishes and utensils kept specifically for this holiday are used.

Stoves and ovens must be scrupulously cleaned before any Passover foods can be cooked on or in them.

The Seders, ceremonial meals on the first two days, are prepared with much symbolism. The table is usually covered with an ornately decorated cloth of rich material.

• Matzoh, unleavened bread, occupies a conspicuous place on the table. And a dish of salt should be readily available so it can be sprinkled on the matzoh before eating.

• A roasted lamb shankbone, symbol of the Paschal lamb sacrificed at the temple in ancient times, is placed near the matzohs. (A roasted chicken neck can be substituted for the shankbone.)

• A roasted egg—token of grief for the destruction of the temple—is also used.

• Bitter herbs, usually horseradish, are available as a reminder of the bitterness of slavery.

Ɔ Charosis—a mixture of chopped apples, nuts, cinnamon, and/or ginger—is moistened with wine to a pasty consistency. This symbolizes the mortar used by Egyptian Jews to hold bricks together.

• Also on the table are karpas—sprigs of parsley or celery leaves— and a dish of salt water in which the karpas can be dipped before eating. The salt water is a symbol of the tears of slavery.

• Wine is an essential part of the Passover Seder, and must be drunk four times during the meal.

The Passover meal is lavish and, by tradition, always includes fish, chicken soup with "knaidlach," and poultry, and/or meat roasts.

Shevuoth

This two-day holiday is known as the Festival of the Torah. Usually celebrated in May, it commemorates the date upon which the Lord gave Moses the Tablets of the Law, which marked the beginning of the Jewish religion.

It is also known as the Feast of Weeks, and/or the Feast of the Pentecost. The former name comes from the fact that it is celebrated seven weeks after Passover, while the latter name, the Feast of Pentecost, means that it occurs the 50th day after the second day of Passover.

On Shevuoth in ancient times, the first fruits of the field were brought to the temple as an offering of thanksgiving. As a result, synagogues and homes are decorated with flowers and foliage symbolizing harvest.

Dairy meals are traditional during these days for two reasons. First, the Law is compared to milk and honey. Second, prior to receiving the Law, Jews did not eat kosher meats but, after receiving it, found that there was not enough time to prepare meals according to the new regulations.

Traditional Sevuoth dishes include: cheese blintzes and kreplach, pirogen, puddings containing cheese and fruit, fruit compotes, fruit tarts, and pastries rich with cream and butter.

Rosh Hashanah

Usually held in September, Rosh Hashanah is considered the "birthday of the world's creation," and is the Jewish New Year.

While these two days are essentially ones for rejoicing, they are also "days of awe" and, as such, are devoted to prayer. The ram's horn, known as the "shofar," is sounded to arouse people to their spiritual shortcomings, and to encourage them to make worthy resolutions to improve their conduct.

Fish, symbol of fruitfulness and plenty, is one of the traditional dishes. Rich and sweet foods, which signify a wish for prosperity, and a sweet new year, are also served.

Challahs are braided and baked in round form to represent a wish for life without end. Years ago, the tops of the challahs were decorated with birds made of dough to indicate the "flying to heaven" of prayers for the new year.

Since bitter and sour foods are avoided, roast meats and poultry are accompanied by sweet vegetable compotes made from carrots, sweet potatoes, white potatoes, prunes, and honey. Taiglach, light dough nuggets cooked in honey and coated with nuts (possibly of Greek origin), are a staple holiday item, as is honey cake.

Yom Kippur

The Day of Atonement is the most solemn and awesome day of the year. This day, which is normally held in late September or early October, is one of penitence and prayer. Consequently, total abstinence from food and drink is required, and smoking is forbidden.

A pre-fast meal must be concluded before sundown the previous day. Since liquids, including water, are not permitted during the feast, the meal is normally underseasoned, and fish and other salty foods are not served, so as not to induce thirst. Soup with kreplach, boiled chicken, simple vegetables, and bland desserts are standard fare. However, this meal must be substantial because it has to sustain an individual for the next 24 or 26 hours.

At the end of the fast, a very bountiful meal is served. It consists of pickled, cooked, and smoked fish variations, cheese blintzes, sour cream, salads, and rich yeast cakes laden with raisins and sweet spices. These foods are prepared the day before the feast so that, with a minimum of heating or other preparation, they can be eaten immediately.

Succoth

Succoth, also known as the Feast of Booths and Festival of the Harvest, is the Jewish Thanksgiving and usually takes place in October.

Booths, which denote the temporary shelters used by the Israelites in their wanderings, are lavishly decorated with fruits of the fields. Grapes, apples, figs, pears, and gourds are hung from the ceiling, or the open roof.

During this holiday, meals are eaten in the Sukkah (booth). In addition to fruits of the harvest, traditional fare includes stuffed cabbage in a sweet sauce, which is served for at least one meal. This symbolizes the products of the earth and the successful food—animal production.

On the ninth and final day, Simchat Torah (rejoicing of the Bible), the richest foods, the finest wines, luscious desserts, and candies are the order of the day.

Chanukah

The Festival of Lights is an eight-day holiday that is usually held in December. It was instituted by Judas Maccabeus to celebrate regaining of the temple, which the Maccabees then rededicated by burning a flask of oil for a full eight days. This led to the practice of lighting special Chanukah candles. Thus, the eight-branched candlestand is a frequent symbol for this holiday, during which gifts are exchanged.

Pancakes are traditionally served, due, no doubt, to the fact that they were the fare for the Maccabee warriors. Because of their thin, flat surface, the speed with which they could be cooked in hot oil, and their effectiveness as hunger quenchers, pancakes were a desirable dish for the warriors.

In various areas where Jews have settled, it has become customary to make the pancakes from rice, corn, and buckwheat—the latter being very popular with East European Jews.

Around the turn of the century, potato pancakes were quite popular with American Jews. Sociologists believe that this was due to the fact that the ingredients were inexpensive, and that the pancakes were an excellent means for warding off hunger. Applesauce and sour cream were later embellishments.

Purim

The one-day celebration of "Lets" is usually in March. It celebrates the deliverance of the Persian Jews from massacre more than 2500 years ago.

Therefore, Purim is a day of jubilation, singing, dancing, and gift-giving. It is intended to show that, although wickedness may temporarily seem to succeed, freedom from persecution will come to those who have faith.

Hamantashen, a three-cornered fruit or poppy seed pastry, is traditionally eaten on this day. There is good-natured rivalry among culinarians to produce the best hamantashen, the best Purim dinner, and to show off their achievements.

Arrangements for Various Functions/13

Catering Clambakes and Barbecues

DATING FROM THE days of the American Indian, clambakes or steams are traditionally a New England happening. Originally a seashore function, today they are held in backyards, parks, and other picnic areas.

To prepare a clambake for 100 or more guests, dig a pit about 3 ft. deep and 4 to 5 ft. in diameter, then line it with large rocks. (In Rhode Island, bakemasters require rocks "as big as a man's head.")

In the next step, place cordwood on top of the rocks and allow it to burn until it is *white hot*. Depending on the size of the stones, pit, and type of cordwood, this procedure could take up to three hours, but from then on the process requires speed.

Embers should be removed and stones swept clean of ashes. About 6 in. of seaweed should then be put on the stones. If seaweed is not available, wet leaves and ferns can be substituted. Next, place a layer of heavy wire mesh over this.

For every 50 guests, add a bushel of well-washed soft-shell clams; with these place one live lobster and two ears of corn for *each guest.* Remove only the silk from the corn. Washed but not pared sweet and/or white potatoes may be added, if desired. As a "topper," add chicken quarters or halves which have been parboiled, buttered, and wrapped in foil. Gutted trout, mackerel, bluefish, or chunks of cod may also be foil-wrapped and used with, or in place of, the chicken.

Top the food with a thick layer of seaweed; then cover the entire area with wet canvas. Weigh down the canvas securely with large rocks or heavy planks, and allow the food to steam from one to two hours.

Although this can be a gala and exciting presentation, it calls for detailed planning and meticulous follow-through. Since all seafood items spoil quickly, they must be properly refrigerated, and given priority attention.

In determining charges for a clambake, a number of unusual conditions must be considered.

1. Do you have the proper tools and personnel available to dig the pit? (This takes considerable time and requires the services of individuals who are physically able to perform the chore. Remember, that at the end of the clambake, the pit must be refilled, smoothed over, and all excess stones and dirt carted away.)

2. Where are you going to get the proper stones? How will you get them to the site of the clambake?

3. Will you be able to get sufficient quantities of seaweed, leaves, or ferns?

4. Will you personally have to pick up the cordwood? Since your order will probably be small, the company from whom you purchase it may not make a delivery.

5. Do you have heavy wire mesh for the base, as well as heavy canvas for the top?

6. If the "bake" is to be held on public land, is a permit required? If it is to be held on private property, will you need written permission from the owner?

7. Ample space must be provided for dirty dishes, as well as for scraping and rinsing (if possible). Because of the informality of this event, be prepared for greater dish loss and breakage. Also, remember that because of the large area to be covered and the unevenness of the terrain, your employees will tire more easily and become more careless with equipment.

8. Disposables, with the exception of dinner plates, should be

used. If disposable dishes must be used for the main course, then select *heavily-coated and rigidly constructed* 10- to 12-in. oval plates.
This is necessary because clams, lobsters, corn, and chicken are heavy,
hot, and ooze liquid.

9. The most inexpensive stainless steel forks, knives, and spoons
should be used. Plastic ware can be substituted, if it is the heavy-duty
type that will not snap or break while in the guests' hands.

10. Rugged paper or plastic tablecloths are particularly appropriate
for a clambake. Provide *mountains of paper napkins* because these
foods are wet and sticky! Also, have a sufficient supply of rubbish
bags, and use the heavy-duty type that will not rip when lobster shells,
clam shells, and corn cobs are packed in them.

BARBECUES

Barbecuing, a form of outdoor cooking, involves both preparation
and presentation skills. Like other types of showmanship, the more
flourishes and props there are, the more effective and impressive the
service.

Props can include showy grilles, decorative and oversized tongs, giant
salt and pepper shakers, colorful sauce bowls, gaudy aprons, extra large
padded gloves and hot pads, plus a beautiful but functional carving
knife, fork, and sharpening steel.   These props should be displayed
prominently and used with flourishes to add to the guests' enjoyment.

When catering a private home barbecue, you can very effectively
use any of the many fabricated barbecue grilles available on the market.
However, their production capability is limited, and the number of
guests that can be served is, therefore, necessarily limited.

In catering home barbecues, you have the advantages of refrigerators, freezers, water, gas, and electricity. And in some homes, you may
find permanently installed grilles, a situation which works to your
advantage.

Home barbecues add much pleasure and diversity to home entertaining. In parts of the country where weather conditions are favorable
and predictable, barbecues are held throughout the year. As a result,
there is a greater variety of equipment available for both the home and
for you, the professional caterer.

Building Your Own Equipment

In some areas, outdoor cooking and dining are only possible about
four months out of the year. Thus, you may not want to buy special
barbecuing equipment. But you can improvise or build your own,
which will then be suited to your particular needs. Even if you do this,

remember that household grilles can be used as *auxiliary units* for producing or holding side dishes, hors d'oeuvres, or small quantities of food.

To build a large, effective charcoal grille, visit a scrapyard or a steel supply house and purchase an iron or steel cellar door grille (or the kind used to protect glass store doors). This grille should have horizontal, vertical, or diamond-shaped spaces no larger than three quarters (3/4 in.) of an inch. (See illustration on following page.)

Next, place two, three, or four pans of equal size, such as old roasting pans or squareheads, on cinder blocks arranged in a shape most suitable to the size of your grille. Thus, the corners of the grille can rest on the cinder blocks or bricks which are placed on the outside corners of the pan arrangements—at whatever height is desired.

Line pan bottoms and sides with heavy foil to reflect heat, speed up cooking, and make them easier to clean. Over this, place one or two inches of gravel (depending on the height of your pans) and top with the coals. The gravel, which allows even heat penetration and distribution, can be washed after repeated uses, dried thoroughly, and used again.

The quantity and type of briquettes needed differ, based on the amount and kind of food to be served. Thick steaks or roasts need a deep bed of coals, while franks or burgers call for shallow fires.

Prior to cooking, rub fat trimmings or bacon over grille rods or wire baskets to prevent sticking. If drippings flare up during the cooking process, sprinkle lightly with water from a plastic squeeze bottle.

Portable Griddles

An average-size (18- by 42-in.) gas-fired restaurant griddle is capable of producing more than 100 orders of griddle cakes or more than 500 orders of franks or hamburgers per hour, and makes an excellent portable cooking unit surface for outdoor barbecues. Second-hand models are often available from restaurant supply houses.

Have a plumber connect a 4- to 6-ft. *flexible brass gas hose* to the gas line on the griddle. If necessary, have it permanently brazed to that spot. The coupling on the opposite end can be fastened to a 20-lb. portable propane gas tank available from most suburban gas companies. Chain an appropriate wrench to this hose so that it will be readily available if and when needed. (See illustration on p. 121.) Buy a sheet of scrap steel larger than the griddle dimensions, and set up the unit on it before placing it in the working area. When completed, test the griddle. Changes in valve openings may be required because they were not originally intended for use with propane gas.

"SQUARE HEADS"

CONCRETE BLOCKS

LARGE SCRAP WIRE GRILLE

Homemade Temporary Outdoor Barbecue for Quantity Production

Size-Flexible--Depending Upon Need and Roasting Pans, or Square Heads or Type and Size of Grille Secured.

Easily Assembled and Disassembled

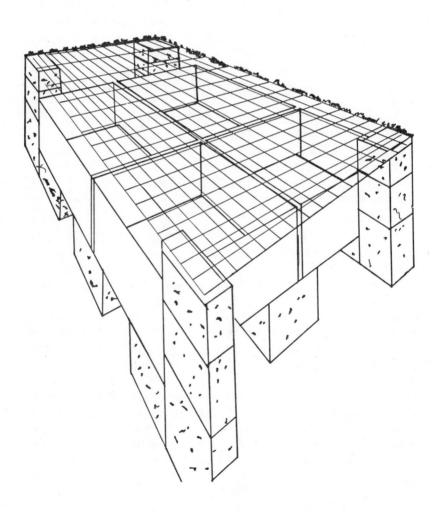

SCRAP SHEET IRON UNDER GRILLE
(To Prevent Heat Transfer)

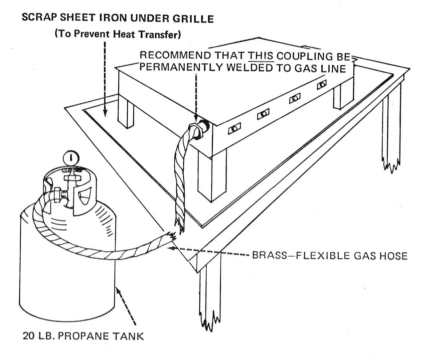

RECOMMEND THAT <u>THIS</u> COUPLING BE
PERMANENTLY WELDED TO GAS LINE

BRASS—FLEXIBLE GAS HOSE

20 LB. PROPANE TANK

This same procedure can be used for setting up a cooking range and oven on a mobile base. Mount the range on a steel-bottomed dolly with heavy capacity wheels. Thus, it can be platform-lifted into or off of a truck and wheeled to the desired area. Using a range in this way will require a portable auxiliary chimney.

It is always advisable, when using propane gas with portable equipment, to carry a spare tank with a gauge showing the amount of gas remaining. If there is no gauge, weigh the tank when full. Then, after each use, weigh it again and mark that weight on a piece of masking adhesive taped to the side of the tank. To better gauge this figure, check with a propane dealer in your area to find out how much the tank weighs when empty.

Building the Fire

When using large barbecue grilles for quantity production, it is essential that you give the "fire area" constant and undivided attention. In this type of set-up, you do not have "finger-tip heat controls," so you cannot get the immediate heat-elevation or heat-reduction responses possible with conventional ranges.

Because of the many variables in outdoor parties, cooking time can only be estimated. Charcoal or compressed fuel packages can take as long as 45 minutes to reach the proper temperature. If you try to rush them, you either burn the food, or undercook it.

To achieve that special "barbecue" flavor in food, you can: (1) brush the food with liquid flavoring; (2) scatter *impregnated* wood shavings on the fire at the proper time; or (3) wrap *dry* shavings in foil that is generously perforated at the top and place the foil-wrapped shavings on the fire in the hope that the resultant smoke will produce the desired "smoky" flavor.

Remember, all meat cookery calls for *glowing coals—no flame!* And the fire should burn until a gray ash film covers the charcoal or briquettes. In home barbecues equipped with crank handles, the proper heat can be achieved by adjusting the grille to a high or low position·

If no thermometer can be placed on grille racks to determine the temperature, you will then have to resort to the "field-mass detection method." To do this, hold your open hand a couple of inches above the grille and count "one and two," "two and three," "three and four," and so on·

If you must remove your hand by the end of the "one and two" count, you know that the fire is very, very hot. In other words, the higher the count, the lower the temperature.

Determining the temperature in ovens without a thermostat can be done in the same way. Insert your hand halfway between the deck and the top of the oven and count one, two, three, and so on, in the same manner, up to eight. If you must remove your hand before reaching the count of eight, you can be certain that the oven is hot enough and ready for roasting.

Starting a good barbecue fire requires practice and skill. The methods which follow are both workable and practical.

1. If using an electric starter, follow the model directions *explicitly.* If liquid starter fuel is used, sprinkle it on the coals *at least a full minute before* applying the starter.

Never, never, never use gasoline or kerosene. And remove all aerosol cans—bug sprays, air fresheners, or other such units—from the vicinity of the grilles.

2. If using canned heat, empty the contents of a small can into a cup fashioned from aluminum foil. Then place it in the fire box, heap charcoal over it in a mound, and ignite. Allow it to burn through and then spread coals over the area desired.

3. Take an empty, 2-lb. coffee can and cut off the top and bottom. With a triangular beverage opener, punch holes in a straight line about 1-1/2 in. apart; bend the tip of the triangles down to form legs and to

allow for drift. Half fill this with charcoal and place it in the center of the fire box. Pour a generous amount of starter liquid over it and cover lightly with charcoal. Allow it to stand for 15 minutes and then ignite *at base.* After it is burning well, add a number of untreated briquettes to nearly reach the top and allow to burn. Next, carefully remove the can and rake the coals over the area desired.

Transporting Equipment

Barbecue and grille equipment require care in packing for transport to and from your commissary. Heavy padded canvas tarpaulins should be used for cover and protection *only* because soot and odors from the equipment can be transferred to other equipment.

Preparing barbecue and grille equipment for return to the commissary is a time-consuming and dirty job. All coal and ashes must be removed from fire boxes and properly disposed of.

Furthermore, *the equipment must be absolutely cold before handling.* Numerous layers of soaking wet newspapers can be placed on grilles to cool them down, and additional water can be poured over them to speed up the process. Access to a hose would be very helpful also.

To clean up pots, skillets, and wire grilles, soap-moistened abrasive pads will be a great aid. However, after returning to the commissary, you should again thoroughly clean all equipment, steaming it, if possible. Then, and only then, can you inspect and repack it for future use.

In catering barbecues, as with other types of parties, proper sanitation and refrigeration cannot be overlooked. All work and serving areas should be inspected, and must be scrupulously clean. While flying and creeping insects may not be bothersome in the barbecuing area, since smoke and heat will drive them away, they could be a source of great annoyance in the service areas. If you must use an insect repellent, do it very carefully; spray it as close to the ground as possible and *do not spray it near any food.*

If the truck you are using does not have refrigeration facilities, then keep all foods in portable foam or fiber glass coolers, using canned freezing pellets or dry ice to keep them at the desired temperature.

Unless proper refrigeration and refrigerated serving facilities are available, it would be inadvisable to serve at a warm weather barbecue any of the following foods: egg and milk mixtures, custards, eclairs, cream puffs, cream-filled cakes, and foods heavy with mayonnaise, such as potato salad, tuna salad, and deviled eggs. These items are particularly sensitive to spoilage.

If you must use salads or dishes containing mayonnaise, take all the ingredients in separate containers under refrigeration and mix them on the job.

Destroy immediately any leftover foods. Do not be big-hearted and give any foods to guests or your client to take home. Strict adherence to this procedure will not only enhance your reputation, but will also protect you from the danger of illness resulting from possible food contamination.

Equipment List For Barbecue Parties
Asbestos gloves
Assortment of wood/bamboo skewers
Brushes—two: one for butter, one for sauce
Canvas gloves—for use in setting up and clean up
Cloth towels and aprons
Fancy carving knife, fork, and steel
Fire extinguisher
First aid kit with burn ointment
Heavy frying pans—cast iron is the most functional material
Hibachis—for use as supplementary grilles for appetizers, side dishes, or small items
Hot pads
Large metal-shielded skewers
Large/showy pepper mill and salt shaker
Large wooden spoons
Long tongs—two: one for meat, one for coals
Long-handled fork, spoon, and turner (spatula)
Meat thermometer
Paper towels
Paring knives
Roast beef slicer
Sturdy work table with cutting boards for food preparation and service
Wire basket grilles—adjustable for the thickness of meat, fish, etc., and having long handles for ease in holding over heat

Variations in Meal Presentation

THERE ARE INNUMERABLE meal presentation possibilities to offer for your client's consideration. While some of these affairs provide normal profit returns, others offer larger profit opportunities. Presentation ideas vary with personal tastes, and although some people are financially able to indulge their desire for extremely lavish affairs, most clients select parties that have standard fare and are served with a modest amount of flourish.

COCKTAIL RECEPTION OR SOCIAL HOUR PRECEDING MEAL
(Standup at reception, seated at dinner)

If the budget allows, a "social hour" may precede an affair. The offerings for the social hour can consist of pre-poured sherry or other appetizer wines, or pre-poured cocktails, such as Manhattans, Martinis, Whiskey Sours, plus an assortment of "nibbles"—potato chips, nuts, bacon crisps, pretzels, and similar items.

BAR PLUS HORS D'OEUVRES
(Standup, with cocktail tables optional; hors d'oeuvres passed butler style)

In addition to bar facilities,* hot and/or cold hors d'oeuvres are usually included, and passed by waiters, hence the term Butler Style.

What you charge depends upon the extent of your involvement. How much did you supply in the way of glasses? Ice? Labor? The value of hors d'oeuvres or any accompaniments, plus the time involved, should be added to the cost of the meal.

BAR PLUS PARTIAL RECEPTION

This involves a fixed and specially decorated table upon which "finger foods" (canapes, cocktail sandwiches, dips, spreads) may be placed. It may also include one hot item from a chafing dish. The food should not be sweet; it should be salty, spicy, and drink-inducing because it is intended to be an appetite-teaser, not an appetite-spoiler.

This type of presentation requires a set-up table for hors d'oeuvres and extra linens, dishes, and decorative units, as well as additional personnel and preparation time. As a result, your cost, and thus the cost to the client is greater.

BAR PLUS FULL RECEPTION
(Generally required for lavish weddings, fund-raising dinners, and VIP testimonials)

This pre-meal reception, which lasts at least one or more hours, necessitates fixed tables with a variety of hot and cold items, plus at least two chafing dish items and additional hors d'oeuvres. In addition to, or in place of, chafing dishes, the client may prefer to have a chef or

*See the first three methods outlined in Chapter 11 under "Liquor Arrangements."

other person(s) carve ham, beef, smoked turkey, or salmon, pastrami, barbecued beef, and countless other exhibition items. Bar offerings should include a wide choice of liquors and a sufficient number of bartenders to ensure fast service.

This type of reception, followed by an equally expensive meal, gives you an opportunity to express fully your artistic and gastronomic abilities; for this you should receive ample compensation.

BASIC OR STANDARD LUNCHEON/DINNER MENU
(Four courses, seated)

> Starter course — Fruit, seafood, soup, etc.
> Main course — Fish, meat, or poultry (or a substantial salad), vegetable, bread, butter, and possibly relish
> Dessert
> Beverage

ADDITIONAL COURSES OR SALADS
(To be added to the basic meal)

Additional courses may be added to make the basic meal more elaborate, or to extend the eating period. Between the first course and the main entree, an additional "petite entree" may also be added. Assuming that fruit is the starter course and roast beef is the main entree, a small fish course such as stuffed fillet of sole or mousse of salmon, or perhaps a soup, can be added. About 40 minutes should be allowed for service of each course.

In some areas of the country, a salad (tossed green, Caesar, avocado) is served as a separate course before the main entree. Each additional course served means more revenue, of course.

INTERMEZZO COURSE

Although gourmets may disagree as to when the intermezzo should be presented, it is an impressive and profitable course. Intermezzo, as the term implies, means intermission—a time lapse before the main course is served.

During this period, which is usually part of a lavish menu, a dish of lemon sherbet (24- or 30-size scoop), topped perhaps with green or white creme de menthe, is served in a silver coupe or sherry glass; the idea is to cool and prepare the taste buds for the main course. Time, labor, and extra glass usage increase presentation costs, but you can still make a handsome profit with this course.

TYPES OF TABLE SERVICE

American

Tables set up for American service include: the complete place settings required by the menu; goblets or glasses of water with ice; rolls (in baskets or on bread-and-butter plates); butter (in iced butter dishes or on bread-and-butter plates); relish trays; cold appetizers (if served) on liners, and salads placed at the tip of each fork. Service plates may or may not be used, depending on the formality of the function being served.

After guests finish the appetizer, waiters should remove appetizer dishes and silver. The main course, completely plated in the kitchen, is then brought on trays to the dining area and served to guests.

If wine is served, the waiters pour it and place the bottles on the tables or in wine coolers next to the table.

When the main course is finished, the tables are cleared completely before the next course is served. No "seconds" on food are offered.

French or Russian

Many party givers object to American-type service because they feel it is too mechanical, too impersonal. They are willing, therefore, to spend more money for either French or Russian service.

Since these services are formal, the tables are usually tastefully decorated with a floral centerpiece and a candelabra. Place settings are geared to menu needs, and attractive service plates are used. No food is served until after guests are seated, and the only time there is no plate before guests is prior to the dessert course. All food is served from the left, beverages from the right. Tables are cleared from the right. Waiters often wear white cotton gloves, particularly for Russian service.

In French service, food is served from a rolling wagon and kept hot on rechaud burners (canned heat or alcohol-burning table stoves). Usually a two-waiter team takes care of a table at a time, with one portioning out the food and the other serving.

In Russian service, food is served from trays, platters, or tureens held by the waiter, with each item served directly to the guest. In addition to the main entree, this same tray may contain the vegetables; if not, another waiter will follow with the vegetables.

Wine is poured by the waiters, and glasses are refilled as needed. Wine bottles are never placed on the table; however, they can be placed in a wine cooler next to the table.

Dessert plates and silver may be removed, but coffee cups should remain, since a second cup of coffee can be offered. Tables are never cleared completely until after guests leave the room.

Both of these services require more and better-trained waiters, as well as more elaborate foodservice equipment. Thus, they command a higher price.

Viennese Tables

This could be *the grand finale,* the piece de resistance to a lavish meal presentation. Since the entire meal will have been served to seated guests, the Viennese table must be presented buffet style.

Most deluxe dinners offer just one dessert; this service, however, can include as many as 50 different desserts! Among these desserts might be elaborately carved fruit pieces offering a melange of melon wedges or balls, cherries, berries, grapes, orange and grapefruit sections with pineapple. Other possibilities are ice cream with various sauces (to make your own sundaes), layer cakes, French pastries, and petits fours. Gelatin desserts, peach or strawberry shortcakes, and puddings are additional considerations. When presented with skillful showmanship, the Viennese table will bring ecstatic responses from the guests.

Most guests will take more than they can eat; therefore, you would be wise to figure three desserts to each guest—for 150 guests have 450 desserts. Consequently, your charges for this should be *no less than four times the cost,* since unconsumed portions and leftovers on the display table represent a waste, as well as additional costs to you. If the client wishes to impress guests with this type of offering, then he/she should not object to the additional charge, which could run from $2.00 to $5.00 extra per guest.

THE BUFFET

The buffet, where foods are presented so guests can serve themselves, is not only popular for receptions and cocktail parties, but can also be a spectacular means for presenting an entire meal. It is particularly appropriate in homes where space is limited, and a large number of people are to be served. The buffet can be elaborate and elegant enough to suit the most sophisticated gourmet tastes and yet can add a special "flair" to the simplest of breakfast, lunch, and/or dinner menus.

Successful buffet catering must use the basic principles of merchandising, since *well-displayed merchandise sells itself.* Your food display, the garnitures, as well as the service ware, enhance the appearance of the table, and act as "attention-getters." As supplementary show-pieces, use ice carvings, flowers, tallow or butter molds, sugar or nougat work. These act as "come-ons" to attract guests to the table.

The buffet table, it can be said, is a miniature market place because its charm, magnetism, excitement, flavor, and food are geared to stimulate the shopper's appetite.

As guests approach the table, their minds subconsciously photograph the entire display; if it is artistically and attractively presented, they are entranced with the picture. Tempted by a wide choice of food beautifully offered, they will become victims of "impulse buying."

No matter how beautiful the table may be, its appearance will be enhanced by either mechanical or human animation. Having employees serve food from chafing or other service dishes is not only a gracious gesture, but one that materially assists in speeding up the service. A chef carving a roast or slicing a salmon has great customer appeal, but one actually cooking a variety of omelets, crepes, or deep-fry specialties kindles a curiosity that is hard to resist, and practically all onlookers are intrigued by the action.

Table-top or "exhibition cooking" should be used when practical. The term "when practical" means after giving serious consideration to the following:

Price

The costs involved in a buffet are higher because the person selected to do specialized cooking will have to spend the entire time at the buffet. Since this person's skill is great, his/her wage rate will be higher; therefore, consider whether your monetary return is sufficient to include this service.

Time

Table-top foods should not take too long to cook because waiting guests could create a traffic jam, interfering with service to others. Small crepes should be prepared in the kitchen, then taken to the buffet for final touches. Each pan should contain at least a dozen crepes so that a number of guests can be hand-served within a short period of time. Filled omelets should be made in a pan large enough for each omelet to be cut into 12-fork portions. Eggs Foo Yung, made in a 12-in. pan, will serve approximately 25 appetizer portions.

Small table-top grilles, capable of being heated by propane gas tubes, can cook from 40 to 60 cocktail franks or 40 cocktail hamburgers, which can be served on finger rolls or cocktail-size bread. A cheese fondue in a 2-qt. chafing dish or fondue pot is enough for at least 50 bread cubes. These suggestions are but a few of the different items that can be prepared quickly, but in quantity.

Equipment

In addition to small table-top grilles, other table-top cooking equipment, such as electric fry pans, waffle irons, chafing dishes, fondue pots, and deep fryers, can be also used effectively for buffet catering.

Table-top deep fat fryers are excellent for "exhibition frying." The most effective and convenient are stainless steel-clad of 4-qt. capacity *(do not use a larger one for buffet service)*, with a rating of no more than 110 volts and 1500 amps. The 1500 amps is important because the electrical system must be able to carry the load, which includes a large number of lights and/or other electrical equipment, without blowing fuses or tripping switches. Before using the fryer at a party, give it a dry run. Also, remember that great care and proper precautions must be taken to guard against accidental spillage.

When using, firmly set the fryer on a table, fill it to the factory-suggested line, using *homogenized shortening,* which is easier to carry and reduces the possibility of spillage.

Products to be deep fried must be free of water and *carefully* lowered into the shortening. Avoid overcrowding; this will allow the product to cook faster and eliminate overflowing of hot grease.

Some items that lend themselves well to table-top frying are: cocktail franks in beer batter; tiny potato puffs; deep-fried ravioli; breaded shrimp; corn puffs; tiny apple fritters; eggplant fingers; fillet of sole fingers; batter-dipped bologna cubes, boneless chicken wings.

Fondue cooking on a buffet is a sure-fire attention getter, and fondue is a comparatively simple dish to prepare. A cheese fondue is the most popular type.

To prepare, shred or dice cheese into small squares; place them in the fondue pot which is over a small fire, add wine, a touch of garlic and seasoning, and stir occasionally to prevent sticking or scorching. When the cheese begins to bubble, reduce the fire so that cheese bubbles only intermittently. Crusted French bread or croutons—each speared by a long bamboo skewer or a two-pronged long fondue fork— are placed on a tray so guests can dip their own. Large paper napkins and 4-in. plates should be available. An attendant should be nearby to replenish fondue or bread.

Space is an important consideration. Can "traffic" move freely? Is there enough space or room on the table to present this service effectively? Will there be sufficient open space around the preparation area so that the heat generated by the unit will not adversely affect other foods?

Safety

Safety is a paramount consideration at all times. Since table-top cooking involves hot liquids, cooking apparatus must be *firmly anchored or tied* to table legs or sides and set on a tray that is at least one-third larger than the unit used. *The table must be rigid and stand steadily on the floor. Never, never use a wobbly table for this purpose.*

If using a "knockdown" or collapsible table, make certain that leg hardware is firmly locked in place. *Then take the additional precaution of tying or wiring the leg hardware* to avoid the possibility of table collapse. When electric wiring is used, *tie the utensil's cord to the table leg* so that if anyone trips over the wire, the grille or fryer will not slide or move. When an extension cord must be on the floor—whether in a traffic area or not—cover it with 4-in. adhesive firmly fastened to the floor; thus, the wire cannot be kicked, and no one can trip over it.

Careless Employees

All precautions will be nullified if you permit a careless employee to do table-top cooking. The efficiency, skill, and adeptness of a qualified employee will add greatly to the effectiveness of your presentation.

Decorative Pieces for the Buffet

WHETHER A SIMPLE affair or a spectacular showcase, the buffet provides you and your staff with an opportune setting for displaying artistic and culinary talents. Ice carvings, tallow work, decorated foods, colorfully garnished food trays, speciality cakes, spun sugar, and nougat designs can be used singly or in combinations to dramatize and individualize buffet tables.

ICE CARVINGS/MOLDS

Because of their size and the effort needed to execute and move them, ice carvings are generally used only for very special occasions, and those held in hotels, clubs, and banquet halls. Furthermore, large unique ice carvings can be done only in an ice-house, or where there is a large walk-in freezer. Smaller ice molds, however, can be made in a commissary/kitchen.

Caviar on Ice

Caviar lends a touch of elegance to a reception or cocktail party buffet. It is most frequently presented in the original can on an ice mold. (See illustration on p. 132.)

To make an ice display for caviar, fill a large gelatin mold, a large, round bowl, or saucepan with water to a depth of 4 in.; place in a freezer until solidly frozen (from two to three days).

To unmold, set pan in hot water for a moment or two, then invert quickly on a tray covered with a plastic doily. (The diameter of the tray should be at least 8 in. greater than the mold.)

Using hot water, half fill a can or pan having approximately the same diameter as the caviar can. Place container of hot water in the center of the ice mold for a few minutes so the ice will melt sufficiently to allow for insertion of the caviar.

Before placing the caviar on ice, fold a small white napkin and place it in the melted area with the can on top. This will prevent the can from rolling or sliding. At this point, decorate the mold with lemon leaves, watercress, or parsley. Hollowed-out serrated lemons, filled with finely chopped, hard-cooked egg whites, or finely minced onions in sour cream, make a very effective garnish. Add lemon wedges or arrange them in a separate dish next to the mold.

Keep a large dry sponge and small pan nearby; about once every half hour, use the sponge to absorb the accumulated melted ice. Squeeze water into the pan. (Do this as unobtrusively as possible.)

Fruited Ice Molds for Punch Bowls

In the bottom of a heart-shaped pan, loaf pan, or ring mold, arrange sliced fruit, or mint leaves with strawberries or cherries. Pour in plain or tinted water, gingerale, fruit juice, or lemonade to a depth of 1/4 in., and freeze. When frozen, fill the mold with additional liquid, then refreeze. To unmold, dip the pan in hot water to the rim, and then invert into punch bowl.

EDIBLE CENTERPIECES

Edible, or partially edible, centerpieces can highlight different sections of the table, or can be most attractive as the focal point on the buffet. For a large elaborate buffet table, they may be supported by an elegant floral arrangement or an ice carving.

Fruited Centerpiece

With florist clay, anchor styrofoam shaped as in the illustration on p. 134, to the inside of a medium or large, silver or glass bowl. Insert bamboo sticks or club toothpicks in the styrofoam, as shown, and "hang" leaves, grapes, pineapple stems, melon balls, strawberries, etc., from them. Fill the bottom of the bowl with shredded coconut, walnut or pecan meats, lemon leaves or other greenery.

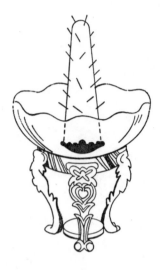

Melon Pieces

Melons, particularly watermelons, can be made into eye-catching centerpieces. Because of their size and shape, watermelons can be arranged either vertically or horizontally, depending upon the amount of display space allowed and the effect desired.

MELON BASKET (VERTICAL)– Scrub entire melon, and dry it well. Scabs and blemishes can be removed by gently scraping the surface. Cut off the bottom (see B in the illustration on facing page) so that melon will stand firmly by itself. Cut away two sections (see A in illustration on facing page) and reserve for slices to surround the base of the melon.

Use an ice cream scoop or large spoon to scoop out the melon flesh to within 2 in. from the bottom, and about 1/2 in. from the walls. Smooth off inner walls before filling with melon balls and more fruit.

Score patterns on the melon surface with a gouging tool (see illustration on facing page) available in hobby shops or art stores. Use french ballers of various sizes to cut "buttons" from the rind. Reverse the "buttons" in each hole for a pleasing effect, or cut "buttons" from orange and/or grapefruit rinds, and place these cutouts in the watermelon rind holes. If the melon must be made far in advance, shrinkage could occur; therefore, it is suggested that the cutouts be anchored with toothpick points.

Serrate handles and edges of melon in any manner desired. Fill the "basket" cavity with cut melon pieces or balls and any additional fruit desired. Make certain that the melon rind surfaces are perfectly dry, then polish with a soft cloth lightly coated with salad oil.

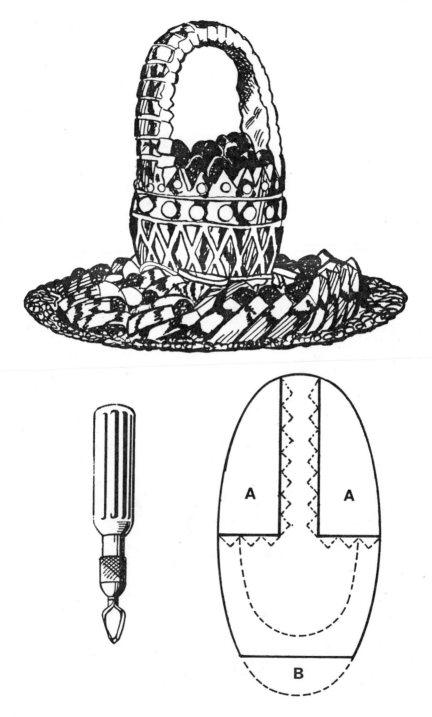

MELON BASKET (HORIZONTAL)—Follow the same procedure as the one used for a vertical basket, but work with the melon placed horizontally. If in cutting out the basket handles, part of the handle breaks off, just even off the broken sides, and add a few decorative finishing touches to make it appear that the design was intentional.

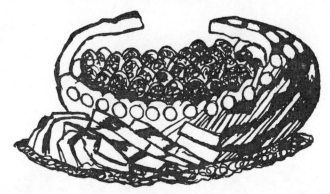

MELON HEAD—Wash the watermelon thoroughly, and let it dry. Using a magic marker, outline the nose, eyes, and lips. Cut through the rind around the marked areas, and carefully pull away the unwanted rind with a paring knife. Smooth off all exposed surfaces, then decorate as desired. For the hat, use stem of a pineapple on a center cut of

pineapple. For the ears, position pineapple rings with toothpicks. Fill centers with red cherries (optional).

ONE PASSENGER AUTOMOBILE— 1. Wash and dry melon thoroughly.

2. Cut as shown below, slicing a piece of the rind from the bottom of the melon so it will rest steadily on a tray.

3. Slice a piece from the thinner end of the melon, and attach a pineapple stem with toothpicks.

4. For the windshield, fit a wedge-shaped slice of melon into a groove prepared in front of the center cut.

5. For the bumper, fit a wedge-shaped slice of melon into a pre-pared groove in the front end of the "automobile."

6. For the head, use a small orange, and cut out features.

7. For the hat, use half of a large orange; scallop the edges, cut out pulp, and top with a cherry "button."

8. For the steering wheel, use a thick, round slice of orange.

9. For backrests and doors, wedge a slice of fresh pineapple into place.

10. For large wheels, use fresh pineapple slices.

11. For smaller wheels or hub caps, use small slices of canned pine-apple, and fill centers with cherries.

12. For the headlights use sliced oranges or lemons with cherries as the centers.

13. Use a scoring tool to add finishing touches. Display on a decora-tive tray.

DECORATED FOOD PRESENTATIONS

Hot foods require only the very simplest of garnishes—sprigs of pars-ley, crisp fresh watercress, paprika-dipped celery curls, pickle fans, carrot curls, parsley-dipped lemon wedges—which are added quickly.

Radish Roses

Using a small, sharp knife, remove the tail from each radish. With point of knife make six or eight, thin, deep cuts in each from top to stem. *Do not cut off.* Place radishes in cold water, and refrigerate for several hours to open "rose" petals. For speed in preparing large numbers of radish roses, you may prefer to use a commercial type of cutter. (See illustration, below left.)

Celery Curls

Cut celery into 3- to 4-in. lengths. Slash lengthwise to within 1/2 in. of leaves or end of celery piece. Or slash both ends, leaving 1/2 in. in center. Place in cold water, and chill until slashed ends curl. Before serving, shake water from celery curls and dip ends in paprika. (See illustration, below right.)

Carrot Curls

Select large crisp carrots; pare or scrape off outer skin. Using a vegetable peeler, cut carrot into lengthwise paper-thin strips. Roll the strips lightly and fasten with a toothpick. Chill for at least an hour in ice water in the refrigerator. Remove toothpicks before serving. (See illustration below.)

Pickle Fans

Cut sweet gherkins into thin lengthwise slices almost to the end of each pickle. Spread slices carefully and press uncut end so fan will hold its shape. (See illustration, below left.)

Accordion Pickles

Slice ends from sweet gherkins. Make thin, crosswise slices almost but not quite through each pickle. Bend pickle gently so the slices separate at the top. (See illustration, below right.)

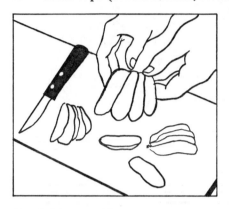 

Turnip/Potato Lilies

To make each lily, cut two, thin turnip or potato slices, and fold to shape flower. Place a carrot stick in the center; fasten with toothpicks. Chill in cold water in the refrigerator.

Cold foods, by their nature, permit more time for garnishing and decorating than do hot foods. At times a simple garnish may be all that is needed. But, for special occasions and certain types of foods, you will want to use more creative and decorative designs.

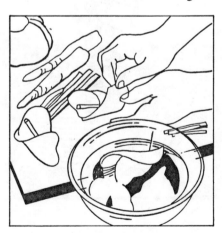

MEAT PRESENTATIONS

Christmas ham, chaudfroid, can be displayed on a mirrored tray with garnishes of stuffed cherry tomatoes and wedges of large tomatoes spread with cheese, reshaped and glazed.

Sliced ham and tongue pates are arranged on a mirrored surface and garnished with decorated and glazed hard-cooked eggs and chopped aspic. The candle and holder are of tallow.

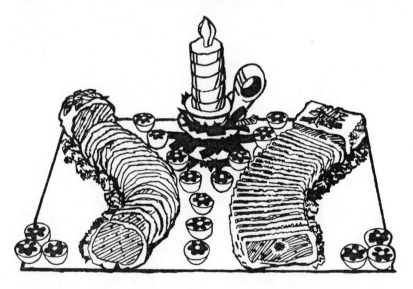

Roast beef and slices of beef can be presented around a parsley and cherry tomato "tree" and garnished with glazed salami cones on artichoke bottoms. The "tree" is made from cone-shaped styrofoam. Toothpicks are used to "hang" the parsley and secure the cherry tomatoes.

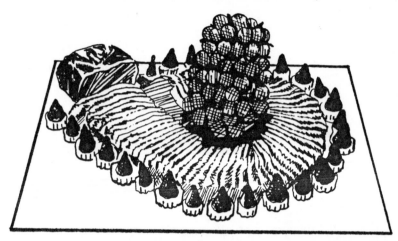

Slices of turkey breast encircle a whole roast turkey, chaudfroid. Poached pears with fresh mint or lemon leaves will make an attractive garnish.

PASTRY PRESENTATIONS

Pastry and other desserts arranged on mirrored trays make beautiful displays. If you make your own mirrored trays, you not only lift the presentation out of the ordinary, but individualize it as well.

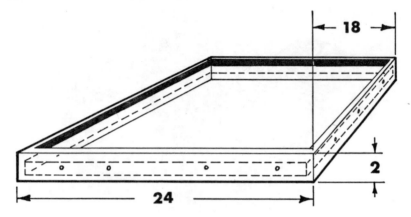

1. Make an 18- by 24-in. frame using 2- by 1/2-in. wood.
2. Fit in a 1-in. plywood sheet to within 1 in. from the top; nail.
3. Cover entire area (sides, inside, top of plywood) with velvet.
4. Measure the inside dimensions of the frame, and have a 1/4-in. mirror cut to fit.

Although the following pastry displays are expensive to execute, they can serve as patterns for less elaborate affairs.

The handled basket filled with miniature brownies is made of "nougat," a type of brittle. The petits fours, consisting of three to four layers, totalling not more than 1-1/4 in. in height, and topped with glazed apricots, cherries, and strawberries, are symmetrically arranged on a mirrored tray. (See illustration on facing page.)

The heart shaped box is made of nougat, topped with ribbons and a rose, both made of spun sugar. The rolled cake slices are filled with butter cream or melba jelly, and covered with a thin layer of patterned and flavored marzipan. (See illustration on facing page.)

Anyone who has mastered the fundamentals of cooking can develop the skills needed to dramatize foods effectively. The intent of this chapter is to stimulate interest in the art of food decoration and presentation. To further develop skills and techniques, practice is necessary. Additional ideas for varying food displays can be found in the many foodservice industry magazines and books such as *The Art of Garde Manger, The Book of Buffets,* and *The Professional Chef.*[1]

1. Published by Cahners Books, Boston.

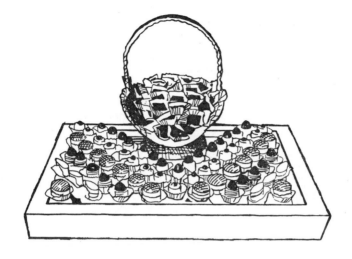

The American
Matrimonial Business

THE AMERICAN matrimonial business generates in excess of $8 billion annually (N.Y. Times, May 31, 1974). Despite the more casual attitude toward marriage today, it is estimated that 8 out of 10 young women still prefer formal weddings. And many of these young women and their parents will be seeking your services!

In discussing plans with prospective clients you will determine the location of the affair, the time of service, number of guests expected, food preferences, general arrangements as well as be prepared to answer any questions concerning etiquette and protocol for the affair the clients may have. You should then prepare and submit a proposal for the menu and desired services for the clients' approval. (See sample proposal on pp. 146-149.)

Although usually a Social Caterer is not involved in the selection of a florist, orchestra, or photographer for a wedding, your client may ask for your recommendations. Certainly, to insure the success of the affair you should be able to suggest people you know whom you will be able to work with smoothly.

Some establishments (hotels, clubs, etc.) may not permit just any florist, orchestra, or photographer to work in their facility. Their reasoning is usually based on past experience—poor performance, abuse of house rules, lack of cooperation. Therefore, they may insist that a "house" florist, etc., be used. You should be aware of such con-

You should be aware of such conditions before making any recommendations to your client.

THE MUSIC

If music is to be used in public halls, hotels, and similar operations, union musicians must be employed. The union determines the size of the orchestra for the occasion, also. Rules vary across the country so check with the local musicians' union before hiring any orchestra or musical group.

The music is an important and integral part of the wedding and reception. The leader announces the "grand entrance" of the newly-weds, their first dance together, and then the first dance of the newly-married couple with their parents. The protocol of a religious ceremony before, during, or after the "feast," the cutting of the cake, and the music associated with this ritual, are also the orchestra leader's responsibility.

Lively and entertaining music contributes immeasurably to the total enjoyment of the affair. It is essential, however, that the orchestra leader coordinate his musical selections with the meal service. Dance music should *not* be played during the service of a food course. The musical selections to be featured during the meal should be planned with the host.

Unless specifically requested by the client, you are not required to serve food to the orchestra. However, if you can afford the expense, it might be prudent to provide a snack for them during one of their "breaks."

THE FLOWERS

Flowers for the wedding and reception are the responsibility of the wedding party. However, you should discuss with the client and the florist the flowers to be used on the buffet and/or head table.

A skilled florist will be able to tint flowers to match or harmonize with the bride's color scheme. Also, he will be able to provide wedding canopies and aisle markers, construct reception and head table backgrounds, and arrange plants and flowers in a variety of decorative settings.

All of the constructed pieces and floral decorations must be removed by the florist following the function, or at a time determined by the florist and the caterer. His area must be cleaned to the complete satisfaction of the supervisor of the premises. If a host-engaged florist neglects his clean-up responsibility, all related cleaning costs will probably be added to the host's bill.

THE PHOTOGRAPHER

A photographer of merit and ability should be employed to record the highlights of the affair. He should be skilled first in spotting, then in capturing on film, those special moments of joy so precious and evident at weddings.

A good photographer works without being too conspicuous or obtrusive. He can pick out suitable backgrounds for posed shots, and is knowledgeable about wedding customs and religious protocol.

Be sure the photographer supplies you with several good pictures of your part of the function: the buffet table, the bride and groom cutting the cake, the head table, and similar activities. These can be invaluable sales promotion tools for both you and the photographer.

THE WEDDING INVITATION

Although your services as a Social Caterer are not required in the selection and sending out of wedding invitations, you must point out to the client that an RSVP is essential if food is to be served. You must know how many guests will attend in order to prepare the proper amount of food.

THE MENU

Wedding dinners should have a printed menu. It is up to you to provide your client with a correct and clearly written menu to give to the printer. Formal menus are usually written in French; however, English is acceptable.

SAMPLE MENU PROPOSAL

JOHN DOE CATERING COMPANY *** 454 MAIN STREET *** HYDE PARK, N.Y.

Menu proposals: Reception and dinner (Wedding)
Mr. Mrs. Joseph Bell
25 Cartright Street
Hyde Park, New York, 12394

To be held at: Knights of Columbus Hall, North Road
New City, N.Y. 00965

Saturday, June 15, 19___
Reception at 3:00 p.m.
Dinner 4:30 p.m. (End by 8:30 p.m.)

To be served from Buffet Table: Choice of four

Deviled Eggs a la Russe	Salmon Roe Caviar	Coronets of Ham and Cheese
Rolled Anchovies on Rye	Pate of Calf's Liver	Shrimps on Horseback
Guacamole Dip	Stuffed Celery with Roquefort Cheese	

To be passed Butler style: Choice of three

Clams Casino	Oysters Rockefeller	Barquettes of Maine Lobster
Cocktail Franks in Batter	Chicken Livers en Brochette	Quiche Lorraine

Choice of two: Bite-size Glazed Corned Beef (sliced to order) on Rye Bread
Chicken a la King on Rice Pilaf   Stuffed Cabbage Rolls (bite-size)

Smoked Turkey (bite-size, sliced to order) on Honey-Nut Bread

Smoked Irish Salmon (sliced to order),　Sweet Onion Rings,　Capers in Dill

Bar Beverages:　Unlimited drinks per guest at bar and at tableside during dinner, including one champagne drink per guest, to toast newlywed couple, according with private arrangements with management of K.C. Hall.

DINNER—CHOICE OF ONE:

Fresh Shrimp Cocktail, Supreme　　Fresh Fruit-Filled Cantaloupe　　Pineapple Basket

Fresh Crabmeat en Avocado　　Broiled Grapefruit with Clover Honey

*

Choice of one:　Vichyssoise with Fresh Chives　　Consomme of Peacock with Game Quenelles

Boneless Brook Trout Filled with Salmon Mousse

Crabmeat-Stuffed Fillet of Sole with Truffles, Fish Veloute and Wine Sauce

*

Optional Courses ($1.00 extra):　Intermezzo;　Fresh Lemon Sherbet, Green Creme de Menthe

Salad prepared table side, House special

MAIN COURSE—Choice of one, served Russian style:

Saddle of Veal, Prince Orloff　　Thick-Cut Roast Rib of Beef

Chicken Kiev on Wild Rice, Brandied　　Beef Wellington, Giant Mushrooms

Filet Mignon (pre-sliced) Bearnaise Sauce

*

(Cont.)

SAMPLE MENU PROPOSAL (Cont.)

Bouquetiere of Fresh Vegetables

*

Iced Revere Bowl of Celery Hearts, Colossal Olives,
Radish Rosettes   Watermelon Rind Pickles

*

Choice of Dessert: Listed on separate sheet submitted.

House Special   Coffee   Tea   Decaffeinated Beverage

WEDDING CAKE: An attractively decorated, 6-tier wedding cake on 4 sets of columns. Will be tied with tulle bows and ornamented on top layer by 3 styrofoam bells (all white). Cake will be served from rolling carts, will be made of pound cake with dark chocolate filling, almonds, and rum flavoring. Entire surface to be decorated with Royal Icing. The price as tentatively agreed upon, plus tax.

CIGARETTES: We will provide 2 packages of assorted popular brand cigarettes per table of 10 guests.

DECORATIONS: We will set up a very attractive display for the center of the main reception table. It will be an il-luminated ice piece with two love birds in a heart ring, flanked by fresh flowers. All other reception tables will have appropriate tallow molds and/or butter molds. Each table will have a very attractive arrangement of fresh pink flowers set into a 4-candle candelabra with 12-in. pink candles.

LINENS: All tablecloths will be pale pink as will be the napkins. Ecru lace cloths over regular cloths, if desired, each table extra.

GRATUITIES: Included for waiters. Included for checkroom and restrooms; no tipping signs to be displayed.

FLOOR PLAN: Floor plan, based upon 150 guests, will be sent upon acceptance of menu items and deposit, as defined on contract.

TABLE CARDS: Will be hand-written, in authentic Spencerian script (extra), or will supply cards typed on I.B.M. Selectric at no extra charge. Guest list must be received no later than one week before affair.

SERVICE ARRANGEMENTS: Waiters, (waitresses) will wear red jackets. Beverage waiters will wear wine chains, and all waiters will wear white gloves.

MUSIC: Your own orchestra; we will coordinate service with leader.

MATCHES AND COCKTAIL NAPKINS: Personalized, and as tentative choice. Charges determined by amount ordered.

PRICE: $ per person; extra charges where so accepted, and initialed by you.

CONTRACT–DEPOSIT: Contract must be signed, and deposit acknowledged, by 14 days from date or by January 15th of 19____.
Our representative, Mr. John Doe, will be very happy to discuss this entire procedure with you, either at your home or at our office, at your convenience.

THE WEDDING CAKE

The wedding cake is not only the focal point of the buffet or dessert table, the cutting of it is one of the featured events of the affair. It is important that you work out the details of the "cutting" ceremony with the host and the photographer so there will not be any last minute confusion to spoil the event.

Although there are many wedding cake designs, traditionally, a wedding cake is always a tiered cake. The tiers are arranged either one on top of the other, or separated by dividers; inverted plastic or glass champagne glasses, plastic or floral columns may be used as dividers.

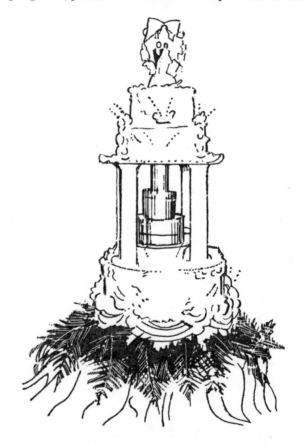

Posed photos of the bride and groom cutting the cake may be taken without disturbing the side of the cake that guests see, or affecting the delicately balanced top layers on a tiered cake. Before the photographer actually takes the picture, the caterer should cut from the rear of the bottom layer two pieces of cake, and place them on a small plate. Conceal these until after the bridal cake-cutting pose is photographed. Then photographs of the bride and groom sharing the pieces of cake may be taken. Your staff will then take over the cutting and serving of the cake.

Cutting the Cake

In certain areas of the country, it is customary to use the wedding cake as the main dessert item for the wedding menu. It is served either by itself or topped with ice cream and such sauces as vanilla custard, pineapple, fruit salad, black cherry, butter-pecan, or any other that appeals to the client.

Other customs dictate that pieces of the cake are bagged or boxed, then given to the guests to take home as a memento (or for single girls to "dream on"). Special bags, with grease resistant liners, appropriately decorated for use as wedding cake souvenir containers are available in stores selling party goods.

Traditionally, the top layer of the cake and the ornament are not cut, but are removed, boxed, and given to the newlyweds to be saved for their first anniversary celebration. The exposed second tier is then sliced and served, before cutting into the next lower tier. The tiers may be cut in a variety of ways to obtain the number of portions needed. (See illustration on following page.)

Decorating the Head Table

THE HEAD TABLE is *the* focal point of the entire dining room. Not only should it have the most effective appearance, but whenever possible, it should be elevated on either a platform or a dais.

Prefabricated platforms are available, and can be built in as many "steps" or rows as you desire. These are often worthwhile investments for permanent establishments, such as hotels and public banquet halls. Before purchasing any of these collapsible platforms, however, be certain to make provisions for storage. And, remember, when elevated arrangements are requested, you are entitled to an additional charge for set-up, use, and break-down.

If a dais is needed, but the facility in which you are serving does not have one, you should be able to supply it. Homemade ones are easy to build; easy to store, transport, and can be set up with the services of just two persons. This equipment also represents a plus factor in terms of the services you can offer. And by charging a fee for use and

CUTTING WEDDING CAKE[1]

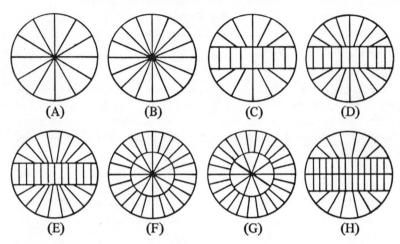

Cutting guide for tiered wedding cake. (A) 8-in., 2-layer cake; yield: 12 servings. (B) 9-in., 2-layer cake; yield: 16 servings. (C) 10-in., 2-layer cake; yield: 20 servings. (D) 11-in., 2-layer cake; yield: 26 servings. (E) 12-in., 2-layer cake; yield: 30 servings. (F) 12-in., 2-layer cake; yield: 36 servings. (G) 13-in., 2-layer cake; yield: 36 servings. (H) 14-in., 2-layer cake; yield: 40 servings.

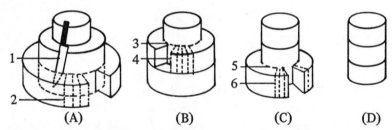

Cutting tiered cakes. (A) Cut vertically through bottom layer at edge of 2nd layer as indicated by dotted line No. 1; then cut out wedges as shown by 2. (B) Follow same procedure with middle layer; cut vertically through 2nd layer at edge of top layer as indicated by dotted line No. 3; then cut wedges as shown by 4. (C) When entire 2nd layer has been served, cut along dotted line 5; cut another row of wedges as shown by 6. (D) Remaining tiers may be cut as desired.

---

1. Reprinted with permission from the American Institute of Baking, *Catering Handbook*, p. 142.

transportation, your construction costs will be self-liquidating; you may, in fact, even show a profit on your investment.

HEAD TABLE CONSTRUCTION

Five portable (4- by 6-ft.) platform sections will hold two 8-ft. by 30-in. tables end to end, seating from 8 to 10 persons, with sufficient room provided behind chairs so that waiters can serve comfortably.

These portable platform sections should be hooked together for safety (see illustration on following page), and be covered with removable rugs, or painted a glossy black, probably the most practical color. Keep in mind that neither the chairs nor the tables should extend to the very edge of the platform.

As a safety feature, and for aesthetic value, place two upright stanchions, at least 36 in. high, screwed into flanges belted to the floor, at the front ends of the platform (see illustration on p. 155.) A plumber or a plumbing supply house can build these in short order.

Brass pipe, chrome or even plain black pipe (painted gold, aluminum, or any other desired color), are also effective but they should be capped with the same metal as the base. Insert screw eyes into each stanchion to hold decorative gold rope or ribbons. Rope or ribbons are available from fabric and trimming stores.

Head tables *should always be draped or skirted.* To serve as a base for the skirts, a "silence cloth," similar to a lightweight blanket, should be positioned first to cover the entire table. This cloth reduces service noise and acts as an anchor for table drapes.

Before draping the table, have the following items on hand (see illustration on p. 156):
A roll of 1-1/2- or 2-in. masking tape
"T" pins of both the 1-1/2- and 2-in. size
Corsage pins (2-in. size)
Thumb tacks with 1/2-in. heads *(Do not use a stapler)*
A steam iron
Draping material

PROCEDURE FOR DRAPING TABLES

Cover the table with the silence cloth, folding it under the table top, where it should be securely taped. Before draping, fold the material to be used in half to find its center; then, pin the center into the middle of the table. Pin the right-hand end of the drape cloth to the table corner at the extreme right; then, repeat this procedure on the left side. (See illustration on p. 157.)

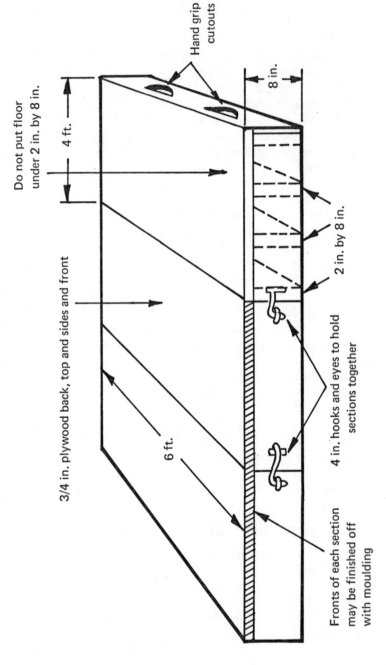

PORTABLE "RISERS" OR DAIS FOR HEAD TABLE

Do not put floor under 2 in. by 8 in.

4 ft.

Hand grip cutouts

8 in.

2 in. by 8 in.

3/4 in. plywood back, top and sides and front

6 ft.

4 in. hooks and eyes to hold sections together

Fronts of each section may be finished off with moulding

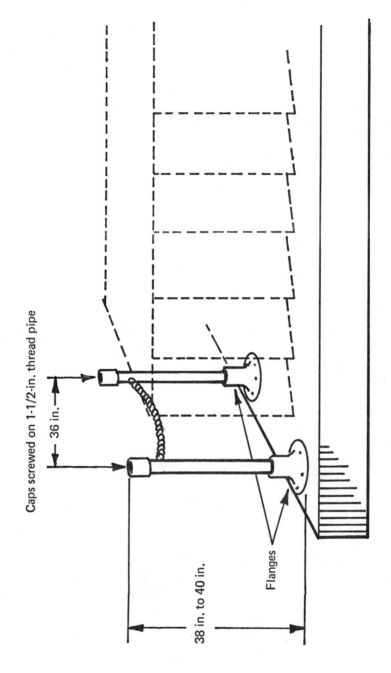

STANCHIONS SUGGESTED FOR EACH END OF HEAD TABLE DAIS

Caps screwed on 1-1/2-in. thread pipe

36 in.

38 in. to 40 in.

Flanges

"TOOLS" FOR DRAPING TABLES

1/2-in. Thumb Tacks

Corsage Pins

1-1/2 in.

Masking Tape
1-1/2 in. to 2 in.

"T" pins

1 in.

1-1/4 in.

1-1/2 in.

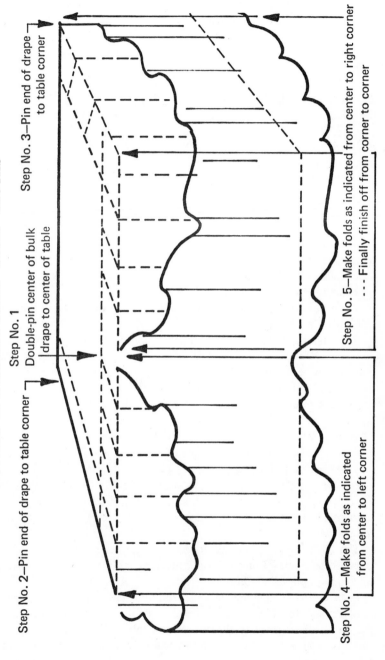

METHOD OF DRAPING USING "BULK" CLOTHS

Step No. 1
Double-pin center of bulk drape to center of table

Step No. 2—Pin end of drape to table corner

Step No. 3—Pin end of drape to table corner

Step No. 4—Make folds as indicated from center to left corner

Step No. 5—Make folds as indicated from center to right corner
- - - Finally finish off from corner to corner

The amount of loosely hanging material will determine how generous you can be with pleats. Pleats must all face in the same direction, and be of equal size. To maintain uniformity, and to mark off pleat widths, use a ruler or a piece of heavy cardboard; then tape or pin each fold to the silence cloth. (See illustration on facing page.) When using pins, do not leave points exposed.

In order to sharpen the folds, use a hot steam iron at the end of the table where the horizontal and vertical lines meet. To relieve pull on the silence cloth while draping, place several upended chairs or other heavy objects on the table opposite the part being draped. Make sure the skirt bottom is even all along the floor. *Do not allow the skirt to touch the floor;* it should be elevated enough so that it will not brush the shoes of anyone standing in front of the table. As a guide for uniform drape lengths, use a heavy piece of cardboard properly marked for that purpose, adjusting to the proper height as you pin or tape.

Table skirts or drapes can be made of synthetic fabrics, but should be of subdued, solid colors rather than patterns. As additional points, remember that the fabric should be:

1. Lightweight so that its weight will not pull down the anchor cloth
2. Opaque, closely woven, and easy to wash or clean
3. Wrinkle-resistant or crushproof so it can be rolled, folded, or hung on skirt hangers
4. Preferably flameproof, a mandatory requirement in some areas

If you know someone who is handy with a sewing machine, have that person hem the edges of one side of the draping material, and put a drawstring through it. Pin the string ends to the opposite corners, and be sure the resulting ruffles are evenly distributed.

To provide for graceful ruffling, as well as for convenient handling, have these units made in 5-yd. lengths. This will result in luxurious ruffling at the front or on the ends of either 6- or 8-ft. tables.

After the drapes are in place, put the top tablecloth over the table. Since seamed edges are not always straight, fold under the front edges to form a perfectly straight fold, or bring the regular seam of the top cloth to the table edge, then pin a 3- or 4-in. ribbon over it from one table corner to the other.

The cloth drop on the guests' side of the head table should be no longer than 8 in. Longer drops interfere with seating and can get tangled with guests' clothes.

Lace cloths, which are placed over the tablecloth and allowed to hang beyond the front skirts to within a foot or so of the floor, will give an air of elegance to the entire head table. They will also save the time involved in trying to match top edges, because the lace cloth hides the slight unevenness.

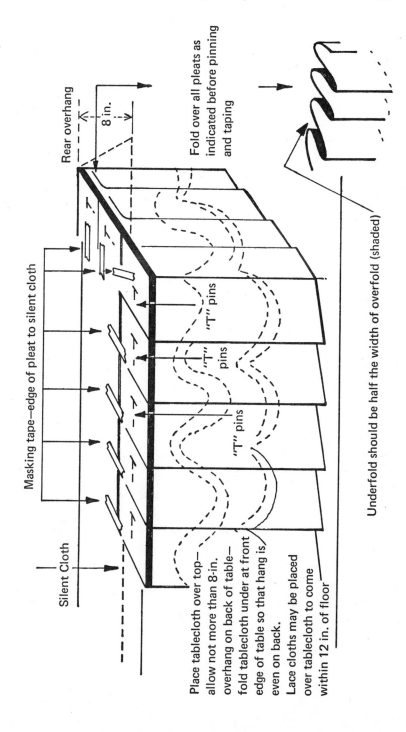

Rear overhang

8 in.

Fold over all pleats as indicated before pinning and taping

Masking tape—edge of pleat to silent cloth

"T" pins

"T" pins

"T" pins

Silent Cloth

Place tablecloth over top— allow not more than 8-in. overhang on back of table— fold tablecloth under at front edge of table so that hang is even on back.
Lace cloths may be placed over tablecloth to come within 12 in. of floor

Underfold should be half the width of overfold (shaded)

Should an occasion call for a particular color scheme and your drapes are inappropriate, you can solve this problem quite simply by ordering additional tablecloths.

Take a cloth, place it on a flat surface and press in folds or pleats with a steam iron (see illustration on p. 161). Hang this as a pre-pleated drape, using the regular draping procedure. Since these "emergency drapes" are shorter, it is advisable to overlap edges from 3 to 4 in. to prevent gaps between cloths.

Another very effective way of adding interest to the head table is to fold napkins (see illustration on p. 162) and, then, turn them over and put them in between each fold. You can use cloths and napkins of contrasting colors to make an intriguing arrangement.

The front of the head table can be garlanded with ferns, smilax, lemon, huckleberry leaves, or natural string smilax, all of which may be obtained from your florist. Natural string smilax is, of course, the most elegant. However, permanent string smilax of plastic or other synthetic material is now available; it is of very fine quality, decorative, delicate, and very difficult to distinguish from the natural.

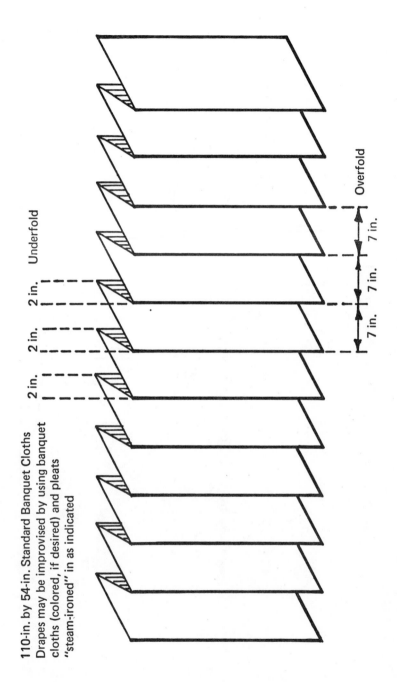

110-in. by 54-in. Standard Banquet Cloths
Drapes may be improvised by using banquet
cloths (colored, if desired) and pleats
"steam-ironed" in as indicated

Underfold

2 in. 2 in. 2 in.

Overfold

7 in. 7 in. 7 in.

DECORATIVE DRAPING FOR BUFFET OR HEAD TABLE

Colored napkin

Fold opposite corners

Reverse napkin and place between folds as indicated

Wine and Bar Service/14

EVERY STATE (and many counties) has its own rules and regulations regarding the sale of alcoholic beverages. If wise, you will check with your local Liquor Control Board before purchasing liquor for resale.

A liquor license is required for all liquor service except when it is served in a private home. In such a case, your client will purchase the liquor to be served to guests.

If you are an on-premise caterer, you can install a permanent bar in your banquet hall after getting a liquor license. When a liquor license is not obtainable, a special one may be available to permit the sale of beer, wine, and champagne only. Whenever you are catering and alcoholic beverages are served, be very careful; do not sell or serve them to minors. If you do, you will not only jeopardize your license, but may find yourself in serious difficulty.

Although your client will supply the alcohol for a private home party, you must provide the bartender, a portable bar or a long table, the necessary glasses and bar service equipment, mixes, and the ice. The number of glasses you will need will depend upon the type and time of function, length of time the bar is to be open, and the type of guest (age and sex) to be served. Generally, you should plan on providing approximately 10 to 15 percent more glasses than the number of guests expected, which will alleviate the need for on-the-job washing. Many attractive disposable "glasses" are available today, and you may consider using them for certain types of functions. However, be sure the client knows your intentions, and is in agreement.

BASIC BAR EQUIPMENT

Bar strainer
Bottle opener
Can opener
Cloth or absorbent paper towels
Corkscrew
Eight-inch round cutting surface
Glass stirring rod or long spoon for mixing, stirring
Large pitchers (with good pouring lips for water, juice, etc.)
Measuring spoons
One jigger measure—with an accurate scale for half and quarter-ounces
Paring knife—for peeling and cutting fruit
Precision pourers to replace corks or caps
Sturdy mixing glass or shaker
Vacuum-type ice bucket with tongs
Waste basket
Wooden muddler—for mashing mint, herbs, and fruits
Zester—for cutting shreds of lemon, lime, or orange

STANDARD BAR MEASURES

1 Dash	1/8 teaspoon (1/32 ounce)
1 Teaspoon (bar spoon)	1/8 ounce
1 Pony	1 ounce
1 Jigger (bar glass)	1-1/2 ounces
1 Wine Glass	4 ounces
1 Split	6 ounces
1 Cup	8 ounces
1 Miniature	1, 1.6, or 2 ounces
1 Half Pint	8 ounces
1 Tenth (4/5 pint)	12.8 ounces (1/10 gallon)
1 Pint (1/2 quart)	16 ounces
1 Fifth (4/5 quart)	25.6 ounces (1/5 gallon)
1 Quart	32 ounces (1/4 gallon)
1 Imperial Quart	38.4 ounces

STANDARD BAR MEASURES (Cont.)

1 Half Gallon	54 ounces
1 Gallon	128 ounces

Wine or Champagne Sizes
(NOTE: Called "pints" or "quarts" in the trade but not true contents)

Split	(1/4 bottle)	6 to 6-1/2 ounces
Pint	(1/2 bottle)	11 to 13 ounces
Quart	(1 bottle)	24 to 26 ounces
Magnum	(2 bottles)	52 ounces
Jeroboam	(4 bottles)	104 ounces
Tappit-Hen	(1 gallon)	128 ounces
Rehoboam	(6 bottles)	156 ounces (1.22 gallons)
Methuselah	(8 bottles)	208 ounces (1.625 gallons)
Salmanazar	(12 bottles)	312 ounces (2.44 gallons)
Balthazar	(16 bottles)	416 ounces (3.3 gallons)
Nebuchadnezzar	(20 bottles)	520 ounces (4.07 gallons)
Demijohn		627.2 ounces (4.9 gallons)

BOTTLE INVENTORY

When liquor is delivered to the bar, you (or the bartender) and your client should inventory the number of bottles. Such an inventory can later save much embarrassment, and avoid possible suspicion developing that some liquor is missing. At the end of the party, your client and the bartender should again count all bottles, including empties, unopened, and broken bottles. The number, of course, should be the same as originally inventoried.

THE COCKTAIL HOUR

In planning a cocktail hour/reception that precedes a dinner, your client and you must agree in advance as to when the bar will open and close. Do not prolong serving drinks beyond the agreed time, or your carefully planned dinner may not be up to your usual high standards.

During the cocktail hour, waiters can pass hors d'oeuvres or, if a buffet set-up is used, they can replenish it as needed. These same waiters will also serve the dinner that follows.

An experienced bartender should be knowledgeable in the proper mixing and dispensing of drinks. Nevertheless, have a good basic bartender's guide book available for ready reference, if needed. In addition to dispensing drinks preceding the dinner, a bartender should pour the wine or champagne during the meal, and be available for bar service later in the evening, if the client so desires.

GUIDE FOR DETERMINING PARTY BEVERAGE REQUIREMENTS

The following is a reference only. For safety purposes, use quarts instead of fifths.

Number of Guests	For Cocktails	Amount Needed	Buffet or Dinner	Amount Needed	After Dinner Party
4	10 to 16 drinks	1 fifth	8 cocktails 8 glasses, wine 4 liqueurs 8 highballs	1 fifth 2 bottles 4/5 pint 1 fifth	12 to 16 drinks
6	15 to 22 drinks	2 fifths	12 cocktails 12 glasses, wine 8 liqueurs 18 highballs	1 fifth 2 bottles 1 fifth 2 fifths	18 to 26 drinks

8	18 to 24 drinks	2 fifths	16 cocktails	1 fifth	20 to 34 drinks
			16 glasses, wine	3 bottles	
			10 liqueurs	1 fifth	
			18 highballs	2 fifths	
12	20 to 40 drinks	3 fifths	24 cocktails	2 fifths	25 to 45 drinks
			24 glasses, wine	4 bottles	
			16 liqueurs	1 fifth	
			30 highballs	3 fifths	
20	40 to 65 drinks	4 fifths	40 cocktails	3 fifths	45 to 75 drinks
			40 glasses, wine	7 bottles	
			25 liqueurs	2 fifths	
			50 highballs	4 fifths	

Rule of thumb for quick computation:
1 case/12 fifth whiskey: 240 drinks; Quarts: 300 drinks per case
1 case wine or champagne (fifths): 96 to 100 drinks per case

WINE AND CHAMPAGNE SERVICE

The selection of wines for any occasion is, of course, up to the client, but it is to your advantage to make suggestions whenever possible.

The most commonly used guide is: red wine with red meats, game, and hearty dishes; and white wines with fish, seafood, omelets, chicken, and veal. Roses, champagnes, and other sparkling wines go with any foods—appetizers, the main course, or desserts.

Red wines should be served at a cool room temperature (60° to 65°F.). White wines, roses, and champagnes should be chilled to 50° to 55°F.

The amount of wine to be served depends on the size of the glass used. A large glass should not be filled more than half-full, while a small glass should be filled to within one-half or three-quarters of an inch from the top of the glass. For champagne, a four- to five-ounce flute

or tulip-shaped glass is often preferred to the traditional saucer-shaped glass, because it helps retain the wine's effervescence longer.

To pour wine, remove the foil or lead seal *just below the cork* so that it will not come in contact with the wine. Some wines have a ring on top of the cork; if this is the case, remove the ring, then twist and pull the cork from the bottle.

In wine bottles where the cork is inserted into the neck, and flush with the bottle top, a corkscrew will be required. Use the corkscrew gently and patiently to get a firm bite into the cork, then work the tip in without crumbling the cork. A good corkscrew is an essential component of your "tool box."

To pour champagne, remove the wire hood, but make sure the cork remains securely in the bottle. Grasp the cork in one hand, and hold the lower part of the bottle in the other hand at a 45-degree angle, and *away from you and any nearby guests. Twist the bottle, not the cork* (see illustration on facing page), to allow the internal gas pressure to push the cork out. Once the cork has been removed, keep the bottle at the 45-degree angle for a few seconds to prevent the champagne from bubbling over.

Champagne is poured in two motions. First, pour it into a *dry glass* (moisture will kill bubbles) until the bubbles reach the brim of the glass. Stop pouring until bubbles subside, then fill the glass two-thirds to three-quarters full. Elevate the neck of the bottle slightly and turn it slowly, to prevent dripping. (See illustration on facing page.) Return the bottle to the cooler to keep the champagne cold, and retain its effervescence. Do not pour the champagne in advance, and allow it to stand.

WINE PUNCHES

Wine punches (see Chapter 16 for recipes) are popular for wedding and anniversary receptions, large tea parties, open houses, and similar occasions. Served from silver, glass, or decorated metal/plastic punch bowls, with matching ladles and trays, they can be very festive and less expensive than straight champagne. An ice ring or ice block decorated with fruit may be floated in the punch for added eye appeal.

Punch cups should be used in serving wine and champagne punches. Be sure to have enough on hand to serve all guests expected to attend the affair.

Wine or champagne punches served from a flowing fountain make an elaborate display for a large party. (See illustration on following page.) Keep the fountain filled; this will allow the guests to serve themselves.

This large champagne or punch fountain holds approximately 6 gal., has concealed lights, and offers a constant flow from four attractive spouts. It is approximately 32-1/2 in. high with 21-in. bowl diameter and therefore would only fit on a rather large buffet table.

IN PLANNING MENUS for a catered affair, you must be flexible. Keep in mind such things as the budget, facilities for service, season of the year, age, and type of guest, your own specialties, and other important factors. Your menus should be designed to fit the occasion, and should offer as wide a selection as possible.

One popular buffet menu contains the following items: Iced Relish Trays—Celery, Olives, Carrot Sticks, Pickles, Radishes. Assorted Cheese Platters—American, Swiss, Cheese Dip. Salads—Jellied Rainbow Fruit Salad, Maraschino Dressing; Potato Salad; Old-Fashioned Coleslaw; Mixed Green Salad, Oil and Vinegar Dressing; Fresh Shrimp Salad. Hot Dishes—Choice of two: Braised Tenderloin Tips; Swedish Meat Balls; Chicken Tetrazzini; Pan Fried Chicken Leg. Cold Assorted Meats—Roast Beef; Corned Beef; Baked Ham; Liverwurst. Condiments—Mustard Dish; Horseradish; Catsup. Bread (with Butter)—Hard Rolls, Pumpernickel. Beverage—Individual choice of: Milk, Orange, Coffee, Tea, or Iced Tea. A choice of desserts is also offered.

LUNCHEON MENU
(Minimum of 75 guests)

Choice of One

Supreme of Fresh Fruit
Soup du Jour   Miniature Antipasto   Spiced Tomato Juice
Eggs Romanoff

*

Sesame Sticks   Flaky Croissants   French Bread

*

Choice of One

Baked Karakas Ham, Champagne Sauce
Creamed Chicken and Mushrooms with Fleurons
Breast of Chicken a la Kiev
Yankee Style Pot Roast with Potato Pancakes
Sliced Turkey over Wild Rice, Mushroom Giblet Gravy
Baked Boston Scrod, Lobster Sauce
Broiled English Sole, Creamy Tartar Sauce
Individual Chef's Salad Bowl with Julienne of
Stilton Cheese, Chicken, Ham, Garlic Croutons

*

Choice of Vegetable or Individual Small Salad

Choice of Potatoes

Potato Croquette in Corn Flake Crumbs

Baked, with Sour Cream and Fresh Chives, or with Crumbled Bacon

Duchesse Potatoes   Au Gratin Potatoes

Lyonnaise Potatoes

*

Celery Sticks   Carrot Curls   Cranberry Relish

*

Choice of Desserts

Three-Layer Strawberry Shortcake

Linzer Torte   Creme de Menthe Frappe

Nesselrode Pie   Warm, Deep Dish Apple or Blueberry Pie

Flaky Hungarian Strudel

Preserved Pear Halves with Chocolate Sauce and Pignolias

*

Choice of Beverage

Coffee   Tea   Milk   Decaffeinated Beverage

LUNCHEON MENU
(For Small Groups of 20 to 30 Guests)

Choice of Appetizer

Fresh Fruit Cup   Chilled Orange Juice
Soup du Jour   Chopped Liver on Tomato Slices

Choice of One Entree

Roast Half Spring Chicken, Dressing and Country Gravy
Sauteed Sirloin Tips of Beef, Mushrooms and Peppers on Pilaf
Fried Deep Sea Scallops or Stuffed Shrimp
Broiled Sirloin Steak (8 oz.)
Pot Roast of Beef, Jardiniere
Grilled Ham Steak, Pineapple Ring
Broiled Fresh Ground Sirloin, Mushroom Sauce, Onion Rings
Sliced Sirloin of Beef on Toast, Sauce Jardiniere
Broiled Halibut or Boston Scrod with Lobster Sauce

*

Tossed Green Salad, Bleu Cheese Dressing or Choice of Vegetable

*

Choice of Potato

Baked Stuffed Potato, Bacon-Flavored Bits
Boiled Red Potatoes, Parsley Butter   French Fried Potatoes

Choice of Desserts

Cheese Cake, Graham Crust   Mint Frappe
Choice of Pies   Chocolate Eclair

Choice of Beverage

Coffee   Tea   Decaffeinated Beverage   Milk

BUFFET LUNCHEONS
(Menu to be decided about 5 days in advance—100 guest minimum)

HOT FOODS

Choice of One   (Poultry)
Fried Chicken Tidbits   Stewed Chicken and Dumplings
Chicken a la Cacciatore   Chicken Creole

PLUS, Choice of One   (Beef)
Beef Bourguignonne   Beef Stroganoff
Beef Roulades   Salisbury Steaks (miniature)
Meat-Stuffed Cabbages
Hand-sliced Sirloin of Beef, or Baked Ham ($0.00 extra)

PLUS,   Choice of one Hot Vegetable in Chafing Dish

PLUS,   Choice of Au Gratin Potatoes, or Western-Style Fried Potatoes

PLUS,   Green Salad, with all the trimmings

PLUS,   Sliced Cold, Poached Salmon or Halibut, Choice of Dressings
Combination Tray of Cold Corned Beef, Turkey, and Ham

PLUS,   Assorted Cheeses, Crackers

PLUS,   Fruit Bowl   Assorted Pastries   Three Varieties of Pie

PLUS,   Slice-your-own-breads and choice of sweet or salted butter

PLUS,   Coffee   Tea   Milk   Decaffeinated Beverage

WOMEN'S CLUB LUNCHEON MENU
(Menu to be determined 5 days in advance—50 guest minimum)

Choice of One

Fruit-Topped Grapefruit Half   Cranapple Juice
Fresh Shrimp Cocktail   Avocado Stuffed with Crabmeat
Vichyssoise

Choice of One

Chef's Special Salad   Fresh Fruit Cocktail with Cottage Cheese
Broiled Swordfish Steak
Crepe Filled with Chicken, Seafood, or Mushrooms
Pot Roast of Beef, Jardiniere   Breast of Chicken a la Kiev
Tuna Salad with Deviled Eggs
Grape Leaves Filled with Rice and Macadamia Nuts

*

Choice of Salad or Vegetable

PLUS Choice of Potato or Additional Vegetable

*

Choice of One

Eclairs   Toasted Pound Cake
Bar-le-Duc with Crackers   Banana Cream Pie
Lemon Sherbet, Creme de Menthe Sauce

*

Choice of Beverage

Coffee   Tea   Decaffeinated Beverage

FASHION SHOW OR DESSERT BRIDGE
DESSERTS AND BEVERAGES ONLY

DESSERT SELECTIONS—Choice of One
Assorted French or Danish Pastries (one tray per table)
Ice Cream Cake Roll (Waiters to offer choice of sauces)
Choice of Parfait (served with cookies)
Assorted Petits Fours
Fresh Fruit Tarts (Bowl of whipped cream on each table)
Large Fruit Cup (Fresh fruits only)
Eclairs Filled with Whipped Cream, Hot Fudge Sauce to be passed
Cream Cheese Cake, Choice of Toppings
Strawberry Shortcake or Special Cream Pies
(will be made for a minimum of 60 portions)
*

Bottomless Carafe of Coffee, each table
(Tea or Milk for individual requests)
*

Three-hour maximum. Host-supplied cards
Bridge tables $0.00 each table extra
*

Mints, candies, cigarettes, if furnished, will be set out in our
dishes—no extra charge

SERVICE CLUB LUNCHEON MENU

APPETIZER—Choice of One

Fresh Fruit Cocktail   Tomato Juice   Soup du Jour

*

Variety Breads   Miniature Dinner Rolls

*

CHOICE OF ENTREE

Baked Virginia Ham, Champagne Sauce   Pot Roast of Beef, Jardiniere

Half, Batter-Fried Boneless Chicken   Chicken Pot Pie with Short Crust

Sliced Flank Steak with Mushrooms, Horseradish Sauce

Hungarian Beef Goulash, Noodles   Grilled Ham Steak with Prune and Raisin Sauce

Broiled Halibut Steak, Maitre d'Hotel   Baked Fillet of Sole Stuffed with Crabmeat

*

CHOICE OF VEGETABLE

Broccoli Polonaise   Timbale of Spinach

Green Peas with Cocktail Onions   or   Cherry Tomatoes and Lettuce, Cream Dressing

*

CHOICE OF POTATO

Lyonnaise Potatoes   O'Brien Potatoes

Boiled Potatoes with Parsley Butter   Shoestring Potatoes

*

CHOICE OF DESSERT

Apple Pie with Stilton Cheese   Gruyere Cheese with Toasted Crackers

Orange Sherbet, Mandarin Sauce   Baked Apple with Peppermint Sauce

Half Grapefruit

*

CHOICE OF BEVERAGE

Coffee   Tea   Decaffeinated Beverage   Milk

MICROPHONE AND LECTERN SUPPLIED

Remote mike supplied, if desired. . . . . extra charge.

Dining area available from 11:30 a.m. Speaker and remainder of program must be completed by 1:45 p.m. or hourly penalty will be imposed.

HORS D'OEUVRES FOR COCKTAIL PARTY

Tiny Potato Pancakes, Applesauce
Cocktail Franks with Spiced Mustard
Swedish Meatballs
Barbecued Chicken Wings
Shrimps in Beer Batter
$0.00 extra per guest

ASSORTED COLD CANAPE TRAY
$0.00 per tray of 72 units

(Above hor d'oeuvre items may be purchased by
the dozen at $0.00 per dozen)

HORS D'OEUVRES FOR A RECEPTION

Barbecued Chicken Wings   Deep-Fried Won Tons
Swedish Meatballs   Shrimp in Beer Batter
Barbecued Pork Spareribs   Chicken Livers in Bacon
Quiche Lorraine   Pizza Slices
Deviled Eggs   Stuffed Celery

($0.00 per guest—minimum or 100 guests)

OPTIONAL
CHEDDAR CHEESE LOG WITH CRACKERS $0.00

CHEESE DIP WITH CRISPS . . . $0.00 per quart

BUFFET SELECTIONS PRECEDING FORMAL
DINNER OR WEDDING
(An excellent selection of Hot and Cold Hors d'Oeuvres)

Barquettes of Caviar
Tiny Roulades of Smoked Salmon
Sliced Smoked Sturgeon
Cocktail Frankfurters   Cocktail Meatballs
Clams Casino
Oysters Rockefeller

Bowls of Shrimp on Horseback, Spicy Cocktail Sauce
Glazed Virginia Ham (sliced to order served on small slices of potato bread)
Diced, Imported Cheddar Cheese
Smoked Fancy Turkey
Cocktail Rye   New York Style Pumpernickel
with
Trays of Assorted Open-Face Canapes
Cocktail Frankfurters
Cocktail Meatballs   Oysters Rockefeller
Clams Casino

Finest Imported Caviar
Presented on Illuminated, Sculptured Ice Socle
with full garniture consisting of
Blinis Freshly Made Toast Sour Cream, Chopped Onions, Drawn Butter
Sides of Smoked Salmon
Sides of Smoked Sturgeon (sliced to order)
with Trays of Assorted Open-Face Canapes
Plus Cocktail Frankfurters, Cocktail Meatballs, Oysters Rockefeller

DINNER MENU

Relish Tray

Celery, Olives, Gherkins, Radishes, etc.

Choice of Appetizer

Fresh Fruit Cup   Chilled Orange Juice

Marinated Herring   Onion Soup au Gratin

Chilled Vichyssoise

Choice of One Entree

Yankee Pot Roast, Jardiniere   Broiled Fresh Halibut or Scrod

Boneless Breast of Capon, Gravy   Roast Turkey, Giblet Gravy, Jelly

Baked Stuffed Giant Shrimp   Sliced London Broil, Mushroom Sauce

Roast Sirloin of Beef au natural   Broiled Boneless Sirloin Steak

Sirloin Steak (12-oz.)

Roast Prime Rib of Beef au jus   Broiled Filet Mignon, Mushroom Sauce

*

Tossed Green Salad, House Dressing

(Fresh vegetable may be substituted)

*

Choice of Potato
Baked, with Sour Cream and Chives
French Fried   Lyonnaise   Roesti Potatoes
Potato Croquette in Corn Flake Crumbs

*

Bread Basket Consisting of
Sesame Seed Rolls   Dark Pumpernickel
Banana Bread   Mini-Bagels   Butterflake Rolls

*

Choice of Dessert
Old-Fashioned Strawberry Shortcake   Choice of Pies
Chocolate Parfait   Orange Sherbet, Mandarin Sauce
Cheese Cake with Blueberry topping

*

Choice of Beverage
Coffee   Decaffeinated Beverage   •   Tea   Milk

CUB SCOUTS OR LITTLE LEAGUE MENU

Fresh Fruit Cocktail
or
Soup du Jour

Fried Chicken, Cranberry Sauce
Broiled Chopped Steak
Meatballs with Spaghetti
Roast Turkey, Giblet Gravy
Fried Fillet of Sole
Baked Ham with Sliced Pineapple

*

Choice of Vegetable and Potatoes

*

DESSERTS—Choice of One

Apple, Peach, Cherry, Blueberry, or Pineapple Pie
Ice Cream with "Make Your Own Sundaes Fixins"
Strawberry Shortcake

Milk   Chocolate Milk   Fruit Drink

Meat Balls with Spaghetti

THREE BUDGET BUFFET PRESENTATIONS
(For 75 or more guests)

No. 1

Tossed Green Salad, Dressing
Celery Sticks, Radish Roses, Olives
Roast Sirloin of Beef, sliced to order
Baked Country Ham
Swedish Meat Balls
Barbecued Chicken Wings
Deep-Fried Shrimp
Chinese Mushroom Chow Mein
Delmonico Potatoes *and*
    Potato Salad
Assorted Pastries *and* Pies
Tea, Coffee, or Milk

No. 2

Tossed Salad, Dressings
Celery Sticks, Radishes, Olives
Roast Sirloin of Beef, to order
Roast Turkey, Sage Dressing
Fried Chicken Tidbits
Swedish Meat Balls
Deep-Fried Shrimp
Chinese Mushroom Chow Mein
Delmonico Potatoes *and*
    Potato Salad
Assorted Pastries *and* Pies
Tea, Coffee, or Milk

No. 3

Tossed Salad, Dressings
Celery Sticks, Radishes, Olives, Gherkins
Steamship Round of Beef, sliced to order
Roast Turkey, Sage Dressing
Baked Virginia Ham, Champagne Sauce
Chinese Chicken Chow Mein, Long Grain Rice
Deep-Fried Shrimp
Poached Fillet of Sole, Lobster—Cream Sauce
Tiny Italian Meat Balls with Pasta Shells, Marinara
Vegetable Gelatin Mold
Tiny Spiced Crabapples
Cauliflower Potatoes au Gratin
Three-Layer Strawberry Shortcake
Plus Petits Fours and Cookies
Tea, Coffee, or Milk

CASH BAR SET UP IN THIS AREA (Extra Charge)
UNLIMITED CHAMPAGNE PUNCH OR BOTTLED BEER—
Extra charge of $0.00 per person

SPECIAL BUFFET DINNER

(Cash Bar in area throughout the entire dinner)

At Bar Area

Onion Dips   Cornucopias of Salami

Pickled Eggs   Cheese Cubes   Pretzel Sticks

AT PLACE SETTING FOR EACH GUEST

Choice of One

Fresh Fruit Cocktail   Mini-Shrimp Cocktail

Eggs a la Russe   Cold Icelandic Sea Trout, Mustard Sauce

*

FROM BUFFET TABLE

Seafood Creole   Fried Wickford Clams

Fried Chicken Tidbits   Cornish Hen Quarters in Orange Sauce

Chinese Pepper Steaks   Beef Bourguignonne

Baked Stuffed Pork Chops   Rice Pilaf

Noodles with Caraway Seeds   Paprika Fried Potatoes

Cold Sliced Turkey, Cranberry Relish   Cold Sliced Corned Beef, Horseradish Mustard

*

Assorted Pickles   Olives   Relishes   Gelatin Molds

*

AVAILABLE AT EXTRA COST–CARVED BY UNIFORMED PERSONNEL

Steamship Round, carved to order   Standing Prime Ribs of Beef, carved

Carved Skirt Steaks or Brisket Beef

*

DESSERTS

Individual French and Danish Pastries

An assortment of 5 Pies and 4 Layer Cakes   Fresh and Preserved Fruit Medley

*

BEVERAGES

Coffee   Tea   Decaffeinated Beverage to be SERVED

NOTE: The above is *an organized buffet dinner*. Guests will be advised as to what tables they are assigned by the use of *table tent cards at the entranceway*. Their starter course will be on the table. Our Head Waiter will explain the procedure over the microphone. He will then call upon *each table* to proceed to the buffet tables. This avoids long lines. *Beverages will be served at the tables*. When guests go to the buffet, waiters will clear their starter dishes.

This menu may also be used as a Prom Menu. House bars will only service guests with *proof of age* (identification card). Self-service areas will be furnished with wine or champagne punch during the entire affair. Colored linens at no extra charge.

DINNER DANCE MENU

Celery Sticks   Ripe and Green Olives   Carrot Curls
*

Choice of One

Fresh Fruit Cocktail   Fresh Shrimp Cocktail
Avocado Half Stuffed with   Soup du Jour
Crabmeat

*

Choice of One

Double Breast of Boneless Chicken, Jubilee
Roulade of Turkey, Giblet Gravy
Roast Sirloin of Beef, Mushroom Sauce
Pot Roast of Beef with Red Cabbage
London Broil, Mushroom Sauce
Deep-Fried Half of Boneless Chicken
Broiled Swordfish Steak, Maitre d'Hotel
Rolled Leg of Veal en Croustade
Roast Prime Rib of Beef

*

Choice of Vegetable and Potato
*

Banana Bread   Mini-Muffins   Parker House Rolls
*

Choice of One

Black Forest Cake   Cheese Cake with Strawberry Sauce
or COMPOTE OF PASTRIES—(one tray per table)

*

Coffee   Tea   Milk   Soda

Bud vase of flowers supplied each table.

WEDDING BREAKFAST
(Minimum 50 guests)
(Available only from 8 a.m. to 11 a.m.—in private area.
Party must end by 11:00 a.m.)

Fresh Orange Juice
*

Scrambled Eggs
*

Choice of One

Canadian Bacon   Sausage Patties
Rasher of Bacon or Grilled Ham
OR Poached Eggs and Ham On Muffins a la Brennan
(extra)
*

Hashed Brown or Roesti Potatoes
*

| Toasted | *AND* | White Toast, |
| Corn Cakes | * | Orange-Butter Spread |

Warm Danish Pastries (extra)
*

Coffee   Hot Chocolate   Tea   Milk

NOTE: The above breakfast may be served *Buffet Style With*
Each And Every Item As Listed
for *$0.00 Extra* per guest.

ALSO AVAILABLE
Wine (for toast) @ $0.00 per glass
Champagne (toast) @ $0.00 per glass
Bottles of Blended Whiskey, Scotch, Bourbon @ $0.00 per bottle

WEDDING PACKAGE PLAN
(For 100 or more)

Choice of One

Fresh Fruit Cup, Grenadine
Chilled Melon   Chilled Orange and Grapefruit Sections

Sardines on Tomato Slices and Stuffed Egg Wedges

*

Nutted Fruit Breads   Butterflake Rolls

*

Choice of One

Soup du Jour   or   Onion Soup, Toast Points

*

Choice of One

Sliced Flank Steak, Sauce Jardiniere   Roast Stuffed Breast of Capon   Roast Turkey, Country Dressing

*

Individual Salad Bowl or Choice of Vegetable

*

Choice of One

Potatoes au Gratin   Baked Potato, Sour Cream   Potato Croquettes

*

COMPLIMENTARY HOUSE DRINK OF CHILLED SAUTERNE, CHABLIS, OR BURGUNDY
(Champagne in place of the above $0.00 extra)

Choice of Dessert

Three-Layer Strawberry Shortcake   Ice Cream Cake Rolls

Creme de Menthe Parfait

*

Coffee   Tea   Decaffeinated Beverage   Milk   plus Tray of Cookies

The above meal includes
WINE TOAST

THREE-PIECE ORCHESTRA FOR FOUR HOURS

WHITE WEDDING CAKE WITH ROYAL ICING AND *ORNAMENT*

HOSTESS TO SLICE AND BAG WEDDING CAKE TO BE GIVEN TO EACH GUEST

CANDELABRA AND FLOWERS FOR HEAD TABLE ONLY

HOST OR HOSTESS TO SUPERVISE AND GIVE GUIDANCE

NOTE: ALL WEDDING PRICES APPLY TO THE FOLLOWING SCHEDULE

Day Weddings — 11 a.m. to 4 p.m.

Evening Weddings — 5 p.m. to 11 p.m.

If weddings overlap these two periods, there will be an added charge of $0.00 per person.
If cash bar is desired, there is a $0.00 for each bartender.

WEDDING MEAL SUGGESTIONS
(Minimum of 100 guests)

Choice of One

Fresh Fruit Cup, Grenadine   Chilled Melon (in season)
Sardines on Tomato Slices   Stuffed Egg Wedges

Chilled Orange and Grapefruit Sections

*

Nut and Fruit Breads   Butterflake Rolls

*

Choice of One

Soup du Jour   or   Onion Soup, Toast Points

*

Choice of One

Sliced Flank Steak, Sauce Jardiniere
Roast Stuffed Breast of Capon
Roast Turkey, Country Dressing

*

House Salad Bowl

or

Choice of Vegetable

*

Choice of One

Potatoes au Gratin   Baked Stuffed Potato   Potato Croquettes

*

COMPLIMENTARY HOUSE DRINK OF CHILLED SAUTERNE, CHABLIS, OR BURGUNDY

(Champagne in place of the above $0.00 extra)

*

Choice of One

Three-Layer Strawberry Shortcake   Creme de Menthe, Frappe   Ice Cream Cake Rolls

*

Coffee   Tea   Milk   Decaffeinated Beverage

KOSHER WEDDING MENU

Tropical Whole Pineapple au Kirsch
Diced Pineapple Marinated in Kirsch—plate to be
decorated with galax leaves, small fruits
(cherries, green and red grapes, plum, peach)

Iced Hearts of Celery   Colossal Ripe and Green Olives
Radish Roses   Sweet Gherkins   Spiced Watermelon Rinds

Salted Jumbo Peanuts and Almonds

Chicken Consomme Double with Mondels
Mock Cheese Straws

Baked Fillet of Sole with Supreme Sauce
Parisienne Potatoes

Roast Breast of Capon on Tongue, under glass, Mushroom Sauce
Wild Rice Croquettes

Cranberry and Orange Relish in Orange Baskets en Parade
(Orange baskets to be decorated with white ribbon
and orange blossoms)

Kishkie, to be passed on silver platters

Kentucky Limestone Lettuce with Hearts of Palm
Artichoke Bottoms, Pimiento Strips, Vinaigrette Dressing

Pastry Swans, filled with mock ice cream
Brandied Peach Sauce

Petits Fours Glace

Black Coffee   or   Tea with Lemon

4-tier wedding cake to be all white with pale pink sugar ribbons
and flowers. Between first and second tier, place white gardenias.
Upper tier to have sugar swans.

BARBECUE MENU

Choice of Two

Sirloin Steak	Turkish Steaks
Marinated Lamb Steaks	Broiled Hamburger Steaks
Pork Spareribs	Grilled Chicken
Grilled Fish	Grilled Canadian Bacon

Choice of One

Fresh Corn on the Cob   Foil-Baked Potatoes
Baked Yams or Sweet Potatoes Baked Beans

Choice of Two

Assorted Relishes   Coleslaw
Tossed Green Salad with Assorted Dressings

Choice of Two

Hot Corn Bread   Hot Biscuits   French Bread

Choice of One

Chocolate Cake   Fruit Pie

Beverage

Coffee   Tea   Soft Drinks   Beer

TRINIDADIAN DINNER MENU

Cocktail Hour   Rum Punch

Pineapple Basket
Callaloo Soup

Manzanilla Shark, Toco Sauce
Fried Caroni Plantains

Claret   Coconut Sherbet

Curried Laventille Goat
Pigeon Peas and Mango Rice

Avocado Tropical Salad with Hearts of Palm

Bol di Rum

Coffee   Tea
After Dinner Drink—Poor Man's Liqueur

CHINESE BUFFET

Hot Dishes
Barbecued Spareribs   Chicken Egg Roll
Roast Pork   Fried Dumplings
Four Color Sho-My (steamed)
*

Cold Dishes
Salt Boiled Chicken   Roast Pickled Duck
Fine Spiced Beef   Smoked Spicy Fish
Chinese Sausage   Abalone
Sauteed Shrimp   Spiced Bean Curd
Sugared Walnuts   Pickled Chinese Cabbage
Fine Spiced Mushrooms
*

Desserts
Kumquats on Ice   Vanilla Ice Cream with Coconut Sauce
Macaroons
*

Beverage
Green Tea   Jasmine Tea

MEDITERRANEAN BUFFET

Olives   Baby Eggplants   Feta Cheese   Relish Tray
        Greek Salad   Marinated Chick-Peas

Hummus bi Taheeni (Sesame Chick-Pea Dip)

Moutabel (Sesame, Lemon Eggplant Dip)

Tabooley (Cracked Wheat, Tomato, and Fresh Mint Salad)

Tarator (Cold Cucumber, Yogurt, and Walnut Soup)

Spanakopetes (Spinach and Filo Pie)

Kreakopita (Lamb Pie)

Warak Mashi (Stuffed Grape Leaves with Garlic Mint Sauce)

Garides Me Saltsza (Shrimp in Tomato, Garlic Feta Cheese)

Moussaka (Baked Eggplant, Tomato, and Lamb Cake)

Couscous a la Marga (Lamb, Chicken, and Vegetable Stew with Semolina)

Shish Tavuk (Skewered Marinated Broiled Chicken)

Souvlakia Mi Arni (Broiled Lamb Kabobs)

Sigari Bouregi (Feta Cheese Pastry)

Khobaz (Arabic Bread)

Baklava (Filo and Nut Rolls)

Gelato Boureka (Filo and Pastry Cream Rolls)

Coffee

FRENCH BUFFET

FROID

Timbales de Sole, Sauce Aurore
Maquereaux au Vin Blanc
Homard en Bellevue
Terrine de Lapin
Pate Maison
Poulet Rose de Mai
Salade Parisienne
Salade de Concumbres

Aloses ou Anguilles en Gelee
Saumon Poche, Sauce Vincent
Rillette de Tours
Galantine de Canard
Mousse de Foie de Volaille
Jambon de Bayonne
Champignons a la Grecque
Celeri Remoulade

Salade d'Endives et Betteraves Rouges

CHAUD

Cassoulet Toulousain

Boeuf Bourguignonne

DESSERTS

Chocolate Sabayon Torte
Charlotte Russe
Frangipane Tarts

Linzer Torte
Petits Fours
Macaroons

The two menus that follow are examples that can be used by caterers planning for special events. These dinners were served to special groups at the Culinary Institute of America. The cover for the menu appearing on pages 200-202 is shown below.

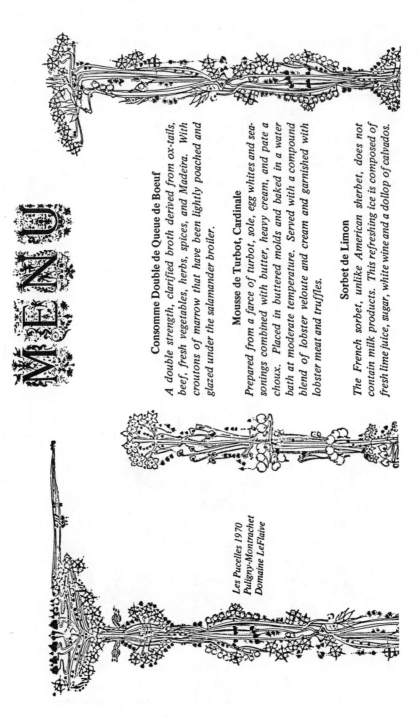

MENU

Consomme Double de Queue de Boeuf

A double strength, clarified broth derived from ox-tails, beef, fresh vegetables, herbs, spices, and Madeira. With croutons of marrow that have been lightly poached and glazed under the salamander broiler.

Mousse de Turbot, Cardinale

Prepared from a farce of turbot, sole, egg whites and seasonings combined with butter, heavy cream, and pate a choux. Placed in buttered molds and baked in a water bath at moderate temperature. Served with a compound blend of lobster veloute and cream and garnished with lobster meat and truffles.

Sorbet de Limon

The French sorbet, unlike American sherbet, does not contain milk products. This refreshing ice is composed of fresh lime juice, sugar, white wine and a dollop of calvados.

Les Pucelles 1970
Puligny-Montrachet
Domaine LeFlaive

Dodine de Canard a l'Ancienne

This is an old, classical term referring to a method of preparation and service of game birds. It has no distinct parallel but has similarities to both ballotines and galantines. Ducks are completely boned and a forcemeat of duck, veal, pork, porkfat and seasonings prepared. Boned portions are placed together. . .filled with the forcemeat and slices of duckling and rolled and secured to form compact bundles. They are oven-roasted during which time they are basted frequently. When cooked, they are allowed to rest briefly before slicing and presentation. Served with Sauce Armagnac and accompanied by flavorful chanterelle mushrooms aux fines herbes and braised hearts of lettuce.

Corton du Roi 1962
Drouhin

Fromages

A selection of choice cheeses. . .depending on market availability and state of ripeness.

Bombe Institute

Rich but light. . .chocolate savayon on delicate sponge cake. . .flavored with pear brandy and covered with an extremely thin layer of marzipan.

Winzenheimer Berg 1967
Trockenbeerenauslese Kabinett
Originalabfüllung
Reichsgraf von Plettenbery

Cafe et Liqueurs

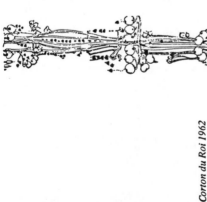
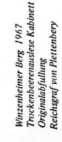

CHEFS DE CUISINE
RECIPIENTS OF THE ESCOFFIER CHAIR

ANDRE BERTIN: Chef Instructor, The Culinary Institute of America; L'Ecole Superieure de Saint-Jean, Lyon, France; L'Ecole Hoteliere LaMartiniere, Lyon; Restaurant Morateur and Carlton Hotel, Lyon; Sauce Chef, Roosevelt Hotel, Waldorf Astoria, Savoy Plaza, New York; Sous-Chef, Carlton Hotel, Washington, D.C.; Head Chef, Gourmet Restaurant; Executive Chef '1 2 3' Club, Wee Burn Country Club, Darien, Conn.

BRUNO ELLMER: Chef Instructor, The Culinary Institute of America; Educated in Europe, Apprenticeship, Hotel Post, Radstadt, Austria. Rotisseur, Grand Hotel St. Wolfgang, Austria; Chef, Hotel Weissmayr, Hotel Bellevue, Badgastein, Austria; Hotel Gold Hirsch, Salzburg, Austria; Castle Hotel Moenchstein, Salzburg; Kurhotels, Warmgad-Villach, Austria; Executive Chef, Hotel Intercontinental, Amman, Jordan; Hotel Summit, New York City.

ARNO SCHMIDT: Executive Chef, The Waldorf-Astoria Hotel, New York City; Supervising Chef, The Culinary Institute of America; Executive Chef, Hotel Regency; Executive Chef, Sheraton Corporation, New York City; Executive Chef, Restaurant Associates; Chef Poissonier, Hotel St. Regis, New York City; Experience in Canada, South America, Switzerland, Austria, Ireland, Holland and Sweden.

WALTER SCHREYER: Pastry Chef, The Culinary Institute of America. Apprenticeship Cafe Conditorei Lohr, Baden-Baden, Germany; Patissier, Hotel Metropole, Wengen, Switzerland; Hotel St. Gotthard, Lucerne; Chef-Patissier, Grand Hotel, Jersey, England; Cake Decorator, various shops, New York City; Pastry Chef, King's Grant Inn, Point Pleasant, New Jersey; Executive Pastry Chef, The Manor Restaurant, West Orange, New Jersey.

FREDERIC SONNENSCHMIDT: Instructor, Buffet Catering, The Culinary Institute of America; Restaurant Rollandseck, Munich, Germany; Hotel Bayerischer Hof, Muncish, Germany; Chef Saucier, Piccadilly Hotel, London, England, Grosvenor Hotel, London, England. Chef, El Dorado, New Rochelle, New York; Executive Chef, Sheraton Motor Inn, New York City; Chef de Partie, Claridge House, London.

DIRECTOR OF SERVICE

EDMOND G. FONTAINE: Maitre d'Hotel Instructor, The Culinary Institute of America; graduate, Ecole Hoteliere; Ritz Carlton, Vichy; Hotel Mamounia, Marrakech; Hotel de L'Europe, Avignon; Manager, Birchwood Country Club, Westport, Conn., restaurant manager, Rotisserie Normande, New Haven. Conn.; Maitre d', Fox Hill Restaurant, Brookfield, Conn.

Dîner Amical

Confrérie de la Chaîne des Rôtisseurs

Baillage de Connecticut

at

The Culinary Institute of America

New Haven, Connecticut

February 21, 1970

Réception

Moet et Chandon Brut
Impérial, 1964

Macon Blanc 1964
Réserve des Mousquetaires
(Sichel)

Kir - Crème de Cassis
L'Héritier-Guyot (Kobrand)

Le Diner

Sercial Madeira -
Blandy's

Pouilly Fuissé (1967)
Louis Jadot (Kobrand)

Castel Roubine 1964
Cru Classé - Côtes
de Provence (Sichel)

Menu

Les Amuses Bouches

Caviar—With blini and lemon wedges, and no other irrelevancies.

Champignons Farcis aux Escargots—Mushroom caps stuffed with snails and topped with Green Goddess dressing.

Longe de Porc Fume Braise au Champagne—Boneless loin of Canadian bacon, braised in Champagne and glazed.

Cuisses de Grenouilles Farcis aux Crabes—**Tiny**, boned frogs legs blended with crabmeat, reformed around a single, small bone. Breaded and deep fried. Served with a light mustard sauce.

Bifteck-Tartare—The classical raw chopped steak (bottom round), seasoned with salt and pepper. We suggest trying it with some of the pressed caviar.

Consomme Mandarin—A double strength peacock consomme served in a carved melon, with miniature won ton, melon pearls, and an Oriental garnish.

Mousse d'Homard en Turban de Truite—Delicate lobster mousse in a turban of fresh Colorado trout, mounted on a puff paste round spread with tomalley butter, enhanced with a sauce of lobster bits and morel mushrooms.

Ris de Veau Braise en Nid de Nouilles Perigueux—Braised sweetbreads with julienne of tongue and truffles in a crisp fried noodle nest. Served with Perigueux sauce.

Trou de Milieu

Glace Chinoise de Quatre Tresors—Four treasure ice in the Chinese manner, made with Lichee wine, loquats, kumquats, and mangoes.

Caille a l'Orientale—Boneless quail with a stuffing of bulgur wheat, sauteed macadamia nuts, mild lamb, and scallions. Served on a truffled crouton and dressed with a sauce prepared from the quail. Accompanied by crisp, freshly prepared Chinese vegetables.

In Europe, the term "quail" is applied to a number of game birds of the pheasant family. In the United States, quail is a term used for several kinds of grouse and partridge. The bobwhite quail, as presented this evening, ranges from southern Canada to the Gulf states and is the only quail native to the area east of the Mississippi. A plump, but small bird, averaging only six ounces en plumage, the bobwhite is delicate in flavor and highly esteemed by gourmets.

Château Petit Village

Pomerol 1964

Ginestet

(Kobrand)

Puree de Foie Gras aux Truffes Blanches et Noires—Fresh goose liver blended with white and black truffles, cognac, and special seasonings. Served with Port wine aspic and French bread Melba.

⌒∽

Fromages—A Brie cheese which we hope will be "a point" to justify its title of King.

Chambertin 1961
Louis Latour

An unusual cheese from Switzerland—a "Tilsit" similar to Tete de Moine.

Served with Baguettes.

⌒∽

Harveys Tawny Port

Souffle au Citron—An individual lemon souffle with a sauce of macadamia nuts, honey and liqueur.

⌒∽

Digestifs:
  Cognac Hennessy VSOP Resérve
  Green Chartreuse   *Cafe de l'Institut*
  Anisette Marie Brizard
  Creme de Menthe Marie Brizard

⌒∽

Mignardises

Les Chefs des Cuisine	*Le Chef Patissier*	*Le Maitre d'Hotel*
LeRoi A. Folsom	Joseph Amendola	John Dodig
Jean Nicolas		
Frederic Sonnenschmidt		

Bailli Délégué des U.S.A. — Edward H. Benenson

Bailli Délégué de New York — Jules J. Bond

Bailli de Connecticut — Jacob Rosenthal

∾

LES INVITÉS

Mr. Joseph Amendola
Mr. Jules J. Bond
Mrs. William C. Celentano
Mrs. Bernard L. Conte
Mr. and Mrs. LeRoi A. Folsom
Mr. Reuben A. Holden
Mr. Peter Jantz
Mr. and Mrs. Frederick R. Lack
Mr. Adolph J. Macina
Mr. Alphonse S. Marcello
Mr. William A. J. Marino
Mr. and Mrs. William F. May
Mr. and Mrs. Kirt Meyer

Mr. and Mrs. Charles S. Mueller
Miss Beth Muir
Mr. and Mrs. Richard Patton
Mr. Ronald W. Peterson
Mr. and Mrs. Morton Reifer
Mrs. Natalie A. Robbins
Miss Sara Rosenberg
Mr. and Mrs. Jacob Rosenthal
Mr. and Mrs. Warren J. Rubin
Mr. Paul A. Sakal
Mr. John E. Smith
Mr. and Mrs. John Sprague
Dr. and Mrs. Paul Weinstein

LES INTRONISÉS

Chevalier	*Dame*	*Cadets*
Frederic Sonnenschmidt	Natalie A. Robbins	Peter Jantz
		Garry Peabody
		Ronald W. Peterson
		Paul A. Sakal
		Edwin F. Schmidt

HÔTES

LeRoi A. Folsom   Joseph Amendola

A Collection of Recipes/16

A COLLECTION OF standardized recipes is a "must" for every Social Caterer. The collection, in addition to the tried and true "basics," should include a variety of specialty dishes that have been thoroughly tested and individualized.

For handy reference have one or more good general cookbooks of family-size as well as quantity recipes always available in the catering office. An avid recipe collector, as all caterers should be, will find magazines and newspapers are also good sources for recipes.

Set Up Recipe Cards

Tested recipes should be typed on special cards (5- by 8-inch or 4- by 6-inch are good sizes), with notations made as to preparation, yield, serving tips, costs. Any changes made in the recipe must always be noted on the recipe card.

For added convenience file recipe cards alphabetically by category such as appetizers, breads, desserts, salads, etc.

In testing or developing recipes, standard measurements should be used.

Measurements	Scoops	Ladles
3 tsp. = 1 tbsp.	No. 6 = 2/3 cup	2 oz. = 1/4 cup
4 tbsp. = 1/4 cup	No. 8 = 1/2 cup	4 oz. = 1/2 cup
2 cups = 1 pt.	No. 12 = 1/3 cup	6 oz. = 3/4 cup
2 pt. = 1 qt.	No. 16 = 1/4 cup	8 oz. = 1 cup
4 qt. = 1 gal.	No. 20 = 3-1/5 tbsp.	
	No. 24 = 2-2/3 tbsp.	
	No. 40 = 1-3/5 tbsp.	

RECIPE CONVERSION

Modern technology has produced pocket-sized calculators that accurately resolve the most complicated problems. On the assumption that a calculator may not be available when it is necessary to convert a recipe into greater or lesser quantities, the following formula will be helpful.

Assume that a standard pie crust formula for 50 units consists of the following ingredients.

FLOUR, sifted	3 lb. 12 oz.
SHORTENING	2 lb. 4 oz.
SALT	2 oz.
WATER	3/4 qt.

STEP ONE: Convert all of the units into ounces.

Flour, 3 lb. 12 oz.	= 60 oz. (16 oz. to 1 lb.)
Shortening, 2 lb. 4 oz.	= 36 oz.
Salt	= 2 oz.
Water, 3/4 qt.	= 24 oz. (32 oz. to 1 qt.)

STEP TWO: Assuming that only 32 crusts are needed, divide the required number (32) by the number of the original recipe (50).

$$
\begin{array}{r}
.64 \ = \ \text{(multiplier factor)} \\
50\ \overline{)\ 32.00} \\
\underline{30.00} \\
2\,00 \\
\underline{2\,00}
\end{array}
$$

STEP THREE: Using .64 as the factor, multiply all ingredients by this number.

60 oz. flour	x .64 =	38.4 oz.	or 2 lb. 6-1/2 oz.
36 oz. shortening	x .64 =	23.04 oz.	or 23 oz.
2 oz. salt	x .64 =	1.28 oz.	or 1-1/4 oz.
24 oz. water	x .64 =	15.36 oz.	or 15-1/2 oz.

The following recipe is for 25 portions of ROAST BEEF HASH.

ONION, finely diced	1 lb.	=	16 oz.
CELERY, finely diced	1/2 lb.	=	8 oz.
OIL	5 oz.	=	5 oz.
POTATOES, cooked, diced	6-1/2 lb.	=	104 oz.
ROAST BEEF, coarsely chopped	4-1/2 lb.	=	72 oz.
SALT and PEPPER	to taste		

Number of portions needed = 110.

STEP ONE: DIVIDE   4.4 = multiplier factor

```
        4.4
25 | 110.0
     100.
      10.0
      10.0
```

STEP TWO:

Onion	16 x 4.4	=	70.4 oz.	or 4-1/2 lb.
Celery	8 x 4.4	=	35.2 oz.	or 2 lb. 3 oz.
Oil	5 x 4.4	=	22 oz.	or 1 lb. 6 oz.
Beef	72 x 4.4	=	316.8 oz.	or 19 lb. 13 oz.
Potatoes	110 x 4.4	=	484 oz.	or 30 lb. 3 oz.

APPETIZERS

DIPS AND DUNKS, HORS D'OEUVRES, PUNCHES

ANCHOVY COCKTAIL "DUNK"

INGREDIENTS

CREAM CHEESE*	1 lb.
PAPRIKA	1/8 tsp.
CELERY SEED	1 tsp.
LEMON JUICE	2 tbsp.
ANCHOVY PASTE	4 tbsp.
CREAM	4 tbsp.
ONION, minced	4 tsp.

*Blue cheese thinned with a little yoghurt may be substituted for cream cheese.

PROCEDURE
1. Cream the cheese until smooth.
2. Add remaining ingredients and blend until fluffy.

TUNA-CHEESE "DUNK"

INGREDIENTS

TUNA	2 7-1/2 oz. cans
CREAM CHEESE	1/2 lb.
DRY WHITE WINE	1/2 cup
MAYONNAISE	1/2 cup
PARSLEY, chopped	2 tbsp.
ONION RELISH, well-drained	1/2 cup
LIQUID HOT PEPPER SEASONING	dash
SALT	1/2 tsp.
GARLIC SALT	1/2 tsp.

PROCEDURE

1. Drain tuna and blend with cream cheese.
2. Add remaining ingredients and blend well.

DIPS OR DUNKS
For informal buffet-type presentation

ADJUNCTS TO DIPS OR DUNKS

1/2-inch rounds of crusty french or italian bread

Swedish bread	Celery chunks
Breadsticks	Radishes
Crisp crackers	Scallions
Toasted thin corn bread	Cucumber fingers
Potato crisps	Raw cauliflower buds
Raw carrot sticks	Avocado chunks, dipped in
Fresh or canned pineapple chunks	lemon juice
Apple and pear wedges, dipped in	
lemon juice	

CELERY WHIRLS

YIELD: about 18 slices

Carefully remove full-length individual stalks from fully trimmed bunch of celery. Clean each stalk thoroughly and drain on absorbent paper.

Make a mixture of 1 cup crumbled blue cheese with 3 oz. package softened cream cheese and 1 tbsp. mayonnaise. Beat until mixture is smooth and creamy, then blend in 2 tsp. lemon juice, 1 tsp. onion juice, 1/4 tsp. garlic salt, 1/8 tsp. monosodium glutamate, and 1/2 tsp. celery or caraway seeds (optional). Beat until thoroughly blended.

Fill full length of celery strips and rearrange stalks into natural shape of celery bunch. Wrap tightly in aluminum foil or plastic wrap and refrigerate for several hours. Cut crosswise into 1/2-in. slices and arrange on tray.

PICKLED EGGS

*Excellent as "nostalgia"—keep in jar at bar area
or display in liquid on buffet tables.*

YIELD: 30 portions

INGREDIENTS

DRY MUSTARD	4-1/2 tsp.
CORNSTARCH	4-1/2 tsp.
WHITE VINEGAR	3 pt.
SUGAR	6 tsp.
TURMERIC	1-1/2 tsp.
EGGS, hard-cooked	30

PROCEDURE
1. Blend dry mustard and cornstarch with water.
2. Add vinegar and spices.
3. Boil 12 min.
4. Remove from heat; let rest 15 min.
5. Add eggs.
6. Refrigerate overnight.

DEVILED EGGS

YIELD: 12 halves

INGREDIENTS

EGGS, hard-cooked	6
MAYONNAISE	1/4 cup
SALT	1/4 tsp.
PEPPER	
PREPARED MUSTARD	1/2 tsp.
ONION, minced	1 tsp.
LIQUID HOT PEPPER SEASONING	a few drops
MONOSODIUM GLUTAMATE	1/8 tsp.
YELLOW FOOD COLORING	2 drops

PROCEDURE

1. Split shelled eggs lengthwise. Carefully remove yolks (use stainless steel spoon).

2. Force yolks through strainer; blend in other ingredients.

3. Pipe blended yolks through pastry bag into hollows of egg whites.

4. Garnish with pimiento, olives, parsley, or capers.

To glaze: place filled and garnished eggs on wire rack and pour cooled liquefied clear gelatine over each. (This enhances the appearance and prevents discoloration.) Chill in refrigerator.

Deviled eggs may be served as an hors d'oeuvre in bar area; as salad; as garnish on cold meat platter.

Variations

Eggs may be "topped off" with red or black caviar or strips of anchovy; fill cavities with flaked smoked whitefish and garnish with yolk puree; garnish with tiny shrimp or one large shrimp; sieve a few slices of smoked salmon or anchovy together with egg yolks; top hard-cooked egg halves with russian dressing or thick tartar sauce; blend a teaspoon of white horseradish with a little whipped cream and add to egg yolk mixture before filling whites.

STEAK TARTARE

YIELD: 50 little balls

INGREDIENTS

TOP ROUND of BEEF, LEAN, ground twice	2 lb.
ONION, minced	2 tsp.
PARSLEY, minced	2 tsp.
WORCESTERSHIRE SAUCE	2 tsp.
PREPARED MUSTARD	1/2 tsp.
SALT	1 tsp.
BLACK PEPPER, freshly ground	1/2 tsp.
LETTUCE, PARSLEY or WATERCRESS	
ANCHOVY FILLETS, cut in half	
DILL PICKLE, thinly sliced	
PUMPERNICKEL or RYE BREAD, thinly sliced rounds	

PROCEDURE

1. Combine meat with onion and next 5 ingredients. Mix well; form into about 50 little balls.

2. Cover; refrigerate until well chilled.

3. Arrange on lettuce on serving plate.

4. Serve on rounds of bread. Provide additional chopped onion, anchovy, and dill pickle slices as accompaniments.

FOR ANTIPASTO

Anchovies	Stuffed eggs	Celery
Sardines	Pickled artichokes	Chick-peas
Tuna	Sliced prosciutto	Pickled eggplant
Pimientos	Salami	Lettuce
Pickled mushrooms	Olives	Scallions
Cherry tomatoes or	Radishes	Ricotta cheese
Tomato wedges	Pickled beets	Cold sausage
Onions	Bologna	
Melon wedges	Raw green peppers	

No less than 6 items should be used at one time. Remember to contrast flavors—spicy, sharp, bland—as well as color.

CHOPPED LIVER

YIELD: 50 portions as first course; 100 plus as spread

INGREDIENTS

CHICKEN FAT (rendered) or VEGETABLE OIL	2 cups
CHICKEN LIVERS or LIGHT COLORED STEER LIVER	8 lb.
ONIONS, MEDIUM SIZED, sliced	15
EGGS, hard-cooked	16
SALT	8 tsp.
BLACK PEPPER, freshly ground	1/2 tsp.
GARLIC POWDER	1/2 tsp.
MONOSODIUM GLUTAMATE	1 tbsp.
SUGAR	1 tsp.

PROCEDURE

1. Saute onions in fat or oil until light brown.

2. If chicken livers are used, saute them until they have lost color. Cover and steam 5 min. If steer liver is used, broil the liver until just done. Allow to cool.

3. Put all ingredients through grinder three times.

4. Add all seasonings, monosodium glutamate, and mix thoroughly. Add a little oil if too dry. For a first course, serve with a No. 16 scoop on lettuce and garnish with cherry tomatoes or red radishes.

If used as a spread, the liver can be molded in any shape desired (as a pineapple or chicken). Chopped egg whites may be sprinkled generously over entire mold.

MEATLESS CHOPPED LIVER

YIELD: 50 portions

INGREDIENTS

ONIONS, MEDIUM, thinly sliced	12
OIL	3 cups
MUSHROOMS, FRESH	12 lb.
EGGS, hard-cooked, thinly sliced	18
MONOSODIUM GLUTAMATE	1 tsp.
SALT	to taste
PEPPER	to taste
GARLIC POWDER (optional)	

PROCEDURE

1. Saute onions until limp, add mushrooms; cook until tender and onions are browned.

2. Put through grinder twice or put through Buffalo chopper until very finely minced.

3. Season to taste. Serve in the same way as chopped chicken or steer liver.

MATZO BALLS

YIELD: 100 portions

INGREDIENTS

SHORTENING	3 lb. 8 oz.
MATZO FLOUR	4 lb.
EGGS	50
SALT	4 tbsp.
NUTMEG	a pinch
PEPPER	1 tsp.

PROCEDURE

1. Mix shortening in blender. Add matzo flour.

2. Gradually blend in the eggs. Add seasonings. Mix thoroughly.

3. Cover and let stand in refrigerator overnight.

4. On following day, form into balls slightly larger than golf balls. Place on waxed paper.

5. Bring a pot of salted water to a rolling boil. Add balls and cook, covered, approximately 20 min.

SPICED CHERRY SOUP

YIELD: 20 cups

INGREDIENTS

RED CHERRIES, SOUR	2 lb.
LEMON RIND	from 1 lemon
CLOVES, WHOLE	12
CINNAMON, STICKS	2
SUGAR	1 cup
SALT	1 tsp.
WATER	6 cups
TAPIOCA, QUICK COOKING	6 tbsp.
RED WINE	2 cups
LEMON	12 thin slices
SOUR CREAM	1 pt.

PROCEDURE

1. Wash cherries, remove stems.
2. With vegetable peeler, remove rind from lemon, in strips, and stick cloves into rinds.
3. In saucepan combine cherries, lemon rind with cloves, cinnamon, sugar, salt, and water. Simmer uncovered for 15 min.
4. Gradually stir in tapioca and bring to boil. Remove from heat.
5. Stir in wine and allow to cool.
6. Remove and discard lemon rind, cloves, and cinnamon sticks.
7. Refrigerate until serving time.
8. Ladle into bouillon cups and top each with a lemon slice and a spoonful of sour cream. The sour cream may also be stirred into the soup.

MUSHROOM BARLEY SOUP

YIELD: 24 7-oz. portions

INGREDIENTS

CARROTS, finely diced	2
ONIONS, finely sliced	2
CELERY STALK, finely diced	1/2
BUTTER	1/2 cup
WATER	1 gal.
PEARL BARLEY	2 cups
SALT	1 tbsp.
PEPPER	a pinch
MUSHROOMS, DRIED	4 oz.
WATER	1 pt.
MONOSODIUM GLUTAMATE	2 tbsp.
LIGHT CREAM	1 cup

PROCEDURE

1. Saute carrots, onions, and celery in butter in hot skillet until tender and delicately browned.

2. Add water, pearl barley, salt, and pepper. Simmer gently until barley is cooked.

3. In the meantime cook the dried mushrooms in the pint of water until soft—approximately 30 min.

4. Drain off any excess liquid, and add mushrooms and monosodium glutamate to the barley mixture. Simmer just long enough to blend flavors.

5. Just before serving add the light cream. Taste and adjust the seasonings if necessary.

VICHYSSOISE

YIELD: 25 portions

INGREDIENTS

LEEKS	1 bunch
BUTTER	6 oz.
ONIONS, MEDIUM	3
SALT	to taste
PEPPER	to taste
CHICKEN STOCK	3 qt.
POTATOES, MEDIUM	6
CREAM	1 pt.
CHIVES or PARSLEY	

PROCEDURE

1. Wash leeks and cut finely.
2. Add to hot butter with onions and seasonings. Cover and cook slowly without browning.
3. Add stock and thinly sliced potatoes. Cook until tender.
4. Put all through foodmill or through china cap. Adjust seasoning.
5. Stir in cream and sprinkle with chives or parsley when serving. May be served hot or cold.

COCKTAIL MEATBALLS

YIELD: 75 tiny meatballs

INGREDIENTS

GROUND BEEF	1 lb.
GROUND PORK	1/2 lb.
EGG, slightly beaten	1
ONION, grated	1 large
SEASONED SALT	1 tsp.
BLACK PEPPER	1/4 tsp.
ALLSPICE	1/4 tsp.
CLOVES	1/4 tsp.
FLOUR	1/4 cup
MILK	1/2 cup

PROCEDURE

1. Have beef and pork ground together (have beef ground two extra times).

2. Combine meat, egg, onion, and seasonings. Add flour and beat, using electric mixer, until thoroughly blended and fluffy.

3. Add milk slowly, 1 tbsp. at a time, beating well. Mixture should be like a thick dough.

4. Shape into tiny balls with a melon ball cutter.

5. Fry in butter or salad oil until golden brown. Turn frequently for even browning.

6. Serve with prepared spaghetti sauce in chafing dish.

Note

These meat balls can also be made using all beef.

SHRIMP ON TOAST ROUNDS

YIELD: 36 canapes

PROCEDURE

1. Drain canned jumbo shrimp and marinate overnight in french dressing.

2. With a small round cutter, cut bread rounds the size of the shrimp.

3. Take shrimp from marinade, drain, and place on bread rounds, decorating with mayonnaise and a strip of ripe olive.

SHRIMP CANAPE

YIELD: 36 canapes

INGREDIENTS

SHRIMP, CANNED, or freshly cooked and shelled, chopped	1-1/2 lb.
ANCHOVY PASTE	2 tbsp.
LEMON JUICE	2 tbsp.
MAYONNAISE	1 cup
TOAST ROUNDS (2 in.)	36
EGG YOLKS, hard-cooked, sieved	8
SHRIMP, WHOLE	36

PROCEDURE

1. Mix chopped shrimp, anchovy paste, and lemon juice with mayonnaise. Spread on toast rounds.
2. Top with grated egg yolk and one whole shrimp.
3. Serve with lettuce, tomato wedge, and celery heart for garnishes.

BLEU CHEESE LOG ROLL

YIELD: 4 doz. appetizers

INGREDIENTS

CREAM CHEESE	1 pkg. (8 oz.)
BUTTER	3 tbsp.
BLEU CHEESE DRESSING MIX	1 pkg.
WALNUTS, finely chopped	1/4 cup

PROCEDURE

1. Blend softened cream cheese and butter with bleu cheese dressing mix. Form into a roll about 1-1/2 in. in diameter.
2. Roll in chopped nuts. Wrap in waxed paper; chill thoroughly.
3. Slice thin and serve on toast rounds or crackers.

CURRIED MEATBALLS

YIELD: 10 lb. of meatballs, approx. 2 gal. sauce

INGREDIENTS	
MEATBALLS	10 lb.
SAUCE	
TOMATOES, CANNED WHOLE	1/2 No. 10 can
BEEF GRAVY, thickened	2 gal.
CURRY POWDER	3 tsp.

PROCEDURE

1. Prepare meatballs using your regular recipe, but using only salt and pepper to season. Brown them.
2. Cook sauce ingredients for 2 hr.
3. Add meatballs to sauce, heat to simmer, and serve over hot rice.

EGG CANAPE SPREAD

YIELD: 1-1/2 cups

INGREDIENTS	
EGGS, hard-cooked	4
CELERY, finely chopped	1/2 cup
GREEN ONIONS, chopped	2 tbsp.
SWEET PICKLE RELISH	2 tbsp.
SEASONED SALT	1 tsp.
SEASONED PEPPER	1/4 tsp.
MAYONNAISE or SALAD DRESSING	1/4 cup

PROCEDURE

Chop hard-cooked eggs and place in a small mixing bowl. Add remaining ingredients and mix thoroughly. Refrigerate for several hours.

BEAN DIP CALIENTE

YIELD: 2-1/2 cups

INGREDIENTS

MEXICAN REFRIED BEANS	1 can (1 lb. 4 oz.)
DAIRY SOUR CREAM	1/4 cup
GARLIC SPREAD	2 tbsp.
SEASONED PEPPER	1/2 tsp.
SEASONED SALT	1 tsp.
CHILI POWDER (optional)	1 tsp.

PROCEDURE

1. Combine all ingredients in saucepan and heat until bubbly.
2. Keep hot over candle warmer or in chafing dish while serving.
3. Garnish with minced onion tops or parsley, if desired. (Excellent with corn chips or tostadas.)

CHEESE PATE

"This Cheese Pate recipe is one that is requested and given to buffet patrons almost daily. It is made in the shape of a loaf, and in other attractive motifs, which vary from day to day, are used to decorate it."

INGREDIENTS

BUTTER	2 oz.
CREAM CHEESE	1 lb.
BLEU CHEESE	10 oz.
WORCESTERSHIRE SAUCE	1 tsp.
DRY MUSTARD	1 tsp.
SALT	to season
PEPPER	to season
PARSLEY, chopped	2 tbsp.
PIMIENTO	1
GREEN PEPPER, chopped	1
OLIVES, chopped	3/4 cup

PROCEDURE

1. Cream butter. Blend in the cheeses. Mix well.
2. Add worcestershire sauce, dry mustard, salt, and pepper.
3. Put parsley, pimiento, green pepper, and olives through chopper. Squeeze through cheesecloth to remove any liquid. Add to cheese mixture. Blend thoroughly.
4. Shape in a loaf. Refrigerate.

STUFFED MUSHROOMS

YIELD: 100 mushrooms

INGREDIENTS

MUSHROOMS	100
CELERY	1 stalk
GREEN ONIONS, including green tops, finely chopped	5
CELERY HEART	from stalk
BREAD CRUMBS, rolled	4 cups

PROCEDURE

1. Remove stems from medium-sized mushrooms and chop stems finely.

2. Saute celery, 5 green onions, celery heart, and stems of mushrooms. Season with salt, pepper, garlic salt, and poultry seasoning. Add bread crumbs to the mixture.

3. Saute the mushrooms in butter for 3 min. Stuff with above mixture.

4. To serve, broil stuffed mushrooms, using them as a canape on bread rounds which have been toasted on one side.

MUSHROOMS ITALIANO

PROCEDURE

1. Prepare one 14-oz. jar Italian Dressing Mix for salads according to directions, using dry red wine in place of vinegar.

2. Rinse fresh mushrooms well under running water. Remove stems and drain thoroughly. Canned mushrooms may be used and should also be drained thoroughly.

3. Pour a sufficient amount of dressing over mushrooms to cover. Marinate several hours or overnight. Stir occasionally. Drain and reserve liquid.

4. Serve with cocktail picks.

Note

Use reserved liquid for salad dressing over greens.

HIBACHI APPETIZERS

YIELD: 12 appetizers

INGREDIENTS

CAESAR DRESSING MIX	1 pkg.
WATER	2 tbsp.
BURGUNDY or CLARET	1/4 cup
SALAD OIL	1/2 cup
SIRLOIN TIP STEAK, cut in 1-in. cubes	1-1/2 lb.
MUSHROOM CAPS	as needed
CHERRY TOMATOES	as needed
GREEN PEPPER, cut in 3/4-in. pieces	as needed

PROCEDURE

1. Empty Caesar Dressing Mix into screw-top, pint-size jar. Add water and shake well. Add wine and oil. Shake again, about 30 sec. Pour over cubes of meat and mushroom caps. Marinate about 2 hr.

2. Arrange cubes on skewers, alternating with mushrooms, cherry tomatoes, and green pepper pieces. Grill quickly over charcoal until meat is nicely browned, about 4 to 6 min.

PRAWN HORS D'OEUVRES

PROCEDURE

Buy medium-sized prawns, shell, and devein. Insert anchovy fillet into deveined prawn cavity, wrap with a strip of bacon; broil.

CODFISH CAKES

PROCEDURE

Shape usual codfish cake mixture into tiny balls. Place in frying basket and fry in deep fat until golden brown. Serve as appetizers on toothpicks.

PIGS IN BLANKETS

PROCEDURE

To make pigs in blankets, drop each oyster in a thin half slice of bacon. Fasten with toothpick. Bake in oven at 425°F. about 20 min. or until bacon is crisp. Serve hot.

CARAWAY CHEESE WAFERS

YIELD: 8 doz. 2-in. wafers

INGREDIENTS

BUTTER or MARGARINE	8 oz.
FLOUR	1 lb.
SALT	2 tsp.
CHEDDAR CHEESE, grated	2 lb.
MILK	3/4 cup
CARAWAY SEEDS	as needed

PROCEDURE

1. Combine shortening with sifted flour and salt; cut in shortening until the particles are pea size.
2. Add grated cheese; mix well.
3. Add milk and mix until blended.
4. Form into rolls 2 in. in diameter and wrap in waxed paper. Chill.
5. Cut into thin slices; place on well-oiled sheet pans. Brush with milk; sprinkle with caraway seeds.
6. Bake in oven at 375°F. for 12 min.

COCKTAIL SAUCE

YIELD: approx. 1 qt.

INGREDIENTS

TOMATO CATSUP	2 cups
CHILI SAUCE	1 cup
LEMON JUICE	1/4 cup
HORSERADISH	1 tbsp.
WORCESTERSHIRE SAUCE	1 tbsp.
SUGAR	1 tbsp.
SALT	2 tsp.
LIQUID HOT PEPPER SEASONING	dash

PROCEDURE

1. Blend all ingredients. Mix thoroughly.
2. Pour into jar, cover, place in refrigerator. Shake well before using.

MONKEY BREAD

YIELD: 20 servings

INGREDIENTS

YEAST	1-1/2 cakes
SUGAR	1 tbsp.
MILK	1 cup
BUTTER	1/4 lb.
EGGS, beaten	3
FLOUR, sifted	3 or 4 cups
SALT	1 tsp.

PROCEDURE

1. Soften yeast in small amount of lukewarm water. Add sugar.

2. Scald milk and add butter, allowing it to melt. Cool to lukewarm, add beaten eggs, then add yeast mixture. Add flour and salt and mix well. Place in greased bowl and allow to rise.

3. Roll out to 1/3-in. thickness, and cut with diamond cookie cutter. Place one layer in well-oiled ring. Spread with melted butter, add second layer, spread with melted butter. Continue adding layers and melted butter until mold is 3/4 full. Allow to rise until double in bulk.

4. Bake in oven at 350° to 375°F. for 45 min.

CHILI-CHEESE BALL

YIELD: 48 servings

INGREDIENTS

SHARP CHEDDAR CHEESE, grated	3-1/2 lb.
INSTANT GARLIC POWDER	4 tsp.
CHILI POWDER	

PROCEDURE

1. In large bowl combine cheese with garlic powder; mix lightly.

2. Shape into 8 balls, pressing firmly. Roll each ball in chili powder until well coated.

3. Serve as an hors d'oeuvre with corn chips or crackers.

CHAMPAGNE OR WINE PUNCH

INGREDIENTS

STRAWBERRIES, FROZEN, SLICED, partially thawed	1 lb.
GRENADINE	8 oz.
CHERRY BRANDY	8 oz.
CARBONATED WATER or PALE DRY GINGER ALE	2 qt.
CHAMPAGNE or WINE, inexpensive brand	2 bottles
ICE	small block
SHERBET, LEMON or ORANGE	1 pt.

PROCEDURE

1. Place strawberries in punch bowl; add grenadine and brandy.
2. Put in small block of ice, then add sherbet.
3. Pour carbonated water over contents in circular motion; add champagne in same manner. Stir slowly two or three times ONLY.
4. Add additional sherbet, if desired.

FRUIT PUNCH

YIELD: Enough for 100 people

INGREDIENTS

SUGAR	5 lb.
POMEGRANATE GRENADINE SYRUP	1/5 bottle
LEMON JUICE	3 qt.
PINEAPPLE JUICE	46 oz. can
PEACHES, NO. 10 CAN	syrup only
LIME FLAVORING	to taste
WATER	as needed

PROCEDURE

Pour syrup from peaches; reserve peaches for other use. Make a simple syrup combining all ingredients except the water. Add water to make 4 gallons of punch. At Wann's, 30 servings to the gallon is the usual measure for punch. Food coloring is used to create color combinations.

BOMBAY PUNCH

YIELD: about 70 cups

To 2 cups lemon juice add enough powdered sugar to sweeten. Pour over large block of ice in punch bowl; stir. Then add 1 qt. brandy, 1 qt. sherry, 4-1/2 cups grenadine, 1/2 cup curacao, 4 qt. champagne, and 2 qt. club soda. Stir well; decorate with fruits in season.

BRANDY PUNCH

YIELD: about 35 cups

To 2 cups lemon juice add the juice of 4 oranges, 1 cup grenadine, and 1 qt. club soda. Add enough sugar to sweeten. Pour over large block of ice in punch bowl; stir well. Add 1/2 pt. curacao and 2 qt. brandy.

CARDINAL PUNCH

YIELD: about 45 cups

To 2 cups lemon juice add enough powdered sugar to sweeten. Pour over large block of ice in punch bowl; stir. Add 1 pt. each brandy and light rum, 1 qt. champagne, 2 qt. claret, 1/2 pt. sweet vermouth, and 1 qt. carbonated water.

CLARET PUNCH

YIELD: about 45 cups

To 2 cups lemon juice add enough powdered sugar to sweeten. Pour over large block of ice in punch bowl; stir well. Add 1/2 pt. curacao, 1 pt. brandy, 3 qt. claret, and 1 qt. carbonated water.

MAIN DISHES

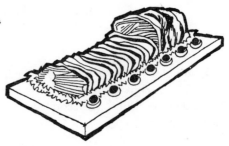

BRAISED SHORT RIBS OF BEEF

YIELD: 6 10-oz. portions

INGREDIENTS

SHORT RIBS (FLANKEN), STRIPS, 10 OZ. EACH	6
MONOSODIUM GLUTAMATE	1 tbsp.
SALT	to season
PEPPER	to season
FLOUR, ALL-PURPOSE, sifted	1 cup
SHORTENING, NONDAIRY	1 tbsp.
ONIONS, LARGE, coarsely cut	3
CARROTS, coarsely cut	3
CELERY STALKS, large pieces	8
BAY LEAF	1
GARLIC CLOVE, minced	1
SOUP STOCK	1 qt.
TOMATO JUICE	1 cup

PROCEDURE

1. Rub short ribs with monosodium glutamate. Season with salt and pepper.

2. Dredge with flour. Cut each strip in two.

3. Brown on all sides in skillet in hot shortening.

4. Place meat in pot with the other 7 ingredients. Cover and simmer slowly 2-1/2 hr., or until meat is tender.

5. Remove meat. Keep hot. Strain sauce.

6. Serve on hot platter with sauce poured over the meat.

Note

Inviting accompanimnets with Braised Short Ribs are peas, carrots, and parsley bouquets.

POTTED CHICKEN WITH VEGETABLES
AND MATZO BALL

PROCEDURE

1. Simmer a 4- to 5-lb. stewing chicken with vegetables, such as carrots, celery, knob celery, parsley, and leeks.

2. When fork tender, remove chicken, and season stock with salt, pepper, and monosodium glutamate.

3. In individual casseroles, place a bed of boiled noodles.

4. Add cooked vegetables, such as carrots, green beans, and peas. Place a matzo ball in center.

5. Add cut-up stewing chicken, and seasoned stock. Serve very hot.

BAKED EGGS IN SOUR CREAM
(May be used as a breakfast dish or light luncheon main course)

YIELD: 8 portions

INGREDIENTS

SOUR CREAM	1 pt.
EGGS	16
CHIVES, chopped or SCALLIONS, minced	2 tbsp.
PARSLEY, chopped	2 tbsp.
BREAD CRUMBS	2 tbsp.
BUTTER, melted	4 tbsp.
SALT	to taste
PEPPER	to taste

PROCEDURE

1. Pour cream in flat, (1 in. deep) oven dish and make indentations with back of bouillon spoon.

2. Break 1 egg into each indentation. Season lightly and sprinkle with chives, parsley, and bread crumbs. Pour melted butter over top.

3. Bake in oven at 450°F. until eggs are set and top is browned.

This may be served with a side dish of asparagus.

KNISHES ⟶

INGREDIENTS
DOUGH

DRY YEAST	1 pkg.
WATER, warm	1/4 cup
FLOUR	2 to 2-1/2 cups
SUGAR	1 tbsp.
SALT	pinch
MARGARINE	2 sticks
EGG YOLKS, large	3

FILLINGS

CHOPPED LIVER (see recipe, p. 215)
POTATO

ONIONS, LARGE, chopped	2
CHICKEN FAT	1/4 cup
POTATOES, mashed, hot	2 cups
EGG, LARGE	1
SALT	to taste
PEPPER	to taste

Saute onions until brown; mix with other ingredients. Chill thoroughly.

GLAZE

EGG YOLKS	2
EGG WHITE, lightly beaten	1 tsp.

Combine.

PROCEDURE

1. Dissolve yeast in warm water.

2. Mix the flour, sugar, and salt in a large bowl.

3. Cut the margarine into the dry ingredients until the pieces are tiny. Add the yeast and the egg yolks.

4. Knead the mixture by hand until it is smooth and holds together.

5. Wrap the dough in wax paper and refrigerate overnight.

6. Divide the dough into 4 equal parts; refrigerate.

7. Place 1/4 of the dough on the pastry cloth and roll out into large rectangle, tissue paper thin. Use a well-floured cloth and rolling pin cover. Dough may be patched if it tears.

8. Place filling on dough in 1-in. strip along the edge closest to you.

9. Pick up cloth and proceed to roll as a jelly roll, resting the seam side down. Cut into 1-in. diagonal slices and place on ungreased cookie sheet; cover. Allow to rest until all the dough has been used.

10. Glaze the knishes with the mixture of egg yolks and whites.

11. Bake in oven at 400°F. for about 20 min. until browned. Remove from sheet; cool.

12. To serve, bake at 400°F. for another 10 or 15 min.

CHICKEN A LA KING

YIELD: 30 portions

INGREDIENTS

BUTTER or MARGARINE	2/3 cup
MUSHROOMS	2 lb.
FLOUR	10 tbsp.
SALT	1 tsp.
PEPPER	few shakes
BROTH or STOCK	2-1/2 cups
CREAM	1 cup
PIMIENTOS, diced	3
CHICKEN, cooked, coarsely diced	4 lb.
SHERRY	to taste

PROCEDURE

1. Melt butter; add mushrooms and saute for 5 min.

2. Stir in flour, salt, and pepper until smooth. Place over boiling water and slowly stir in broth and cream. Cook until thickened.

3. Add pimientos, chicken, and sherry and heat thoroughly.

This dish may be served on toast, waffles, scones, corn muffins, rice, buttered noodles, or chinese noodles, accompanied by mashed or baked potatoes, broccoli or asparagus, or broiled pineapple slices. It may be garnished with croutons, almonds, thinly sliced water chestnuts, and/or incorporated into omelets or scrambled eggs.

This is an excellent dish for ladies' luncheons, teas, etc.

BEEF STROGANOFF

YIELD: 3 servings

INGREDIENTS

BEEF FILLET, cut in thin slices	1 lb.
SALT	as needed
PEPPER	as needed
ONION, diced	1/2 cup
MUSHROOMS, sliced	1 cup
SHORTENING, for braising	as needed
FLOUR	1 tbsp.
SOUP STOCK	1 cup
MONOSODIUM GLUTAMATE	1 tsp.
MOCHA MIX	1 cup

PROCEDURE

1. Season beef with salt and pepper and let stand 2 hr.

2. Braise onion with mushrooms in shortening for 10 min. Add flour, and blend together. Pour in soup stock and let simmer for 10 min. Add monosodium glutamate.

3. Saute beef in shortening until brown and add to sauce. Let simmer 10 min.

4. Before serving, add mocha mix. Serve with broad noodles or rice.

GRILLED SALISBURY STEAK, BELMONT →

YIELD: 20 portions

INGREDIENTS

BEEF, finely ground	9 lb.
ONION, grated	1-1/2 cups
GREEN PEPPER, grated	1-1/2 cups
GARLIC, finely minced	3 cloves
PARSLEY, finely chopped	1/2 cup
PAPRIKA	1 tsp.
SALT	1 tbsp.
PEPPER	1 tsp.
THYME, POWDERED	1 tsp.
FLOUR	1-1/4 cups
SALT	1 tsp.
PEPPER	1 tsp.
OLIVE OIL	1/4 cup

PROCEDURE

1. Combine ground beef, onion, green pepper, garlic, and parsley. Season with paprika, salt, pepper, and thyme.

2. Blend well and shape into 20 steaks or 40 small steaks, 2 for each portion.

3. Sprinkle lightly with seasoned flour and brush with olive oil.

4. Broil 5 to 6 min. on each side or until done.

SAUCE

INGREDIENTS

BUTTER	2 cups
CATSUP	4 cups
LEMON JUICE	1/2 cup
WORCESTERSHIRE SAUCE	4 tbsp.
LIQUID HOT PEPPER SEASONING	3 to 4 dashes
PREPARED MUSTARD	3 tbsp.
MACE	pinch
SALT	to taste
PEPPER	to taste
DRY SHERRY	1-1/2 cups

PROCEDURE

1. Melt butter in a saucepan.
2. Add the catsup, lemon juice, worcestershire sauce, hot pepper seasoning, mustard, and mace. Season to taste with salt and pepper. Blend well.
3. Stir in sherry; heat just to boiling point.
4. Pour sauce over steaks at service time.

LAMB BROCHETTE
(Excellent main dish for dinners, luncheons;
serve mini portions as appetizers)

YIELD: 48 portions

INGREDIENTS

OIL	3 cups
WINE or CIDER VINEGAR	12 oz.
LEMON JUICE	2/3 cup
ONION, minced	1/2 cup
PARSLEY FLAKES	2 tbsp.
SALT	2 tsp.
OREGANO, LEAF	1-1/2 tsp.
BLACK PEPPER	2 tsp.
GARLIC POWDER	2 tsp.
LAMB LEGS, cut into 1 in. cubes	2
TOMATOES, firm, wedges	5 lb.
MUSHROOMS, CAPS	2 lb.

PROCEDURE

1. Combine first nine ingredients to make a marinade and mix well. Pour marinade over lamb cubes and refrigerate 5 to 6 hr., mixing 2 or 3 times.

2. Arrange lamb cubes, tomato wedges, and mushroom caps alternately on metal skewers or on disposable lamb skewers, and broil about 10 min., basting frequently with marinade.

3. Serve on bed of curried or saffron rice pilaf.

Note

Brochettes may be oven-baked at 375°F. for 40 min. in marinade that has been slightly thickened with cornstarch or beurre manie.* Cover with foil for first 20 min. Remove foil cover; turn brochettes, and finish baking.

*Beurre manie—2 tbsp. flour creamed with 2 tbsp. butter.

PALESTINE LAMB CASSEROLE

YIELD: 50 servings (approx. 8 oz. ea.)

INGREDIENTS

ONION, sliced	2 lb.
OLIVE OIL or SALAD OIL	2 cups
LAMB SHOULDER, BONELESS, cubed	12 lb.
SUMMER SQUASH, coarsely chopped	12 lb.
TOMATOES, FRESH	6 lb.
OREGANO	2 tsp.
SALT	1 tbsp.
PEPPER	1/2 tsp.
OLIVES, RIPE, GREEN or BLACK	100 to 150

PROCEDURE

1. Saute onion in hot oil in heavy pot or steam-jacketed kettle until soft. Add cubed lamb and saute until browned.

2. Dip tomatoes in boiling water for 1 min. Remove peel and cut in wedges. Add tomatoes and seasonings, cover and simmer for 20 to 25 min.

3. Add squash and continue to cook until lamb and squash are tender.

4. Add olives. Ladle mixture into 8-oz. casseroles.

PIQUANT STUFFED CABBAGE A LA THELMA

YIELD: 36 portions

INGREDIENTS

CABBAGES, LARGE	2
RICE, UNCOOKED	3/4 cup
HAMBURGER	3 lb.
EGGS, LARGE	2
SALT	1 tsp.
MONOSODIUM GLUTAMATE	1 tsp.
CATSUP	1/4 cup
ORANGE JUICE, FROZEN, thawed, undiluted	1 6 oz. can
TOMATOES, CRUSHED	1 No. 2-1/2 can
TOMATO PUREE	1 No. 2-1/2 can
VINEGAR	1/2 cup
LEMON JUICE	1/3 cup
BROWN SUGAR	1/2 lb.
HONEY	2 lb.
CLOVES, GROUND	1/4 tsp.

PROCEDURE

1. Remove as much of core from cabbages as possible. Place cabbages in boiling water to soften outer leaves.

2. With a two-pronged fork lift the cabbages from the water and remove as many leaves as possible.

3. Return cabbages to water and repeat process until all usable leaves are removed. Drain well.

4. Retain heart leaves and chop finely for use in sauce. Trim the ribs of each leaf until the entire leaf is of the same thickness.

5. Cook the rice until it is soft; cool. Combine with hamburger and next 4 ingredients.

6. Line the bottom of the pan with the chopped cabbage (include finely chopped stems and any remaining cabbage not used in stuffing).

7. Flatten each cabbage leaf with palm of hand; fill each leaf with a No. 16 scoop of meat mixture. Roll up each leaf; place seamside down in baking pan, with sides touching each other. Do not pack more than 3 cabbage rolls high.

8. Mix orange juice and remaining ingredients; pour over cabbages. Liquid should be about 1/2 in. over top layer of cabbage rolls.

9. Cover; bake in oven at 350°F. for 1-1/2 hr.

10. Adjust seasoning; continue baking for 1-1/2 hr. longer. In final stage of cooking it may be necessary to add catsup diluted with water to keep liquid to within 1 in. of top layer of cabbages.

SALMON-MUSHROOM FILLING FOR CREPES

INGREDIENTS

BUTTER	1/2 cup
OIL	1 tbsp.
ONIONS, LARGE, diced	4
MUSHROOMS, sliced	1 lb.
GREEN PEPPER, finely diced	1
SALMON, cooked, cold	6-1/2 lb.
SALT	to taste
WHITE PEPPER	to taste
LIQUID HOT PEPPER SEASONING	to taste
DILL SEED, CRUSHED (optional)	

PROCEDURE

1. Saute onions in butter and oil until limp. Add mushrooms, green pepper, and cook until onions are brown and mushrooms and green pepper are tender. Remove from heat.

2. Skin, flake, and bone the salmon and add to onion mixture. Add to cream sauce.* Season to taste. Chill.

Note

Lobster, shrimp, cod, or any boneless chunk fish may be substituted. It is not recommended that this product be frozen.

*CREAM SAUCE FOR SALMON-MUSHROOM FILLING

INGREDIENTS

BUTTER	1 cup
FLOUR	1 cup
WHITE PEPPER	to taste
SALT	2 tsp.
PAPRIKA	dash
HALF-AND-HALF	1 qt.

PROCEDURE

1. Melt butter over medium heat.

2. Sprinkle flour over butter and whisk until smooth. Season and add half-and-half. Remove from heat.

3. Cover with wax paper, and cool until ready to use.

BAKED GEFILTE FISH
(Serve sliced as first course, or cut into squares for hors d'oeuvre)

YIELD: 30 portions

INGREDIENTS

WHITEFISH, FILLETS	2 lb.
YELLOW PIKE, FILLETS	2 lb.
WINTER CARP, FILLETS	2 lb.
ONIONS, LARGE	6
SALT	12 tsp.
PEPPER	to taste
EGGS, lightly beaten	24
ICE WATER (imperative)	4-1/2 cups
SUGAR	2 tsp.
MATZO MEAL	6 tbsp.

PROCEDURE

1. Grind fish twice with onions, using fine blade. Add remaining ingredients and mix thoroughly, seasoning to taste.

2. Turn mixture into very lightly oiled 9-in. by 5-in. by 3-in. loaf pans. Cover lightly with foil. Bake in water bath in oven preheated to 350°F. for 1 hr., or until tops are firm to touch.

This may be served hot or cold. Accompany with white or red horse-radish, or with sliced hard-cooked eggs.

CAULIFLOWER SEAFOOD CASSEROLE
(Excellent for buffet receptions)

YIELD: 25 to 30 portions

INGREDIENTS

CAULIFLOWER, LARGE	
BUTTER	1/2 cup
FLOUR	1/2 cup
MILK or HALF-AND-HALF	1 qt.
SALT	3 tsp.
LUMP CRABMEAT	4 cups
LEMON JUICE	1-1/2 tbsp.
FRENCH PEAS	2 No. 2 cans
PARMESAN CHEESE, grated	1 cup
BREAD CRUMBS, fine	1 cup

PROCEDURE

1. Separate cauliflower into flowerettes. Cook in boiling salted water for 10 min. Drain thoroughly.

2. Melt butter in saucepan. Stir in flour; when bubbly, slowly add milk, and season with salt.

3. Stir over moderate heat until mixture thickens.

4. Add crabmeat and lemon juice. Blend and remove from heat.

5. Place cauliflower flowerettes in shallow baking dish, add drained peas, and cover with crabmeat mixture. Sprinkle surface with grated cheese and bread crumbs. Bake 20 min. in oven preheated to 350°F.

MUSHROOM SEAFARERS SPECIAL
*(May be used on buffet, or as main course,
or one-dish luncheon with broccoli or asparagus)*

YIELD: 30 portions

INGREDIENTS

MUSHROOMS, FRESH	5 lb.
FISH, FILLETS (COD, SOLE, etc.)	4 lb.
CHICKEN GUMBO SOUP, CONDENSED	1 No. 5 can
TOMATOES, CRUSHED	3 No. 2-1/2 cans
SHRIMP, deveined	2 lb.
THYME, GROUND	1/2 tsp.
SALT	1/2 tsp.
LIQUID HOT PEPPER SEASONING	1/2 tsp.

PROCEDURE
1. Halve fresh mushrooms.
2. Cut fish fillets into 2-in. chunks.
3. In saucepan bring soup and tomatoes to boiling point. Add mushrooms, fish, and remaining ingredients.
4. Simmer until fish and shrimp are cooked, about 10 min.
5. Serve over rice or extra-wide noodles.

BATTER FOR SCAMPI FRITTERS

INGREDIENTS

FLOUR	1 lb.
SALT	1 tsp.
WATER, tepid	24 tbsp.
SALAD OIL	6 tbsp.
EGG WHITES	8

PROCEDURE
1. Put flour and salt in a bowl and make a well in center.
2. Add water and oil alternately, whipping constantly until batter is smooth and light.
3. Add stiffly beaten egg whites just before using.
4. Dip scampi in batter and deep fry until crisp. May be served with lemon wedges.

BANANA FRITTERS

YIELD: 12 fritters

INGREDIENTS

FLOUR, sifted	1 cup
BAKING POWDER	2 tsp.
SALT	1-1/2 tsp.
SUGAR	1/4 cup
EGG, well beaten	1
MILK	1/3 cup
SHORTENING, melted	2 tsp.
BANANAS	3

PROCEDURE

1. Sift together flour, baking powder, salt, and sugar into mixing bowl.

2. Combine egg, milk, and shortening and add to dry ingredients. Mix until batter is smooth. **DO NOT THIN BATTER.**

3. Peel three firm bananas and cut each into 4 diagonal pieces. Roll in flour and dip into batter, completely coating banana.

4. Deep fry about 6 min. at 375°F. until well browned. Turn fritters to brown evenly.

5. Serve hot. These may be served as a main course or as a dessert with fruit sauce or whipped cream.

CASSOULET
"Menu Maker and Party Planner"
by Elizabeth Hedgecock Sparks
Menu Maker, Kernersville, N.C.

YIELD: 10 servings

INGREDIENTS

NAVY BEANS, SMALL, DRIED	1 lb.
SALT	2 tsp.
HERB BLEND (see procedure)	
ONION, chopped	3/4 cup
SMOKED SAUSAGE LINKS	1 lb.
BEEF or POULTRY, cooked, diced	2-1/2 cup
DRY WHITE WINE	3 cup
TOMATO SAUCE	1 8 oz. can
PARSLEY, minced	3/4 cup
BREAD CRUMBS, fine, dry	3/4 cup
BUTTER	1/3 cup

PROCEDURE

1. Cover beans with cold water and bring to a boil. Remove from heat and soak for several hours.

2. Add salt and blend of herbs—a pinch each of basil, marjoram, thyme, oregano, mace, and savory. Cook until beans are almost tender, adding water as needed. All the water should be gone when beans are finished.

3. In a large casserole, arrange a layer of beans, onion, thinly sliced sausage, and meat. Continue until all ingredients are used.

4. Mix wine with tomato sauce and pour over the top. Mix minced parsley, bread crumbs, and melted butter and spread over the top.

5. Cover and bake in oven at 325°F. for 2 hr.

HAM JAMBALAYA WITH RICE

YIELD: 24 servings

INGREDIENTS

ONION, chopped	1 cup
GREEN PEPPER, chopped	3/4 cup
MARGARINE	6 oz.
TOMATOES, CANNED	1 qt.
RICE, washed	1 lb.
SUGAR	2 tbsp.
SALT	1 tbsp.
PEPPER	1/2 tsp.
PAPRIKA	1 tsp.
GARLIC SALT	1/2 tsp.
MONOSODIUM GLUTAMATE	1/2 tsp.
WORCESTERSHIRE SAUCE	2 tbsp.
HAM, cooked, diced	2 lb.

PROCEDURE

1. Saute onion and green pepper in margarine.

2. Add tomatoes and bring to a boil.

3. Add the rice, cover and cook slowly until the rice is tender. Add small quantities of water from time to time if necessary to prevent burning. Do not stir unnecessarily.

4. When the rice is tender, add the seasonings and diced ham. Cook until thoroughly heated.

PETITE HAM LOAVES WITH GLAZE

YIELD: 30 servings

INGREDIENTS

SMOKED PORK BUTT, ground	3 lb.
BONELESS PORK, ground	4 lb.
EGGS, beaten	5
BREAD CRUMBS, fine, dry	3/4 qt.
MILK	3/4 qt.
BROWN SUGAR	1/3 qt.
VINEGAR	1 cup
DRY MUSTARD	1 tbsp.

PROCEDURE

1. Thoroughly mix the meat, eggs, bread crumbs, and milk. Shape into individual loaves. Each should weigh about 5 oz.   Place in baking pan.

2. Bake in oven at 350°F. for 45 min.

3. Remove from the oven and pour off the excess fat and liquid.

4. Cover with the mixture of brown sugar, vinegar, and mustard. Return to oven and continue baking another 45 min.

BAKED HAM WITH CRANBERRY MANDARIN SAUCE

YIELD: 40 to 45 servings

INGREDIENTS

HAM	1 9 lb.
BROWN SUGAR	1 lb.
CORNSTARCH	3/4 cup
CRANBERRY JUICE	2 qt.
ORANGE JUICE, FROZEN CONCENTRATE	4 oz.
CLOVES, POWDERED	1/2 tsp.
MANDARIN ORANGES, drained	3 cups

PROCEDURE

1. Heat ham according to label instructions. Cool slightly. Slice ham and place in steam table pans.

2. Mix brown sugar and cornstarch in sauce pot. Add cranberry juice, orange juice concentrate, and cloves. Bring slowly to boiling point and simmer until sauce is clear and thick (about 10 min.), stirring occasionally.

3. Add mandarin oranges. Serve a 1-oz. ladle of sauce over each order of ham.

HAM AND SWEET POTATO PATTIES

YIELD: 30 servings (2 patties each)

INGREDIENTS

HAM, cooked, ground	6 lb.
PINEAPPLE, CRUSHED, well drained	1 qt.
SWEET POTATO, mashed	2 qt.
EGGS, slightly beaten	6
SALT (omit if ham is very salty)	1 tbsp.
CINNAMON	1-1/2 tsp.
NUTMEG	1-1/2 tsp.
CORN FLAKE CRUMBS	1 qt.
SHORTENING	8 oz.

PROCEDURE

1. Combine the ham, pineapple, sweet potato, eggs, salt, and spices. Mix well and shape into patties.

2. Turn the patties in corn flake crumbs and brown both sides in hot fat just before serving.

3. Garnish with parsley.

Note

These ham and sweet potato patties have eye and appetite appeal when served with a green vegetable.

LASAGNE IMBOTITE ⟶

YIELD: 50 servings

INGREDIENTS
SAUCE

GARLIC CLOVES, quartered	6
SALAD OIL	1 cup
TOMATO PASTE	4-2/3 cup (7 6 oz. cans)
ITALIAN PLUM TOMATOES	7 qt. (14 1 lb. cans)
CELERY, diced	1-3/4 cups
SALT	4 tsp.
PEPPER	1 tsp.

STUFFING

PORK SAUSAGE MEAT	5 lb.
BROAD LASAGNE NOODLES	3-3/4 lb.
SALT	5 tbsp.
RICOTTA CHEESE	5 lb.
MOZZARELLA or SCAMORZE CHEESE, cubed	7-1/2 cups
PARMESAN CHEESE, grated	7-1/2 cups

CHICKEN ITALIANO

YIELD: 20 servings—2 pieces chicken, approx. 3 tbsp. sauce

INGREDIENTS

CHICKEN PARTS	40 4 oz. pcs.
FLOUR	2/3 cup
SALT	2 tsp.
CONDENSED TOMATO SOUP	1 3 lb. 3 oz. can
OREGANO, LEAF, crushed	1-1/2 tsp.
INSTANT GRANULATED GARLIC	1/4 tsp.

PROCEDURE

1. Dust chicken with seasoned flour. Brown in shortening until golden; drain well.

2. Combine soup, oregano, and garlic; heat to simmer to blend flavors. Arrange chicken in two steam table pans (12-in. by 20-in. by 2-1/2-in.) Ladle on hot sauce. Bake in preheated oven at 350°F. for 45 to 60 min. or until done.

PROCEDURE

1. To prepare sauce, cook garlic in oil in a heavy saucepan until it is golden brown, about 3 min. Remove garlic from oil. Add tomato paste, tomatoes, celery, salt, and pepper to oil. Mix thoroughly. Cover. Simmer 2 hr. stirring occasionally.

2. To prepare stuffing, brown sausage in heavy skillet until pink disappears. Pour off drippings.

3. Cook noodles with salt in boiling water, about 15 min. or until tender, but not soft. Drain. Combine cooked sausage meat, ricotta, and mozzarella cheese.

4. In each of 5 baking pans (13-in. by 9-1/2-in. by 2-in.) pour 1/2 cup of tomato sauce. Cover with a layer of noodles, then a layer of sausage-cheese mixture, a layer of sauce, and a layer of parmesan cheese. Repeat layers until all the ingredients are used. The top layer should be sauce and parmesan cheese. Bake in oven at 375°F. about 45 min. or until bubbly. Cut into squares and serve with additional cheese.

Note

For American-style lasagne use 7 1-lb. 12-oz. cans of tomatoes instead of plum tomatoes; 7 lb. of dry cottage cheese instead of ricotta.

To prevent noodles from sticking together, immerse in cold water until ready to use. For ease in serving, let lasagne stand for 10 min. before cutting. The lasagne may be combined ahead of time and refrigerated until ready to bake. Increase baking time about 1/2 hr.

SAVORY CHICKEN DIVAN

YIELD: 100 servings

INGREDIENTS

STUFFING CROUTONS, HERB-SEASONED	3 lb. 2 oz.
WHITE SAUCE, MEDIUM	1-3/4 gal.
BROCCOLI SPEARS, cooked, drained	6 2-1/2 lb. pkg.
CHICKEN or TURKEY, white meat, sliced	12 lb. 8 oz.
PARMESAN CHEESE, grated	1 lb. 12 oz.

PROCEDURE

1. Place 1/2 cup croutons for base of each serving in casserole.

2. Ladle 1 oz. white sauce over croutons. Arrange 2 broccoli spears over croutons and sauce, top with 2 oz. sliced chicken; cover with 1 oz. white sauce, sprinkle with 1 tbsp. cheese. Repeat process for each serving.

3. Bake in oven at 350°F. about 20 min. or until thoroughly heated. Garnish with a sprig of parsley.

CHICKEN AND SPAGHETTI LOAF

YIELD: 30 servings

INGREDIENTS

SPAGHETTI	1 lb.
CHICKEN, cooked, diced	2 qt.
BREAD CRUMBS, dry	1 qt.
CHEDDAR CHEESE, grated	1 lb.
PARSLEY, chopped	1/4 cup
GREEN PEPPER, chopped	1 cup
PIMIENTO, chopped	1/2 cup
SALT	2 tbsp.
EGGS, beaten	12
MILK	2 qt.

PROCEDURE

1. Break spaghetti into 2-in. pieces. Cook until tender in boiling salted water.

2. Drain and rinse with cold water.

3. Place in a mixing bowl and combine all ingredients, mixing well.

4. Place mixture in oiled loaf pan and bake in oven at 325°F. for 1 hr.

5. Heat canned mushroom soup and use as a sauce when serving the loaf, sliced into appetizing portions for hearty eating. Unusual taste and texture of loaf is certain to have wide appeal.

LEMON BUTTER BAKED CHICKEN

YIELD: 50 portions

INGREDIENTS

CHICKEN (1-1/2- to 2-lb. broilers, split, or	
2-1/2- to 3-lb. fryers, quartered)	
BUTTER	1-1/2 lb.
LEMON JUICE	1 cup
VINEGAR	1 cup
WATER	1 pt.
SALT	3 tbsp.
SUGAR	1 cup
LIQUID HOT PEPPER SAUCE	1 tbsp.
WORCESTERSHIRE SAUCE	2 tbsp.
CORNSTARCH	6 tbsp.

PROCEDURE

1. Sprinkle chicken lightly with salt.

2. Combine remaining ingredients except cornstarch, bring to a boil and simmer for 1 min.

3. Dip chicken pieces into sauce and lay them skin side down in steam table pans. Pour remaining sauce evenly over chicken. Bake, uncovered, in oven at 375°F. for 30 min.

4. Turn skin side up and bake another 20 to 30 min., until pieces are golden brown.

5. Pour sauce off chicken into saucepot and thicken it with cornstarch mixed in a little cold water. Pour this thickened glaze over the chicken. Serve 1/4 or 1/2 chicken.

SCALLOPED TURKEY AND DRESSING

YIELD: 50 servings

INGREDIENTS
FOR DRESSING

WHITE BREAD, stale, cubed	6 lb.
PEPPER	1/2 tsp.
SALT	1 tbsp.
POULTRY SEASONING	2-1/2 tbsp.
ONION, finely chopped	1 qt.
CELERY, finely chopped	1 qt.
WATER	2-1/2 qt.
SAUSAGE or BACON FAT, melted	1 cup

FOR CREAMED TURKEY LAYER

FAT	12 oz.
FLOUR	12-1/2 oz.
SALT	1-1/2 tbsp.
MONOSODIUM GLUTAMATE	1 tsp.
TURKEY BROTH	4 qt.
TURKEY, cooked, diced	5 lb.

FOR TOPPING

BUTTER or MARGARINE	8 oz.
BREAD CRUMBS, fine, dry	12 oz.

PROCEDURE

1. Combine all the ingredients for the dressing. Mix thoroughly. Divide into 2 oiled baking pans.

2. Make a gravy of the fat, flour, salt, monosodium glutamate, and turkey broth. When thick and smooth, add the diced turkey. Pour over dressing.

3. Melt butter or margarine, mix with crumbs and sprinkle over layer of creamed turkey.

4. Bake in oven at 350°F. for 45 min. If the dressing is preheated, the baking time can be shortened.

5. When ready to serve, mark in squares as a guide for uniform portions. The quantity of turkey can be varied according to cost, if desired. Chicken can be used instead of turkey.

CHESTNUT STUFFING

PROCEDURE

To vary basic dry bread stuffing for turkey:

1. Prepare 1 lb. raw chestnuts by immersing them in cold water to cover. Bring to a boil. Simmer gently 15 to 20 min. Drain, shell, skin. Or, cut a cross in the flat side of each chestnut. Mix with oil and bake in oven at 450°F. for 20 min. or saute in oil. Cool, shell, and, with a sharp knife, remove brown skins.

2. Chop chestnuts coarsely and add to dry bread cubes before adding other ingredients. Minced bacon or cubed ham may also be added.

TURKEY VERONIQUE

YIELD: 50 servings

INGREDIENTS	
BUTTER or SHORTENING	1 lb.
CELERY, finely diced	1 cup
ONION, minced	1/2 cup
MUSHROOMS, diced	2 lb.
GREEN PEPPER, diced	2 cups
FLOUR	3 cups
MILK, hot	3 qt.
CHICKEN STOCK, hot	1 qt.
SALT	2 tbsp.
WHITE PEPPER	1 tsp.
TURKEY, cooked, diced	6 qt.
RED GRAPES, pitted, halved	2 lb.
SHERRY	1/2 cup
CREAM	1/2 cup

PROCEDURE

1. Melt butter. Add celery, onion, mushrooms. Saute lightly.

2. Blanch green pepper 5 min. Add to pot and cook on slow fire until vegetables are glazed (but not brown).

3. Add flour. Stir in well.

4. Add the hot milk, stock, and seasonings, blending well with wire whip until smooth. Cook 15 min. on a slow fire, stirring occasionally.

5. Add turkey and grapes. Simmer slowly another 10 to 15 min.

6. Stir in sherry and cream and remove from fire. Serve in toast cups.

CREAMED TURKEY WITH PINEAPPLE AND ALMONDS

YIELD: 30 servings

INGREDIENTS

MARGARINE	8 oz.
FLOUR	5 oz.
TURKEY BROTH	1-1/2 qt.
MILK or THIN CREAM	1 qt.
SALT	2 tsp.
PEPPER	1/4 tsp.
ONION, grated	2 tbsp.
TURKEY, cooked, diced	4 lb.
PINEAPPLE, CANNED or FRESH, shredded, drained	3 cups
ALMONDS, SLICED, toasted	6 oz.

PROCEDURE

1. Melt margarine, add flour, and stir until blended.
2. Add broth and milk, stirring constantly over low heat until mixture is uniformly thickened. Place over hot water.
3. Add seasonings and turkey and heat thoroughly.
4. Just before serving, stir in pineapple and almonds.
5. Serve over noodles, rice, toast, or baking powder biscuits.

CHICKEN OR TURKEY CACCIATORE

YIELD: 52 servings

INGREDIENTS

FRYER CHICKENS, quartered	13
ONION, sliced 1/4 in.	3 lb.
GARLIC CLOVES, minced	2
TOMATOES, WHOLE	1-1/2 No. 10 cans
TOMATO PUREE	1/2 No. 10 can
OREGANO, CRUSHED	2 tbsp.
CELERY SEED	2 tbsp.
BAY LEAVES	10
A LA KING SAUCE MIX	2-1/2 lb.
WATER, cold	1-1/2 gal.

PROCEDURE

1. Brown chicken until half done.

2. Saute sliced onion and garlic; add to whole tomatoes and puree. Add oregano, celery seeds, and bay leaves. Add chicken and simmer in oven at 350°F. for approx. 30 min.

3. Prepare A La King Sauce following package directions, using the 1-1/2 gal. water. Add sauce to chicken mixture and continue baking for 30 more min. or until "forkdone."

4. Serve a quarter chicken per portion with sauce ladled over top.

BARBECUED DRUMSTICKS

YIELD: 30 servings

INGREDIENTS

DRUMSTICKS, 5 to 6 OZ. EACH	30
FLOUR	8 oz.
SHORTENING	1 lb.
SAUCE	
SALAD OIL	4 oz.
ONION, chopped	3/4 cup
GARLIC, minced	2 cloves
HOT PEPPER SAUCE	1/4 tsp.
LEMON JUICE	1/2 cup
WORCESTERSHIRE SAUCE	1/3 cup
SALT	1-1/2 tsp.
PEPPER	1/4 tsp.
MONOSODIUM GLUTAMATE	1 tsp.
SUGAR	2 tbsp.
CHILI POWDER	1-1/2 tsp.
OREGANO	1/2 tsp.
WATER	2 cups
CATSUP	1 cup

PROCEDURE

1. Flour drumsticks and brown in hot fat. Place in baking pans.

2. Saute onion and garlic in hot oil until transparent.

3. Add all other ingredients. Cover and cook gently for 10 min. If necessary, more water can be added at the end of the cooking time.

4. Pour about half the sauce over the drumsticks. Cover and bake in oven at 375°F. for about 30 min. Add remaining sauce, and bake uncovered 20 min.

SWEET AND PUNGENT SHRIMP ON RICE

YIELD: 2 gal., 32 servings—1 cup shrimp, 1/2 cup rice

INGREDIENTS

SHRIMP, UNCOOKED	7 lb.
GREEN PEPPER	1 lb. 8 oz.
WATER	2-1/2 qt.
BOUILLON CUBES	10
APPLE SLICES	1 No. 10 can
CORNSTARCH	3-3/4 oz.
SOY SAUCE	1/4 cup
CIDER VINEGAR	1 pt.
DARK BROWN SUGAR, firmly packed	2 lb.
SALT	2 tsp.
RICE, cooked	6 lb. 8 oz.
FRIED CHINESE NOODLES	1 lb.

PROCEDURE

1. Cook shrimp in boiling water for 5 min., drain; shell, cut shrimp lengthwise, and clean.

2. Cut green pepper in wide strips.

3. Heat water; add bouillon cubes, stir until dissolved.

4. Add shrimp, green pepper strips, and apple slices. Simmer 5 min.

5. Combine cornstarch, soy sauce, vinegar, sugar, and salt; blend well and stir into shrimp mixture. Cook until thickened, stirring occasionally.

6. Serve over hot rice with fried noodles.

Note

Chicken or vegetable stock may be used in place of water and bouillon cubes. Cooked or canned lobster or chicken may be substituted for shrimp.

FISH CHOWDER

YIELD: 4 gal.

INGREDIENTS

BACON, diced	3 lb.
ONION, diced	2 lb.
SALAD POTATOES, cooked, peeled, or	8 lb.
WHOLE POTATOES, CANNED	1 No. 10 can
TOMATOES	2 No. 10 cans
CORN, WHOLE KERNEL	1 No. 10 can
SALT	1/4 cup
PEPPER	1 tbsp.
MONOSODIUM GLUTAMATE	3/4 cup
FISH FILLETS (skinless perch, whitefish,	
haddock or fish of your choice)	12 lb.
BAY LEAVES	4

PROCEDURE

1. Fry bacon and remove from pan. Saute onion lightly in bacon fat.
2. In a 5-gal. stock pot put the potatoes, tomatoes, corn, including the juice; add the bacon, onion, salt, pepper, monosodium glutamate, and the fish.
3. Place bay leaves in a cloth bag or lay on top of chowder. Simmer until fish are cooked. Remove bay leaves when finished.
4. Taste, adjust to desired flavor and serve.

BLEND LEMON AND SEAFOOD

Lemon Supreme Sauce: Bake this simple flavor mixture right into a salmon steak. Place fish on foil-lined baking dish and pour over it this mixture: equal parts of fresh lemon juice and butter, chopped green onions (tops and all), salt, and pepper.

Butter 'n Nutmeg Sauce: Suggested as a savory accompaniment to fresh fish is this blend of 1/3 cup butter softened in fresh lemon juice plus 1 tsp. nutmeg. Add mixture to fish as it browns in butter.

SEAFOOD NEWBURG

YIELD: 50 servings

INGREDIENTS

SCALLOPS	4 lb.
OYSTERS, shucked	3 lb.
SHRIMP, cooked	3 lb.
LOBSTER MEAT, cooked	4 lb.
BUTTER	2 lb.
BREAD FLOUR	20 oz.
MILK, warm	4 qt.
LIGHT CREAM, warm	2 qt.
PAPRIKA	4 tsp.
SHERRY	10 oz.

PROCEDURE

1. Wash scallops and cut in 3/4-in. pieces. Poach in boiling water 5 min. Drain.

2. Saute oysters in 3 oz. butter until edges curl.

3. Clean shrimp and cut in 3/4-in. pieces.

4. Clean lobster meat, removing bones and veins; cut in 3/4-in. pieces.

5. Melt 20 oz. butter, add bread flour, cook 10 min., do not allow to brown. Add heated milk and cream a little at a time, stirring until thick and smooth.

6. Saute lobster in remaining butter until lobster gives a pink color to butter; add shrimp and cook until warm. Remove from fire, add paprika and stir in well.

7. Add all seafood to sauce, stir in gently until well mixed.

8. Add sherry, finish seasoning with salt and a pinch of cayenne.

PRAWNS CREOLE

INGREDIENTS

BUTTERFLY PRAWNS, 31 to 40 SIZE	10 lb.
OLIVE OIL	2 cups
PARSLEY SPRIG, FRESH, chopped leaves	1
ROSEMARY, DRY	1 tsp.
GARLIC CLOVES, chopped	4
SALT	1 tbsp.
PEPPER	1 tsp.
TOMATO PUREE	1 No. 10 can
BAY LEAVES	3
CHEDDAR CHEESE, grated	

PROCEDURE

1. Shell and devein prawns.

2. Heat olive oil until warm in saucepan, adding parsley, rosemary, and garlic. Simmer until garlic is golden brown.

3. Add salt and pepper, tomato puree, and simmer for 20 min.

4. In a separate pan pour boiling water to cover prawns. Add bay leaves, bring to a boil, then strain and add stock to tomato sauce. Simmer for 30 min.

5. Just before serving, add prawns to sauce. Serve over steamed rice to which a little sauce has been added and blended until rice has a light orange color. Top with cheddar cheese.

FRIED STUFFED SEA SCALLOPS, ROQUEFORT

YIELD: 150

INGREDIENTS

SEA SCALLOPS, JUMBO, FRESH	10 lb.
WHITE PEPPER	
ROQUEFORT CHEESE	1-1/2 lb.
SAUTERNE	about 1/4 cup
EVAPORATED MILK	1 cup
COMMERCIAL BREADING, FULLY SEASONED	1-1/2 cups

PROCEDURE

1. Drain scallops on clean linen cloth. When thoroughly dry, slice across the grain, being careful not to cut all the way through, to make shell-like form. When all are cut, open by raising top slice. Season lightly with white pepper.

2. Cream roquefort cheese, adding sauterne as needed. With No. 1 star tube on pastry bag, put enough cheese mixture inside each scallop to form closing adhesive. Refrigerate at 38°F. for 1/2 hr. to completely set and chill.

3. Dip chilled scallops into evaporated milk; coat with commercial breading. Place on waxed paper-lined pans. Let stand about 1/2 hr. Fry one layer only in basket in fat at 350°F. for 3-1/2 min., or until golden brown and firm to touch. Drain on brown paper. Put into chafing dish.

EGGS STUFFED WITH MUSHROOMS

YIELD: 30 servings

INGREDIENTS

MUSHROOMS, finely chopped	2-1/2 lb.
ONION, finely chopped	1/4 cup
MARGARINE	1/4 cup
EGGS, hard-cooked	30
SALT	1-1/2 tsp.
PEPPER	1/2 tsp.
PAPRIKA	1/2 tsp.
PREPARED MUSTARD	2 tbsp.
WHITE SAUCE, MEDIUM	2 qt.
CRUMBS, buttered	1 pt.
CHEESE, grated	1 cup

PROCEDURE

1. Saute chopped mushrooms and onion in margarine.

2. Cut eggs in half lengthwise and remove the yolks. Rub the yolks through a sieve; add the mushrooms, onion, and seasonings.

3. Refill the egg white halves with the yolk mixture and line up in baking pan. Cover with cream sauce. Top with buttered crumbs and grated cheese mixed together.

4. Bake in oven at 375°F. only until crumbs are brown (approx. 15 minutes).

SEAFOOD SECRETS

Complement the mild flavor of fish with a tart relish, such as pickled or harvard beets, coleslaw, green pepper and celery relish, marinated cucumbers, onion relish, etc.

For variety use a barbecue sauce when baking fish such as bass, trout, whitefish, swordfish, etc. The barbecue sauce blends with the natural flavor of the fish to give added eating pleasure.

BEEF BOURGIGNONNE

YIELD: 50 servings

INGREDIENTS

SALT PORK, parboiled, diced	1/2 lb.
BEEF CHUCK, LEAN, bite size, dredged in flour	12 lb.
OIL or SHORTENING	1/2 cup
PORK FAT	
SALT	2 tbsp.
PEPPER	1/2 tsp.
GARLIC, minced	2 to 3 cloves
ONIONS, MEDIUM, finely chopped	4
THYME)	
BAY LEAF) BOUQUET GARNI	as needed
PARSLEY)	
BURGUNDY	1 qt.
BROWN STOCK (to cover)	1-1/4 gal.
MUSHROOMS	2 lb.
BUTTER	1/2 lb.
LEMON JUICE	2 tbsp.
WHITE ONIONS, SMALL	96
SUGAR	1 cup
FLOUR	3/4 cup
PARSLEY	1/2 cup

PROCEDURE

1. Saute diced salt pork until lightly browned. Remove and reserve.

2. Saute beef in shortening and fat from sauteed salt pork. Season with salt and pepper; add garlic, onions, bouquet garni, wine, and stock. Cook about 2 hr.

3. Saute mushrooms in 1/2 of the butter, and lemon juice; glaze small white onions in remaining butter and sugar with a little water, until lightly browned. Add onions and cook until tender (both beef and onions should be ready). Remove bouquet garni. Correct seasoning and thicken with flour as needed. Add mushrooms and salt pork. Sprinkle with chopped parsley.

BEEF MARIA*

The Complete Book of Entertaining by Nata Lee, Inc.
Hawthorn Books, Inc., New York City

YIELD: 6 servings

INGREDIENTS

FLANK STEAK	2 lb.
BUTTER	4 tbsp.
GARLIC CLOVES	4
PARSLEY, chopped	1/4 cup
THYME	1/4 tsp.
SALT	1/2 tsp.
TOMATO PUREE	1 small can
BASIL LEAF	1
DRY RED WINE	1 cup
MUSHROOMS, MEDIUM	12
ROSEMARY	1/2 tsp.
OREGANO	1/2 tsp.

PROCEDURE

1. Trim fat from flank steak; slice 1/4 in. thick, cross grain.
2. Brown meat in butter in dutch oven.
3. Add garlic, parsley, thyme, salt, tomato puree, basil leaf, red wine and cook slowly until meat is almost tender—about 15 min., depending on size of pieces.
4. Add cut up mushrooms, rosemary, and oregano. Continue cooking until tender.

Note

May be made ahead and frozen.

MEATBALLS IN SOUR CREAM GRAVY

YIELD: 32 servings (3 medium-sized meatballs each)

INGREDIENTS

GROUND BEEF	7 lb.
BREAD CRUMBS, fine, dry	3 cups
EGGS, slightly beaten	1-1/2 cups
SALT	1 tbsp.
PEPPER	1/8 tsp.
OREGANO	1 tbsp.
MARJORAM	1 tsp.
ROSEMARY, SMALL NEEDLES, crushed	20 (approx.)
MILK	3 cups
ONION, sliced	1 lb.
SHORTENING	8 oz.
BEEF BROTH	1 qt.
SOUR CREAM	1-1/2 qt.
LEMON JUICE	1/3 cup

PROCEDURE

1. Combine ground beef, crumbs, eggs, salt, pepper, herbs, and milk. Mix well and shape into balls.

2. Brown the sliced onion in the hot fat. Remove onion and set aside.

3. Brown the meatballs, turning until they are uniformly brown. Add beef broth. Cover and cook slowly for about 30 min. or until the meatballs are thoroughly cooked. Remove the meatballs and keep in a warm place.

4. Thicken the liquid remaining in the pan with a flour and water mixture until it becomes a fairly thick gravy.

5. Add the browned onion slices, sour cream, and lemon juice. Heat thoroughly but do not boil. Pour over the hot meatballs and serve.

QUICK LASAGNE

YIELD: 36 servings

INGREDIENTS

WIDE EGG NOODLES, cooked	1-1/2 lb.
BUTTER or MARGARINE, melted	1/2 cup
GROUND BEEF, LEAN	4 lb.
SALT	2 tsp.
PEPPER	1/4 tsp.
TOMATO SAUCE	1 qt.
CREAM CHEESE	1-1/2 lb.
SOUR CREAM	1/2 cup
COTTAGE CHEESE	1-1/2 lb.

PROCEDURE

1. Cook noodles in large quantity of boiling, salted water. Drain and rinse. Place in steam table pan and add melted butter.

2. Brown ground beef. Add salt, pepper, and tomato sauce. Let simmer for a few minutes.

3. Soften cream cheese with sour cream. Blend in cottage cheese and mix well.

4. Spread cheese mixture over noodles. Top with ground beef and tomato sauce.

5. Bake in oven at 350°F. for 30 min. or until heated thoroughly. Serve with parmesan cheese if desired.

GROUND BEEF STROGANOFF

YIELD: 32 servings

INGREDIENTS

ONION, finely chopped	3 cups
GARLIC, minced	3 cloves
BUTTER or MARGARINE	1/2 cup
GROUND BEEF, LEAN	6 lb.
FLOUR	3/4 cup
SALT	2 tbsp.
PEPPER	1/4 tsp.
PAPRIKA	2 tsp.
MUSHROOMS, SLICED, drained	3 8 oz. cans
CONDENSED CREAM of CHICKEN SOUP	3 10-1/2 oz. cans
CONDENSED CREAM of MUSHROOM SOUP	3 10-1/2 oz. cans
SOUR CREAM	1-1/2 pt.
PARSLEY, finely chopped	1/2 cup

PROCEDURE

1. Saute the onion and garlic in butter or margarine. Add ground beef and brown.
2. Add flour, salt, pepper, paprika, and mushrooms. Cook 5 min.
3. Add soups, simmer for 10 min.
4. Add sour cream and heat thoroughly but do not boil.
5. Sprinkle with chopped parsley and serve on hot noodles.

VEAL NEW ORLEANS

YIELD: 20 servings, 3 oz. sauce

INGREDIENTS

VEAL CUTLET	5 lb. (20 pc. 4 oz. ea.)
FLOUR	1 cup
PAPRIKA	1 tbsp.
SALT	1 tsp.
WHITE PEPPER	1/2 tsp.
ONION, chopped	1 cup (5 oz.)
GARLIC, minced	2 cloves
SHORTENING	2 tbsp.
CONDENSED CREAM of MUSHROOM SOUP	1 3 lb. 2 oz. can
WATER	2 cups
TOMATO PASTE	2/3 cup (6 oz. can)
WORCESTERSHIRE SAUCE	1 tbsp.
PARSLEY, chopped	1/4 to 1/2 cup

PROCEDURE

1. Dredge veal in mixture of flour, paprika, salt, and pepper. Fry veal in deep fat (350°F.) for about 2 min. or until lightly browned; drain well; arrange in 12-in. by 18-in. by 2-in. baking pan.

2. Saute onion and garlic in shortening. Add soup; stir until smooth. Blend in water, tomato paste, and worcestershire sauce. Pour sauce over veal.

3. Bake in preheated oven at 400°F. for 30 to 35 min. or until sauce is bubbling. Serve with generous garnish of parsley.

JELLIED VEAL LOAF

YIELD: 24 slices, 3/4-in. by 3-in. by 2-in.

INGREDIENTS

BONELESS VEAL SHOULDER, cooked, finely diced (approx. 1-1/2 qt. diced)	4 lb.
VEAL STOCK	1-1/2 qt.
GELATINE, UNFLAVORED	1-1/4 oz.
COLD WATER	1 cup
ONION JUICE	3 tbsp.
VINEGAR	1/3 cup
SALT	1-1/2 tbsp.
PEPPER	1/4 tsp.
EGGS, hard-cooked, sliced	6
STUFFED OLIVES, sliced	1/2 cup
PIMIENTO, diced	1/2 cup
EGGS, chopped	3
PARSLEY, chopped	1/4 cup

PROCEDURE

1. Cook veal in salted water for about 2 hr. or until well done. While cooking add an onion, a stalk of celery, and a tsp. of pickling spices. When the veal is tender, remove it, cool, and dice finely.

2. Cook the broth down until only 1-1/2 qt. remains. Strain it and, while it is still hot, add to it the soaked gelatine.

3. Add the onion juice, vinegar, salt, and pepper. Allow to cool but not to set.

4. In the bottoms of loaf pans, arrange slices of egg and olives. Cover with the gelatine mixture. Chill until congealed before filling further.

5. Mix the parsley with the veal. Place a layer of this over the congealed layer, then a layer of chopped eggs and pimiento. Top with another layer of veal and cover all with the gelatine mixture. Chill until firm. Slice and serve.

LAMB RAGOUT EN CASSOLETTE

YIELD: 24 servings—8 oz. stew, 1/2 cup noodles

INGREDIENTS

LAMB CUBES	5 lb.
FLOUR, seasoned	1 cup
SHORTENING	1/2 cup
CONDENSED CONSOMME	1 3 lb. 2 oz. can
SAUTERNE	1 cup
GARLIC, minced	1 clove
ROSEMARY, crushed	1/2 tsp.
CARROTS, 1-in. sticks	2 lb.
GREEN BEANS, CUT	1-1/2 lb.
CORNSTARCH	1/2 cup
WATER	1 cup
NOODLES, MEDIUM, cooked	12 cups (1-1/2 lb. uncooked)

PROCEDURE

1. Dust lamb with seasoned flour. Brown well in shortening. Add consomme, sauterne, garlic, and rosemary; cover; cook over low heat 1 hr.

2. Add carrots, green beans; cover; cook about 45 min. or until vegetables are tender.

3. Pour off broth and measure. Add enough water to make 2 qt. Pour into separate saucepan. Heat to boiling. Make paste of cornstarch and water; pour into simmering broth stirring constantly until thickened. Add to lamb.

4. Serve 1 cup stew over 1/2 cup noodles.

VEGETABLES

DUCHESSE POTATOES

INGREDIENTS

POTATOES	3 lb.
BUTTER	6 oz.
PEPPER	to taste
SALT	to taste
NUTMEG	to taste
EGG YOLKS, beaten	6
MILK	as needed
EGG	as needed
BREAD CRUMBS	as needed

PROCEDURE

1. Cook potatoes in salted water, drain, and allow to dry for a few min., then sieve them.

2. Return them to the pan, add butter, pepper, salt, and nutmeg.

3. Remove pan from the heat and add egg yolks; milk may also be added if the potato mixture is going to be piped.

4. Shape the duchesse potatoes or pipe them, as required, brush with beaten egg and bake in oven at 450°F. until golden brown. Or, shape the mixture as desired, coat with egg and bread crumbs, and fry in deep fat.

POTATO PANCAKES

YIELD: 20 to 24 servings

INGREDIENTS
POTATOES, WHITE, raw, EP	6 lb.
ONIONS, MEDIUM	2
EGGS	6
FLOUR	1-1/2 cups
SALT	2 tsp.
BAKING POWDER	1/2 tsp.

PROCEDURE

1. Grate or grind potatoes and onions very fine. Pour off any liquid that accumulates.

2. Add eggs and blend well.

3. Stir in the flour mixed and sifted with the salt and baking powder.

4. Heat oil or shortening in skillet. Drop potato mixture by heaping tablespoons into hot skillet.

5. Fry until crisp and golden brown on the underside. Turn and brown on the other side.

6. Serve with sour cream or applesauce.

RICE PILAF

YIELD: 35 servings

INGREDIENTS
BUTTER	8 oz.
ONION, finely chopped	6 oz.
RICE, UNCOOKED	3 lb.
CHICKEN STOCK, hot	1 qt.
SALT	1 tsp.

PROCEDURE

1. Melt butter in 5 qt. saucepan. Add onion; cook until onion is transparent.

2. Add rice and saute 5 min., stirring often.

3. Add hot chicken stock and salt.

4. Cover tightly and bake in oven at 350°F. for 35 to 40 min., until all liquid is absorbed and rice is dry and fluffy.

TANGY RED CABBAGE WITH CHESTNUTS

YIELD: 30 servings

INGREDIENTS

RED CABBAGE, MEDIUM SIZE	4
WATER, boiling	
BACON DRIPPINGS or CHICKEN FAT	1/2 cup
APPLES, GREEN, LARGE, peeled, cored, diced	4
WATER	4 cups
RED WINE VINEGAR	1-1/2 cups
SUGAR	4 tbsp.
SALT	to taste
PEPPER	to taste
RAISINS, soaked in sweet wine	1 cup
CHESTNUTS*, cooked	1-1/2 cups
ROUX	
FAT or DRIPPINGS	4 tbsp.
FLOUR	4 tbsp.

*Water chestnuts, coarsely sliced, make an excellent substitute

PROCEDURE

1. Cut cabbage in wedges and pour boiling water over to wilt. Drain thoroughly.

2. Saute cabbage and apples in drippings for 10 min.

3. Add water, vinegar, sugar, and seasonings. Bring to boiling, reduce heat; cover and cook until tender, about 20 min.

4. Make brown roux from flour and drippings. Whisk in cabbage liquid until smooth.

5. Add cabbage, raisins, and chestnuts. Simmer 10 min. longer. Adjust seasoning.

BANANA SCALLOPS
(Serve as pass-around with duck sauce)

YIELD: approx. 24 cuts

INGREDIENTS

FAT or SALAD OIL	
SALT	1-1/2 tsp.
EGG, slightly beaten	1
or EVAPORATED MILK, UNDILUTED	1/2 cup
BANANAS, firm, green-tipped	4
CORN FLAKES, fine crumbs,	1/2 cup
or CORN MEAL	1/2 cup

PROCEDURE

1. Heat 1 in. of shortening or oil in frying pan.
2. Add salt to egg or milk.
3. Peel and slice bananas into 3/4-in. cuts.
4. Dip bananas into egg or milk. Drain and roll in crumbs or corn meal.
5. Shallow fry in hot (375°F.) fat for 1-1/2 to 2 min. until brown and tender.
6. Drain well and serve hot.

FRIED BANANAS A LA CORRAL

YIELD: 12 servings

INGREDIENTS

GREEN BANANAS	6
NUTMEG	dash
SALT	dash
COMMERCIAL BREADING, FULLY SEASONED	1 cup
SUGAR	1/2 tsp.
CINNAMON	1/8 tsp.
POWDERED SUGAR	
MARASCHINO CHERRIES, chopped	

PROCEDURE

1. Split bananas lengthwise, then cut in half, yielding 4 pieces per banana. Place cut side down on clean damp napkin. When all are cut, turn and sprinkle lightly with nutmeg and salt.

2. Mix breading, sugar, and cinnamon. Coat bananas with breading mixture, patting gently but do not press. Place 1/2 in. apart on wax paper-lined tray. Let stand 5 min.

3. Fry 6 banana pieces at a time in 350°F. fat for 3 min. or until golden brown. If bananas are to be served off-premises, fry 1-1/2 min. in 375°F. fat. Drain on brown paper. Put on serving tray or chafing dish. Sprinkle with powdered sugar and chopped maraschino cherries.

FRESH VEGETABLE CASSEROLE EPICURE

YIELD: 50 servings

INGREDIENTS

GARLIC, finely minced	2 tsp.
POTATOES, bite-size	1 gal.
CARROTS, large dice	1 gal.
WHITE TURNIPS, bite-size	1 qt.
ONION, large dice	1 gal.
CELERY, large dice	2 qt.
CABBAGE, large dice	2 qt.
GREEN PEPPER, julienne	1 qt.
FRESH TOMATOES, large dice	3 qt.
STEW BEEF, large dice	12 lb.
BUTTER (optional)	1/4 lb.
STOCK	1 gal.
BASIL LEAVES	1 tsp.
WHITE PEPPER	1 tsp.

PROCEDURE

1. Prepare the first nine ingredients. The potatoes, carrots, and turnips may be turned on the machine. Refrigerate.

2. Brown the beef in hot fat. Discard the fat. Add the butter (if desired) and the stock; cook until tender.

3. Add the first eight ingredients (reserving the tomatoes), add seasonings, cover tightly, and cook for 20 min.

4. Add the tomatoes and cook 5 min. more.

5. Serve in a large casserole with about 4 oz. beef and some of the broth.

CABBAGE ROLLS WITH SOUR CREAM SAUCE

YIELD: 25 1-roll servings

INGREDIENTS

GROUND BEEF	6 lb.
ONION, diced	1 cup
MEAT DRIPPINGS	1/2 cup
CELERY, diced	2 cups
RICE, cooked	4 cups
HORSERADISH	1 tbsp.
PREPARED MUSTARD	1/4 cup
EGGS, well beaten	4
CABBAGE LEAVES, large	25
TOMATO SAUCE	3 qt.

SOUR CREAM SAUCE (made from 7 oz. sour cream
  sauce mix and 1 qt. cold, whole milk, according
  to directions on pkg.)

PROCEDURE

1. Using a heavy skillet over hot heat, brown meat and onion in meat drippings. Remove from heat. Thoroughly blend in the celery, rice, horseradish, mustard, and eggs.

2. Cook cabbage leaves in boiling, salted water for approx. 3 min.; drain.

3. Place approx. 4 oz. of meat mixture on each cabbage leaf. Roll leaf and fasten with toothpick.

4. Place rolls close together in a greased baking pan. Pour tomato sauce evenly over top; cover and bake in oven at 350°F. for approx. 30 min.

5. Remove from oven, and place rolls in suitable steam table container to "hold."

6. Pour Sour Cream Sauce into liquid remaining in baking pan and blend well. Ladle mixture over individual cabbage roll prior to serving.

WHITE BEANS ST. FRANCIS

YIELD: 16 8-oz. servings

INGREDIENTS

NAVY (PEA) BEANS	2 lb.
HAMBONE	1
BOUQUET GARNI*	1
SALT	1-1/2 tbsp.
BUTTER	4 tbsp.
ONION, chopped	1
TOMATOES, FRESH, peeled, chopped	4
or	
TOMATOES, CANNED	1 qt.
SALT	as needed
PEPPER	as needed

*To make a bouquet garni, tie in cheesecloth two small pieces celery or celery leaves, leeks, a few parsley branches, a bay leaf, two cloves, a little thyme, and, if desired, a clove of garlic.

PROCEDURE

1. Soak beans in cold water overnight.
2. Add more water to make 3 qt. Add hambone, a bouquet garni,* and 1-1/2 tbsp. salt. Bring to boiling, skim, cover, and boil until well done. Remove hambone and the bouquet garni; drain off water.
3. In a casserole, put butter and chopped onion and simmer until yellow. Add peeled and chopped fresh or canned tomatoes and simmer for 30 min.
4. Add beans, season with salt and pepper, and simmer altogether 15 min.

BOUQUETIERE OF VEGETABLES

PROCEDURE

Arrange the following vegetables on a silver tray:

Tomato halves, broiled and sprinkled with parmesan cheese, topped with a sprig of parsley

Green Broccoli

Cauliflowerettes

Green Beans which have been marinated in oil and vinegar dressing

Glazed Carrots

White Asparagus Spears, served on artichoke bottoms and topped with pimiento strips, can be added for a note of luxury. Offer a choice of sauces with the vegetables.

SWEET POTATO WALNUT PUFFS

YIELD: 50 puffs

INGREDIENTS

SWEET POTATOES	9 lb. AP
EGGS, beaten	10
NUTMEG	1 tsp.
SALT	1 tbsp.
WALNUTS, chopped	1 lb.
CORN FLAKES, rolled fine	8 oz.

PROCEDURE

1. Cook the sweet potatoes until done. Peel and mash.
2. Add the beaten eggs, seasonings, and chopped walnuts.
3. Using a No. 12 scoop, shape puffs and place on well-oiled sheet pans. Sprinkle generously with corn flake crumbs. Bake in oven at 350°F. for 35 to 40 min.

BAKED TOMATO SLICES

YIELD: 180 slices, 90 servings

INGREDIENTS

TOMATOES	30 lb.
SALT	3-1/2 oz.
SUGAR	8 oz.
PEPPER	1/2 tsp.
BREAD CRUMBS	2-1/4 lb.
MARGARINE	8 oz.
CHEESE, grated	8 oz.

PROCEDURE

1. Wash firm tomatoes; remove stem end. Cut tomatoes into 1/2-in. slices (if tomato is small, cut into halves).
2. Place cut slices on greased 12-in. by 20-in. pans. Sprinkle each slice with salt, sugar, and pepper.
3. Mix bread crumbs and margarine. Scatter over top of each tomato; add 1 tsp. grated cheese.
4. Brown in oven at 375°F. for 25 to 30 min.

CHUCK-WAGON BAKED BEANS

YIELD: 25 servings

INGREDIENTS

BACON, diced	5 oz.
ONION, chopped	1/2 cup
PORK and BEANS	1 gal.
DRY MUSTARD	1/2 tsp.
SALT	1/2 tsp.
BROWN SUGAR	2 tbsp.
SORGHUM MOLASSES	2 tbsp.
BARBECUE SAUCE	1 cup

PROCEDURE

1. Slowly cook bacon for a few minutes; while it is still limp, drain off excess fat and add onion.

2. Cook onion slowly until clear, but not brown.

3. Add pork and beans. When warm, add mustard, salt, brown sugar, and molasses. When well heated through, place beans in baking pan and pour barbecue sauce (recipe below) thinly over the beans. Bake in oven at 325°F. for 50 min.

BARBECUE SAUCE

INGREDIENTS

CATSUP	1 cup
LEMON JUICE from	1/2 lemon
LIQUID HOT PEPPER SAUCE (more if wanted)	4 dashes
SPECIAL SPICED SAUCE	1 tsp.
LIQUID SMOKE	1 tsp.
BLACK PEPPER	dash

PROCEDURE

Combine ingredients; mix well.

EGGPLANT DELUXE

YIELD: 50 servings

INGREDIENTS

ONION, finely diced	3 lb.
MUSHROOMS, FRESH, diced	4 lb.
BUTTER or SHORTENING	1 lb.
PARSLEY, chopped	1 cup
BROWN SAUCE	1 cup
SALT	3 tbsp.
WHITE PEPPER	1 tsp.
LEMON JUICE, fresh	1/4 cup
BREAD CRUMBS, soft	1 qt.
EGGPLANT	10 lb.
HAM, 3-OZ. SLICES	10 lb.
PARMESAN CHEESE, grated	1 pt.
PAPRIKA	1/4 cup

PROCEDURE

1. Lightly saute onion and mushrooms in 1/4 of the butter or shortening. Add chopped parsley and brown sauce, salt, pepper, lemon juice, and 1/2 cup bread crumbs. Reserve.

2. Peel eggplant and cut in 1/2-in. slices. Roll in oil. Season lightly with salt and pepper and grill 3 or 4 min. on each side.

3. To prepare for service, spread ham in pan and cover with seasoned onion and mushroom mixture. Place a slice of grilled eggplant on top.

4. Combine the remaining bread crumbs, parmesan cheese and paprika. Mix well, sprinkle over eggplant.

5. Drop remaining butter over top and heat in oven at 350°F. for 10 min. If necessary, brown under broiler.

FRESH GREEN VEGETABLE CASSEROLE

YIELD: 50 servings

INGREDIENTS

SNAP BEANS, PEAS, BRUSSELS SPROUTS,	
BROCCOLI, freshly cooked, seasoned, combined	8 lb.
NUTMEG	1 tsp.
BUTTER	1/2 lb.
SUPREME SAUCE	3 to 4 qt.
PARMESAN CHEESE (optional)	1/2 lb.

PROCEDURE

1. Season vegetables with nutmeg.
2. Saute lightly in 1/4 lb. butter, being careful not to break up vegetables.
3. Add sauce and blend in.
4. For large scale service, put into two large steam table pans. Dust with parmesan cheese. Pour the remaining butter, melted, over the top and glaze in broiler or oven until golden brown.

Note

If about 1 cup of bread crumbs is mixed with cheese, a firmer crust will result.

HARLEQUIN RICE

YIELD: 50 1/2 cup servings

INGREDIENTS

ONION, sliced	2 qt.
DRIPPINGS	2/3 cup
TOMATOES	1 No. 10 can
APPLE JUICE	2 cups
SALT	8 tsp.
PEPPER	2 tsp.
LIQUID HOT PEPPER SAUCE	1/2 tsp.
GARLIC, minced	3 cloves
RICE, UNCOOKED	1-1/2 qt.
OLIVES, RIPE, SLICED	1 cup

PROCEDURE

1. Brown onion in drippings. Add remaining ingredients and pour into shallow baking pan. Cover.
2. Bake in oven at 350°F. for 40 to 50 min. until rice is tender. Twice during last 20 min. of cooking, toss rice mixture lightly with fork.

ROMAN PIZZA DELIGHT

YIELD: 13 lb. 13 oz.—50 servings of 1 large slice or 2 small slices

INGREDIENTS

BITE-SIZE CORN CEREAL, crushed to 2-1/2 qt.	1 lb. 2 oz.
EGGPLANT, peeled, sliced 1/4 in. thick	3 lb. 13 oz. EP
EGGS, well beaten	11 oz.
TOMATO SAUCE	4 lb. 10 oz.
WATER	3 lb.
SALT	2 tbsp.
OREGANO, POWDERED	2 tbsp.
BASIL, POWDERED	1 tbsp.
PARMESAN CHEESE	2-3/4 cup

PROCEDURE

1. Place 3/4 of the corn cereal crumbs in each buttered No. 5 steam table pan. Place peeled eggplant slices on crumbs.

2. Pour beaten eggs on eggplant. Sprinkle 3/4 cup crumbs over each pan of eggplant.

3. Combine tomato sauce, water, salt, oregano, and basil. Pour 3 cups sauce over each pan.

4. Bake until tender in oven at 400°F., approx. 30 min.

5. Combine cheese and remaining corn cereal. Sprinkle 1-1/2 tbsp. of the mixture over each serving. Place in broiler 2 min. or until lightly browned.

HOPPING JOHN

YIELD: 20 lb.

INGREDIENTS

BLACK-EYED PEAS, DRIED	7 lb.
SALT PORK BELLY, small cubes	6 lb.
ONION, diced	5 lb.
RICE, UNCOOKED	2-1/2 lb.
SALT	to taste
PEPPER	to taste

PROCEDURE

1. Boil peas, pork belly, and onion in water until peas are tender.

2. Cook rice separately, rinse, and add to peas. Bring mixture to boil and remove from fire.

3. Season to taste after cooking is completed.

BEETS WITH ORANGE SAUCE

YIELD: 25 1/2 cup servings

INGREDIENTS

FLOUR	3 oz.
SALT	2 tsp.
CLOVES, WHOLE	2 tsp.
PAPRIKA	3/4 tsp.
BEET JUICE	3 cups
ORANGE JUICE	3 cups
VINEGAR	1/2 cup
MARGARINE	4 oz.
ORANGE RIND, grated	2 tbsp.
SUGAR	5 oz.
BEETS, diced	1 No. 10 can

PROCEDURE

1. Mix dry ingredients.

2. Combine liquids—beet juice, orange juice, and vinegar. Reserve a small amount to mix with dry ingredients and heat. Add margarine or butter.

3. Add paste gradually, stirring constantly. Cook until thickened and clear.

4. Pour sauce on beets and keep hot.

SCALLOPED POTATOES

YIELD: 24 lb., in four 12-in. by 20-in. by 2-1/4-in. pans; recommended serving: 6 oz.

INGREDIENTS

NONFAT DRY MILK	2-1/2 qt. (3-3/4 qt. inst.)
PASTRY FLOUR	1 lb. 6 oz.
SALT	6 oz.
WHITE PEPPER	2 tsp.
WATER	2 gal.
BUTTER	1 lb.
POTATOES, RAW, thinly sliced	24 lb. (approx. 34 lb. AP)

PROCEDURE

1. Combine dry ingredients. Add enough of the water to make a pouring paste.

2. Heat remaining water to a boil. Melt butter in it and remove from heat. Pour paste slowly into water and butter mixture, stirring with french whip until blended.

3. Place drained sliced potatoes in 4 greased counter pans 12-in. by 20-in. by 2-1/4-in. Scale: 6 lb. per pan.

4. Pour sauce over top. Bake uncovered until soft.

Note

Bake according to directions above. Do not bake in deeper pans.

FRENCH BEANS AU GRATIN

YIELD: 100 1/2 cup servings

INGREDIENTS

BUTTER or MARGARINE	14 oz.
FLOUR	1-2/3 cup
SALT	1/3 cup
PEPPER	2-1/2 tsp.
SUGAR	1/3 cup
ONION, finely chopped	3 tbsp.
SOUR CREAM	1 gal.
GREEN BEANS, sliced lengthwise, cooked, drained	3-3/4 gal. (5 No. 10 cans)
SWISS CHEESE, shredded	7 lb. 8 oz.
CORN FLAKE CRUMBS	1 lb. 8 oz.
BUTTER or MARGARINE, melted	14 oz.

PROCEDURE

1. Melt butter; blend in flour, salt, pepper, sugar, and onion.

2. Add sour cream gradually, stirring constantly. Cook at low temperature until thickened, stirring occasionally.

3. Fold in green beans; heat thoroughly. Pour into greased counter pans or individual casseroles.

4. Sprinkle cheese over beans. Combine corn flake crumbs with melted butter; sprinkle over cheese. Bake in oven at 400°F. about 20 min.

PARMESAN POTATO ROSETTES WITH BRAZIL NUTS

"Parmesan Potato Rosettes, except for the topping, can be made in advance and refrigerated. They are excellent for large-party service. They go well with a special chicken dish and a bright-colored vegetable, such as green lima beans with pimiento butter."

YIELD: 24 servings (1 rosette per serving)

INGREDIENTS

POTATOES	8 lb. **EP**
BUTTER or MARGARINE	8 oz.
SALT	to season
WHITE PEPPER	to season
MILK, hot	as needed
TOPPING	
HEAVY CREAM	1-1/2 cups
PARMESAN CHEESE, grated	1 cup
WORCESTERSHIRE SAUCE	1/2 tsp.
LIQUID HOT PEPPER SAUCE	dash
BRAZIL NUTS, sliced	1 cup

PROCEDURE

1. Steam potatoes. Remove to mixer bowl. Whip on power mixer until free from lumps.

2. Add melted butter, seasonings, and just enough milk to hold potatoes together well. (The amount of milk will depend on the potatoes. The mixture should be quite stiff.)

3. On a well-greased and floured baking sheet, shape into individual servings using a pastry bag with a rose tube, or form into nests with a scoop or spoon.

If rosettes are to be placed in refrigerator, brush tops with melted butter to prevent drying. Cover with waxed paper and a damp towel.

4. Whip cream. Fold in the parmesan cheese, worcestershire sauce, and hot pepper sauce. Refrigerate until needed.

5. About 20 min. before serving time, place rosettes in oven at 350°F.

6. When piping hot, remove from oven and top each serving with at least 1 tbsp. topping mixture. Sprinkle brazil nuts over the topping.

7. Place in oven at 400°F. until topping and nuts are delicately browned. Serve immediately.

SALADS

CHICKEN SALAD, EXOTIC

YIELD: approx. 2-1/2 qt.

INGREDIENTS

CHICKEN, cooked, cut in large chunks	5 cups
ONION, grated	2 tsp.
CELERY, 1/2-in. cuts	1 cup
GREEN PEPPER, minced, slightly blanched	1 cup
LIGHT CREAM	1/4 cup
MAYONNAISE	2/3 cup
SALT	1 tsp.
PEPPER	1/8 tsp.
VINEGAR	2 tbsp.
ALMONDS, SLIVERED, toasted	2/3 cup
or PECANS, broken	2/3 cup
GREEN GRAPES, halved, seeded	2 cups

PROCEDURE

1. Combine chicken, onion, celery, and pepper.

2. Mix cream with mayonnaise, salt, pepper; add vinegar and toss with chicken. Refrigerate.

3. To serve, place scoop of chicken salad on lettuce. Garnish with toasted almonds and grapes.

Garnishes: sliced hard-cooked eggs; asparagus tips dipped in lemon juice; carrot sticks; olives; pickled peaches; pineapple chunks; cranberry jelly; or apple or avocado, dipped in lemon juice.

BASIC FRENCH DRESSING

YIELD: 1 qt.

INGREDIENTS

VINEGAR	1 cup
SALAD OIL	3 cups
SALT	
WHITE PEPPER	

PROCEDURE

Add seasonings to vinegar; combine with oil and mix well.

FRUITED FRENCH DRESSING

YIELD: 1-1/2 qt.

INGREDIENTS

BASIC FRENCH DRESSING	1 qt.
FRUIT JUICES	2 cups
SALT	1 tbsp.
SUGAR	2 tsp.
SALAD OIL	2 cups

PROCEDURE

Combine ingredients; mix well.

MUSTARD FRENCH DRESSING

YIELD: 1 qt.

INGREDIENTS

VINEGAR	1 cup
SALT	to taste
PEPPER	to taste
DIJON MUSTARD	1/4 cup
SALAD OIL	3 cups

PROCEDURE

Whip salt, pepper, and mustard into vinegar; then whip oil into the above until well incorporated.

LEMON FRENCH DRESSING

YIELD: 1 qt.

INGREDIENTS

LEMON JUICE	1 cup
SALT	to taste
PEPPER	to taste
SALAD OIL	3 cups

PROCEDURE

Whip salt and pepper into lemon juice, then whip in oil until well incorporated.

RUSSIAN DRESSING

INGREDIENTS

MAYONNAISE	1-1/2 qt.
CHILI SAUCE	3/4 cup

PROCEDURE

Combine ingredients and stir well.

GARLIC AND HERB DRESSING

YIELD: 1 qt.

INGREDIENTS

GARLIC BUD, crushed	1
THYME	1 tsp.
BASIL	1 tsp.
OREGANO	1 tsp.

PROCEDURE

Add to 1 qt. Basic French Dressing.

TOMATO AND HERB DRESSING
GARLIC AND HERB BASE

INGREDIENTS

CHILI SAUCE	1/2 pt.
SUGAR	1 tbsp.

PROCEDURE

Add ingredients to Garlic and Herb Dressing; blend well.

EMULSIFIED MUSTARD-GARLIC DRESSING

INGREDIENTS

SALAD OIL	3 cups
GARLIC CLOVES, finely minced	6
DIJON MUSTARD	1/4 cup
WORCESTERSHIRE SAUCE	1/2 tsp.
LEMON JUICE from	1/2 lemon
WINE VINEGAR	1 cup
SALT	to taste
PEPPER	to taste

PROCEDURE

Combine ingredients and mix thoroughly.

LORENZO DRESSING

YIELD: 1 qt.

INGREDIENTS

VINEGAR	1 cup
OIL	3 cups
CHILI SAUCE, strained	4 oz.
GARLIC CLOVE, finely minced	1
WATERCRESS, finely chopped	1/4 bunch

PROCEDURE

1. Combine vinegar and oil.
2. Add remaining ingredients and mix well.

GREEK DRESSING

INGREDIENTS

OLIVE OIL	3 cups
WINE VINEGAR	3/4 cup
LEMON JUICE	1/4 cup
OREGANO	pinch

PROCEDURE

Combine ingredients and mix well.

SAUCE GRIBICHE
(Excellent for cold fish)

YIELD: 1 qt.

INGREDIENTS

EGGS, hard-cooked	12
PREPARED MUSTARD	4 tsp.
SALT	2 tsp.
PEPPER	1/2 tsp.
OIL (olive oil preferred)	6 cups
VINEGAR	2 cups
SWEET GHERKINS, chopped	12
PARSLEY, chopped	3 tbsp.
CHIVES or TARRAGON, chopped	3 tbsp.

PROCEDURE

1. Separate cooked egg whites from yolks and set aside.
2. Force egg yolks through sieve and make a paste with the prepared mustard, salt, and pepper.
3. Slowly beat in the oil; when smooth, slowly beat in vinegar.
4. Stir in the gherkins, parsley, and chives.
5. With paring knife, slice the whites of the eggs and blend into the sauce.

MEXICAN COLESLAW

YIELD: 25 portions

INGREDIENTS

CABBAGE, shredded	3-1/2 lb.
CARROTS, shredded	6 oz.
ONION, finely minced	2 oz.
CORN, WHOLE KERNEL	1 No. 303 can
or CORN, FROZEN, cooked	1 lb.
GREEN PEPPERS, SMALL, blanched, diced medium	2
PIMIENTOS, LARGE, rinsed, diced medium	2
BASIC FRENCH DRESSING	1 pt.
LETTUCE BASE	2 heads
PARSLEY SPRIGS	for garnish

PROCEDURE

1. Mix cabbage, carrots, onion, corn, green peppers, and pimientos.
2. Combine with Basic French Dressing.
3. Serve on lettuce base; garnish with parsley sprigs.

LORENZO SALAD

YIELD: 25 portions

INGREDIENTS

PEAR HALVES	25
ESCAROLE	3 heads
CELERY, julienned	1/2 bunch
APPLES, peeled and julienned	3
PINEAPPLE, (fresh, if possible), julienned	6 slices
MARASCHINO CHERRIES, finely minced	
WATERCRESS	for garnish

PROCEDURE

1. Place one half canned pear on a bed of escarole.
2. Fill cavity of pear with celery, apples, and pineapple.
3. Garnish with cherries and watercress.
4. Serve cold with French dressing.

PANAMA SALAD

INGREDIENTS
PINEAPPLE, sliced
LETTUCE BASE
ORANGE SECTIONS
GRAPEFRUIT SECTIONS
MARASCHINO CHERRIES, halves
GREEN PEPPER, 1/2 rings or diamond-shaped

PROCEDURE

1. Place slice of pineapple on lettuce base.
2. Alternate orange and grapefruit sections until pineapple ring is covered.
3. Garnish with cherry and green pepper rings (or diamond-shaped).
4. Serve with Fruited French Dressing.

DOCTOR SALAD

INGREDIENTS
LETTUCE BASE
TOMATO, LARGE, sliced
COTTAGE CHEESE, mixed with chives
CREAM CHEESE ROSETTES
WATERCRESS, for garnish

PROCEDURE
1. On lettuce base center tomato slice.
2. Place scoop of cottage cheese on top of tomato.
3. Garnish with cream cheese rosettes and watercress.

PRINCESS SALAD

INGREDIENTS
TOMATO, sliced
LETTUCE
ASPARAGUS TIPS
PIMIENTO STRIPS
GREEN PEPPER, half ring
PARSLEY, for garnish

PROCEDURE
1. Place tomato slice on lettuce bed.
2. Place 5 asparagus tips on top of each tomato slice.
3. Garnish with strips of pimientos, green pepper and parsley.

ONION RELISH

INGREDIENTS

VINEGAR	1 cup
SUGAR	1 cup
SALT	1-1/4 tsp.
WHITE PEPPER	3/4 tsp.
TURMERIC	1 tsp.
MUSTARD SEED	1 tsp.
ONIONS, LARGE, chopped	3
RAISINS	1 cup

PROCEDURE
1. Bring vinegar, sugar, spices to a boil.
2. Add onions and raisins and simmer, covered, for 30 to 40 min.

CORN RELISH

INGREDIENTS

CIDER VINEGAR	1-1/2 cups
SUGAR	1 cup
SALT	1-1/2 tsp.
WHITE PEPPER	3/4 tsp.
TURMERIC	1 tsp.
MUSTARD SEED	1 tsp.
TOMATO, peeled, finely chopped	1
GREEN PEPPER, finely diced	1
ONION, finely diced	1
CORN, WHOLE KERNEL, drained	3 cups

PROCEDURE

1. Bring vinegar, sugar, spices to boil.
2. Add diced vegetables, simmer 10 min., covered.
3. Add corn; simmer 30 min., stirring frequently.
4. Thicken slightly with cornstarch, if necessary.

COTTAGE CHEESE AND CHIVE RELISH

INGREDIENTS

COTTAGE CHEESE	1 lb.
CHIVES, FREEZE-DRIED	1/2 cup
ONION, finely minced	1/4 cup
SALT	1/2 tsp.
WHITE PEPPER	1/4 tsp.
LIQUID HOT PEPPER SEASONING	dash
WORCESTERSHIRE SAUCE	dash

CRANBERRY RELISH

INGREDIENTS

CRANBERRIES	2 lb.
APPLES	4
ORANGES	4
LEMONS	2
WALNUTS, chopped	1/2 cup
SUGAR	1 lb.
SHERRY or MADEIRA (optional)	2 oz.

PROCEDURE
1. Grind fruits and nuts.
2. Mix together with sugar and sherry. Simmer.

KIDNEY BEAN RELISH

INGREDIENTS

SUGAR	1 cup
CIDER VINEGAR	1-1/2 cups
SALT	1-1/2 tsp.
WHITE PEPPER	3/4 tsp.
TURMERIC	1 tsp.
MUSTARD SEED	1 tsp.
ONION, finely diced	1
PIMIENTOS, finely diced	2
CELERY STALKS, finely diced	2
KIDNEY BEANS, drained	3 cans

PROCEDURE
1. Bring vinegar, sugar, spices to boil.
2. Add diced vegetables, simmer 10 min., covered.
3. Add beans; simmer 30 min., stirring frequently.
4. Thicken slightly with cornstarch, if necessary.

MARINATED BEETS

INGREDIENTS

ONION, very thinly sliced	1
BEET JUICE	1 cup
WHITE VINEGAR	1 cup
SUGAR	1-1/4 cups
CINNAMON, STICK	1
THYME	1/2 tsp.
SALAD OIL	1/4 cup
WHITE PEPPER	1/4 tsp.
SALT	1/2 tsp.
BEETS, SLICED	3 cups

PROCEDURE

1. Bring to boil, simmer beet juice, vinegar, sugar, salad oil, spices for 5 min.

2. Add sliced beets and onions to hot marinade; mix well. Refrigerate overnight.

MARINATED MUSHROOMS

INGREDIENTS

ONIONS, finely minced	1-1/2
OLIVE OIL	6 oz.
GARLIC CLOVES, finely minced	2
LEMON JUICE	2 tsp.
LIQUID HOT PEPPER SEASONING	1/4 bottle
WHITE VINEGAR	6 oz.
SALT	2 tsp.
MONOSODIUM GLUTAMATE	1 tsp.
WHITE PEPPER	1 tsp.
BAY LEAVES	2
THYME	1 tsp.
MUSHROOMS, quartered	1 basket

PROCEDURE

1. Slowly saute onions and garlic in olive oil. Do not brown.

2. Add the rest of the ingredients, except mushrooms. Bring to a boil.

3. Add washed and drained mushrooms to marinade; cover and simmer 8 to 10 min. Cool.

4. Remove bay leaves. Serve chilled.

MINNESOTA PICKLE

INGREDIENTS

CUCUMBERS, unpeeled, thinly sliced 1/16th in.	1 qt.
ONION, SMALL, thinly sliced	1
SUGAR	1/2 cup
CIDER VINEGAR	1/2 cup
CELERY SEED	1/2 tsp.
TURMERIC	1/2 tsp.
SALT	1 tbsp.

PROCEDURE

1. Mix sliced cucumbers with onion and salt. Let stand 1/2 hr; wash, drain well.

2. Boil sugar, vinegar, celery seed, turmeric; add cucumbers and onions, simmer 10 min., covered.

3. Pack in sterilized jars immediately.

CAULIFLOWER A LA GRECQUE

INGREDIENTS

ONION, minced	1/2 cup
GARLIC CLOVE, minced	1
BAY LEAVES	2
THYME	1/2 tsp.
CHILI SAUCE	1/4 to 1 cup
SALT	1 tsp.
PEPPER	1-1/2 tsp.
LEMON JUICE from	1 lemon
WHITE VINEGAR	1/2 cup
CIDER VINEGAR	1/2 cup
CAULIFLOWER, sectioned, washed, drained	1 head

PROCEDURE

1. Combine all ingredients except cauliflower; bring to boil.

2. Add hot drained cauliflower, simmer 5 min.

MARINATED CHICK-PEAS

INGREDIENTS

CHICK-PEAS	3 cans
ONION, finely minced	1/2 cup
GARLIC, finely minced	1 clove
SALT	1/2 tsp.
WHITE PEPPER	1/4 tsp.
CHIVES, FREEZE-DRIED	1/4 cup
CIDER VINEGAR	1/4 cup
SALAD OIL	1/2 cup

PROCEDURE

1. Wash and drain chick-peas.
2. Combine all other ingredients; pour over chick-peas, and chill.

FROZEN CREAM CHEESE SALAD

YIELD: 24 servings

INGREDIENTS

GELATINE, UNFLAVORED	1/2 oz.
WATER	1/2 cup
PINEAPPLE, CRUSHED	1 pt.
MAYONNAISE	1 cup
SALT	1 tbsp.
CELERY SALT	2 tsp.
DRY MUSTARD	1 tsp.
PAPRIKA	1 tsp.
GREEN PEPPER, chopped	3/4 cup
CREAM CHEESE	1 lb.
WHIPPING CREAM	1/2 pt.

PROCEDURE

1. Soak the gelatine in cold water for 5 min. Then place over hot water until completely dissolved.
2. Stir this into the combined pineapple, mayonnaise, and seasonings. Stir well.
3. Fold in the green pepper, the softened, whipped, cream cheese, and whipped cream.
4. Place in No. 2 cans or in a long loaf pan and freeze.
5. Slice and serve on watercress or endive.

HOT SPRING SALAD

YIELD: 24 servings

INGREDIENTS

CAULIFLOWER	2 lb.
BROCCOLI SPEARS	2 lb.
CORN	1/2 lb.
GREEN BEANS	1 lb.
PEAS	1/2 lb.
ASPARAGUS SPEARS	1/2 lb.
CARROT STRIPS	1 lb.
CREAM SAUCE, LIGHT	1 qt.
CHEDDAR CHEESE, grated	8 oz.

PROCEDURE

1. Arrange cauliflower and broccoli spears in each end of casserole. Fill bottom of casserole with remaining vegetables.

2. Cover with light cream sauce (recipe below).

3. Sprinkle remaining grated cheese on top; add a dash of paprika.

4. Put in oven at 400°F. until cheese has melted. Serve.

LIGHT CREAM SAUCE

INGREDIENTS

NONFAT DRY MILK, reconstituted	1 qt.
MARGARINE	1/4 lb.
SALT	1/4 tsp.
FLOUR	2 oz.
CHEDDAR CHEESE	6 oz.

PROCEDURE

Mix 4 oz. nonfat dry milk with 3-1/4 cups water for 1 qt. yield. Mix with remaining ingredients.

FRIJOLE SALAD

YIELD: 4 qt., 32 servings

INGREDIENTS

KIDNEY BEANS, CANNED, washed, drained	3 pt.
CABBAGE, shredded	3 pt.
TOMATOES, diced	1 qt.
CUCUMBERS, quartered, sliced	1 qt.
FRENCH DRESSING	1 pt.

PROCEDURE

1. Allow kidney beans to drain while preparing the other ingredients.
2. Combine the vegetables, tossing lightly.
3. Marinate in french dressing at least 30 min. Drain well before serving.

Note

In winter, celery and shredded lettuce may be substituted for the cucumbers.

PEACH AND RASPBERRY MOLD

YIELD: 48 servings

INGREDIENTS

GELATIN, RASPBERRY FLAVOR	24 oz.
WATER, hot	2 qt.
FRUIT JUICES, cold	2 qt.
PEACHES, SLICED, well drained	1 No. 10 can
RASPBERRIES, FROZEN, thawed, drained	2 lb.

PROCEDURE

1. Dissolve the gelatin in hot water. Add cold fruit juice.
2. Arrange peach slices in molds or salad pans. Pour half the gelatin mixture over the peaches. Chill until firm.
3. Add raspberries to remaining gelatin and, when it is almost congealed, pour over the first layer. Chill until firm.

CRANBERRY WALDORF MOLDS (OR SALAD)

YIELD: 100 1/2 cup servings

INGREDIENTS

CRANBERRY JUICE COCKTAIL	6 qt.
GELATIN, LEMON FLAVOR	3 lb.
SALT	1-1/2 tbsp.
APPLES, UNPARED, cored, chopped	4 qt.
CELERY, chopped	2 qt.
WALNUT MEATS, broken	1 qt. (1 lb.)

PROCEDURE

1. Heat cranberry juice cocktail to boiling. Add gelatin and salt. Stir to dissolve. Chill until partially set.

2. Stir in apples, celery, and nuts. Pour into individual molds or large pans. Chill until firm.

MOLDED CRANBERRY SALAD

YIELD: 30 4-oz. molds

INGREDIENTS

CRANBERRIES, FRESH	2 lb.
ORANGES	2
SUGAR	2 lb.
GELATIN, CHERRY FLAVOR	12 oz.
WATER, boiling	1-1/2 qt.
CELERY, diced	2 cups
APPLES, UNPARED, diced	2 cups
WALNUTS, chopped (optional)	1 cup

PROCEDURE

1. Wash cranberries and put through food chopper.

2. Cut whole oranges into sections and put through food chopper.

3. Add the sugar to cranberry and orange mixture and set aside.

4. Dissolve gelatin in boiling water. Chill until it begins to thicken, then add cranberry mixture, celery, apples, and nutmeats.

5. Place in individual molds and chill until firm.

FROZEN FRUIT SALAD

YIELD: 30 servings

INGREDIENTS

GELATINE, UNFLAVORED	1/2 oz.
PINEAPPLE JUICE	1 cup
ORANGE JUICE	2/3 cup
SUGAR	5/8 cup
PINEAPPLE TIDBITS	1-1/2 cups
CLING PEACHES, CANNED, diced	1-1/2 cups
WHITE CHERRIES, pitted	1 cup
MARSHMALLOWS, cut up	1/4 lb.
MARASCHINO CHERRIES, sliced	1/4 cup
PECANS, finely chopped	1/4 cup
CRYSTALLIZED GINGER	1 tsp.
WHIPPING CREAM	1-1/2 cups
MAYONNAISE	1 cup

PROCEDURE

1. Soak gelatine in fruit juice. Dissolve over warm water. Add sugar. Cool.

2. When gelatine mixture begins to congeal, add the drained fruit, marshmallows, cherries, pecans, and ginger. Fold in the whipped cream and mayonnaise.

3. Pour into 5 clean No. 2 tin cans or any other desired molds. Freeze in ice cream cabinets or freezer boxes.

4. Unmold and slice for serving.

Note

Several weeks' supply of this salad may be made at once and kept frozen.

INDIVIDUAL BEET SALADS

YIELD: 50 servings

INGREDIENTS

BEETS, MEDIUM-SIZE, WHOLE, cooked	50
COTTAGE CHEESE	2 lb.
CELERY SEED	2 tbsp.
ONION SALT	2 tbsp.
GREEN PEPPERS, minced	2
SPECIAL SPICED SAUCE	1/3 cup
MAYONNAISE	1 cup

PROCEDURE

1. Remove centers of beets. Chop centers and mix with cheese, celery seed, onion salt, and green pepper. Mix with special spiced sauce and mayonnaise until smooth.

2. Fill centers of beets with the mixture. Chill and serve on lettuce leaves as a salad or as a garnish for roasts.

CIDER SALAD MOLDS

YIELD: 30 4-oz. molds

INGREDIENTS

APPLE CIDER or APPLE JUICE	3 qt.
GELATIN, APPLE FLAVOR	24 oz.
LEMON JUICE	1/2 cup
SALT	1 tsp.
CARROTS, grated	1 pt.
CELERY, finely chopped	1 pt.
APPLES, UNPARED, finely chopped	1 pt.
WALNUTS, chopped	4 oz.

PROCEDURE

1. Heat 1 qt. of cider and dissolve gelatin in it.

2. Add cold cider, lemon juice, and salt.

3. Cool until the mixture begins to congeal. Then add remaining ingredients.

4. Fill molds and refrigerate until firm.

WILLIAM TELL SLAW

YIELD: 52 1/2 cup servings or 48 2/3 cup servings

INGREDIENTS

SALAD DRESSING	1-1/2 qt.
LEMON JUICE	1/3 cup
INSTANT ONION, finely rolled	2 tbsp.
SALT	1 tbsp.
WHITE PEPPER	1/2 tsp.
RED APPLES, UNPARED, quartered, cored	2 lb.
AMERICAN CHEESE, grated	3 lb.
CABBAGE, shredded medium fine	5 lb.

PROCEDURE

1. Combine first 5 ingredients.
2. Dice or slice apples into dressing, stirring often to coat well.
3. Add cheese and cabbage, mixing lightly but thoroughly. Chill.
4. If desired, serve on lettuce leaf in sauce dish garnished with apple wedge.

STAR SALAD

YIELD: 32 servings

INGREDIENTS

GELATIN, LEMON FLAVOR	18 oz.
WATER, boiling	1-1/2 qt.
WATER, cold	1 qt.
CREAM CHEESE	1 lb.
CELERY, finely chopped	1 pt.
GREEN PEPPER, finely chopped	1 cup
JELLIED TOMATO ASPIC	4 1 lb. cans

PROCEDURE

1. Dissolve gelatin in boiling water. Add cold water.
2. Whip the cream cheese; gradually stir in gelatin mixture until the two are well combined.
3. Chill until the mixture begins to congeal, then stir in chopped celery and green pepper. Pour into pans and chill until firm.
4. Cut into squares for serving. Cut stars from slices of canned jellied tomato aspic and top each salad with a star.

RED WINE GELATIN MOLD

YIELD: 30 servings

INGREDIENTS

SWEETENED CONCORD GRAPE WINE	3 qt.
WATER	3 qt.
CINNAMON, STICK	3
CLOVES, WHOLE	3
GELATIN, LIME FLAVOR	12 oz.

PROCEDURE

1. Combine wine, water, cinnamon, and cloves; bring to a boil. Add gelatin and stir until dissolved.

2. Pour into molds which have been rinsed with cold water, but not dried. Chill until set. Serve as a salad.

GOLDEN RICE SALAD

YIELD: 50 1/2 cup servings

INGREDIENTS

SALAD OIL	3/4 cup
VINEGAR	1/3 cup
SALT	4-1/2 tsp.
PEPPER	1/2 tsp.
RICE, cooked in stock (5 cups uncooked rice cooked in 10 cups chicken stock), hot	3-1/2 qt.
OLIVES, RIPE, cut in large pieces	3 cups
EGGS, hard-cooked, diced	6
CELERY, diced	4-1/2 cups
DILL PICKLES, chopped	3/4 cup
PIMIENTO, chopped	3/4 cup
GREEN ONIONS, chopped	1-1/2 cups
MAYONNAISE	1-1/2 cups
PREPARED MUSTARD	1/3 cup

PROCEDURE

1. Blend together salad oil, vinegar, salt, and pepper; pour over hot rice and mix well. Set aside to cool.

2. Add remaining ingredients to cooled rice, toss lightly, and chill thoroughly.

3. Serve on lettuce leaves with crumbled bacon and extra sliced eggs for garnish, if desired.

CORN SHOCK SALAD
AND MINIATURE CHEESE PUMPKINS

YIELD: 72 salads

INGREDIENTS

WATER, boiling	1/2 gal.
GELATIN, LEMON FLAVOR	24 oz.
WATER, cold	1/2 gal.
VINEGAR	2 tsp.
CABBAGE, sliced	12 oz.
PINEAPPLE, CRUSHED, drained	8 cups
CARROTS, shredded	12 oz.
ASPARAGUS, GREEN SPEARS	8 No. 300, 15 oz cans
	OR 1 No. 5 squat can
3-OZ. CONE-SHAPED DRINKING CUPS	72

PROCEDURE

1. Boil 1/2 gal. of water and dissolve gelatin. Add 1/2 gal. of cold water.

2. Add vinegar, cabbage, pineapple, and carrots.

3. Ladle this mixture into the cone-shaped cups which have been placed in water glasses to hold them erect. Cool until congealed.

4. To unmold salad, encircle with a boning knife. This forms the basis for your "Corn Shock."

5. Place 3 or 4 asparagus spears vertically against the Corn Shocks to heighten the resemblance and appeal.

6. Place chopped lettuce around the base and set Miniature Cheese Pumpkins near the shock.

MINIATURE CHEESE PUMPKINS

PROCEDURE

1. For each pumpkin, use 2 tsp. process cheese spread or club cheese. Shape cheese into small pumpkin shape. Place a whole clove on top to simulate the stem.

2. With a toothpick put 5 or 6 grooves vertically on the pumpkin and paint the grooves with liquid yellow food coloring.

JELLIED SALMON, CELERY, AND CUCUMBER SALAD

YIELD: 24 4-oz. molds or 3 large fish molds

INGREDIENTS

GELATIN, LEMON FLAVOR, prepared	18 oz.
WATER, boiling	1-1/2 qt.
GELATINE, UNFLAVORED	2 tbsp.
WATER, cold	1-1/4 qt.
VINEGAR or SWEET PICKLE JUICE	1 cup
SALT	3 tbsp.
PEPPER	1/4 tsp.
ONION JUICE	1 tbsp.
RED SALMON, flaked	3 1 lb. cans
CUCUMBER, diced	3 cups
CELERY, diced	3 cups

PROCEDURE

1. Dissolve lemon flavor gelatin in boiling water. Add unflavored gelatine which has been soaked in 1 cup of the cold water.

2. When it is thoroughly dissolved, add the remaining qt. of cold water, the vinegar, salt, pepper, and onion juice.

3. Allow to cool until the mixture begins to congeal.

4. Mix the gelatin with the flaked salmon, celery, and cucumbers.

5. Mold and chill until firm. Serve on lettuce with mayonnaise.

JELLIED MEAT SALAD

YIELD: 30 4-oz. molds

INGREDIENTS

GELATINE, UNFLAVORED	1 oz.
WATER, cold	1-1/2 cups
MEAT STOCK (or a broth made from a concentrated beef soup base), hot	1-1/2 qt.
ONION JUICE	1 tbsp.
SALT	1 tbsp.
VINEGAR	3 tbsp.
BEEF or VEAL, cooked, chopped (about 3 lb. raw wt.)	1 qt.
PEAS, FROZEN, cooked	1-1/2 cups
PIMIENTO, chopped	1/2 cup
CELERY, chopped	1-1/2 cups

PROCEDURE

1. Soak the gelatine in cold water for 5 min. Then mix it with the hot meat stock and stir until the gelatine is completely dissolved.

2. Add the onion juice, salt, and vinegar. Cool until the mixture begins to congeal.

3. Add meat, peas, pimiento, and celery. Place in molds. Chill until firm.

4. Serve on lettuce with mayonnaise.

CHICKEN ALMOND MOUSSE

YIELD: 32 individual molds

INGREDIENTS

GELATINE, UNFLAVORED	3/4 oz.
WATER, cold	1/2 cup
CHICKEN STOCK, hot	4-3/4 cups
CHICKEN MEAT, cooked, finely diced (approx. 2 lb.)	6 cups
SALT	1 tsp.
PEPPER	1/2 tsp.
HEAVY CREAM, whipped	1 qt.
MAYONNAISE	1 qt.
ALMONDS (optional)	1/2 cup

PROCEDURE

   1. Soak gelatine in cold water for 5 min. Then dissolve in hot chicken stock. Cool.

   2. Add diced chicken, salt, and pepper; chill until mixture begins to set.

   3. Fold in whipped cream and mayonnaise. Cooking sherry may be added, too, if desired. Toasted sliced almonds may also be added for texture interest.

   4. Mold. Chill until firm. Serve on lettuce.

HAM AND POTATO SALAD

YIELD: 20 servings—No. 8 scoop (1/2 cup)

INGREDIENTS

HAM, diced, 1/2-in. cubes	1 lb.
YOUR FAVORITE POTATO SALAD	2 qt.

PROCEDURE

   1. Lightly blend ham into potato salad mixture. Chill thoroughly.

   2. Serve in a nest of crisp lettuce. Garnish with sliced stuffed olives and radish roses.

MOLDED CHEESE RINGS

YIELD: 34 individual ring molds

INGREDIENTS

GELATINE, UNFLAVORED	1 oz.
WATER, cold	1-1/2 cups
CREAM CHEESE	1-1/2 lb.
ROQUEFORT CHEESE	1/2 lb.
SALT	1-1/2 tsp.
HEAVY CREAM, whipped	1-1/2 pt.

PROCEDURE

1. Soak gelatine in cold water for 5 min. Then heat over boiling water until it is completely dissolved.

2. Have the cheeses at room temperature. Cream, add salt and mix them well.

3. Add the gelatine (which has been slightly cooled) gradually and stir until well combined. Fold in the whipped cream.

4. Fill individual ring molds. Chill until firm.

5. Serve on lettuce or other greens and fill the center with fresh fruit.

JELLIED CHERRY AND APRICOT SALAD

YIELD: 40 servings

INGREDIENTS

GELATINE, UNFLAVORED	3 oz.
WATER or FRUIT JUICE	1-1/2 qt.
LEMON JUICE	1-1/2 cups
SUGAR	12 oz.
ROYAL ANNE CHERRIES, pitted	1 qt.
APRICOT HALVES	1 qt.
CELERY, rings, finely cut	3/4 qt.
PECANS, chopped	6 oz.

PROCEDURE

1. Soak the gelatine in 1 pt. of cold water or fruit juice for 5 min. Then dissolve over hot water.

2. Add the remaining juices and sugar. Chill until it is just beginning to congeal.

3. Arrange the fruit attractively in individual molds or in large pan. Add celery rings and nuts. Fill molds with gelatine mixture and chill until firm.

4. Serve with cream mayonnaise or whipped cream dressing.

JELLIED VEGETABLE SALAD

YIELD: 24 servings

INGREDIENTS

GELATIN, LEMON FLAVOR	15 oz.
WATER, hot	1 pt.
WATER, cold	1 pt.
SWEET PICKLE JUICE	1 pt.
LEMON JUICE	1/4 cup
SALT	2 tsp.
ONION, grated	2 tbsp.
SOUR CREAM	1 pt.
CABBAGE, CARROTS, GREEN PEPPER, RAW, chopped	2 qt.
OLIVES, GREEN, STUFFED, sliced for garnish	1/2 cup

PROCEDURE

1. Dissolve gelatin in hot water. Add cold water, pickle juice, lemon juice, salt, onion, and sour cream.

2. Blend well and chill until mixture begins to congeal. Fold in vegetables and chill until firm.

3. Serve on crisp lettuce and garnish with sliced olives.

CABBAGE SLAW

YIELD: 30 servings

INGREDIENTS

CABBAGE, chopped or shredded	5 lb., EP
PARSLEY, chopped	1/2 cup
ONION, chopped	2 tbsp.
or INSTANT MINCED ONION	1/2 tbsp.
CELERY, chopped	2 cups
GREEN PEPPER, chopped	2 cups
PIMIENTO, chopped	4 oz. jar
SUGAR	1-1/2 lb.
VINEGAR	1-1/2 pt.
SALT	1 tbsp.
PEPPER	1/4 tsp.

PROCEDURE

1. Combine cabbage, parsley, onion, celery, green pepper, and pimiento.

2. Dissolve sugar in vinegar. Add salt and pepper.

3. Add vinegar mixture to chopped vegetables and mix well.

4. Keep in cool place. This slaw may be prepared hours in advance of serving time.

TOMATO ASPIC SALAD

YIELD: approx. 28 4-oz. servings per pan

INGREDIENTS	1 Med. Pan	3 Med. Pans	5 Med. Pans
GELATINE,			
UNFLAVORED	2 oz.	6 oz.	10 oz.
TOMATO JUICE	1 qt.	3 qt.	1-1/4 gal.
WATER	1 qt.	3 qt.	1-1/4 gal.
BAY LEAVES	4 (only)	12 (only)	20 (only)
ONION, sliced	6 oz.	1 lb. 2 oz.	1 lb. 14 oz.
CARROTS, quartered	1 lb.	3 lb.	5 lb.
CELERY, tops	2 cups	1-1/2 qt.	2-1/2 qt.
CLOVES, WHOLE	1 tbsp.	3 tbsp.	5 tbsp.
SALT	1 oz.	3 oz.	5 oz.
SUGAR	4 oz.	12 oz.	1 lb. 4 oz.
VINEGAR	1 cup	3 cups	1-1/4 qt.
LEMON JUICE	1/2 cup	1-1/2 cups	2-1/2 cups
TOMATO PUREE	1 qt.	3 qt.	5 qt.

PROCEDURE

1. Sprinkle gelatine into cold tomato juice; stir to prevent lumping. Dissolve gelatine in steamer or bain-marie.

2. Simmer vegetables, spices, and salt in the water until the vegetables are tender. Strain. Add enough liquid to make 1 qt. per pan. Discard vegetables.

3. Add dissolved gelatine, sugar, vinegar, and lemon juice. Add tomato puree, and season to taste. Put 3-1/2 qt. into each medium pan.

Variations

1. *Ribbon Salad:* Put 1-1/2 qt. aspic in bottom of pan and let set until hard. Spread a thin layer of cottage cheese over this (2-1/2 lb. per pan). Cottage cheese will spread more easily if pureed. Then put 1-1/2 qt. aspic over the cheese.

2. *With Cottage Cheese Balls:* Put 1-1/2 qt. aspic into pans and let set until hard. Place on top of this, No. 24 scoops of cottage cheese in rows of 4 by 6, then add 1-1/2 qt. aspic. Top of ball of cottage cheese should show through the aspic.

3. *Tomato Perfection Salad:* Substitute tomato aspic for plain gelatine base in Perfection Salad.

4. *With Deviled or Hard-Cooked Eggs:* When aspic begins to congeal, place deviled eggs in aspic in rows of 4 by 6 so that yolk shows above the surface. Or garnish with sliced eggs, sliced stuffed olives, etc.

5. *With Asparagus Tips:* Put 1-1/2 qt. of aspic in bottom of pan and let harden. Place asparagus tips in even rows; add 1-1/2 qt. aspic.

CURRIED TURKEY SALAD

YIELD: 50 servings

INGREDIENTS

RICE, UNCOOKED	4 cups
ONION, minced	1-3/4 cups
CIDER VINEGAR	1/2 cup
SALAD OIL	1 cup
CURRY POWDER	2 tbsp.
TURKEY, cooked and cubed	14 cups
CELERY, chopped	7 cups
GREEN PEPPER, chopped	1-3/4 cups
SALAD DRESSING	4-1/2 cups
SALT	1 tbsp. or to taste

PROCEDURE

1. Cook rice according to package directions. Cool thoroughly.
2. Combine rice, onion, vinegar, oil, and curry powder; refrigerate for several hrs.
3. Toss together lightly the turkey, rice mixture, celery, green pepper, salad dressing, and salt.
4. Chill. Serve 2/3 cup per portion in crisp lettuce cups.

BLUE CHEESE DRESSING

YIELD: 2 qt.

INGREDIENTS

EVAPORATED MILK, chilled	1 tall can
MAYONNAISE-TYPE DRESSING	1 qt.
BLUE CHEESE, crumbled	10 oz.
GARLIC SALT	few grains

PROCEDURE

1. Whip evaporated milk until stiff. Fold into mayonnaise.
2. Add cheese and garlic salt; blend well.

Note

May be covered, and stored in refrigerator for several days.

POTATO SALAD

YIELD: approx. 100 portions

INGREDIENTS

POTATOES, cooked, peeled, diced	30 lb.
ONIONS, diced	6 large
CELERY, diced	4 stalks
PIMIENTO	1 can
EGGS, hard-cooked, sliced	4 doz.
EVAPORATED MILK	2 cans
VINEGAR	1/3 cup
SUGAR	4 oz.
SALT	2 oz.
MUSTARD	1 cup
SALAD DRESSING	3-1/2 qt.

PROCEDURE

1. Lightly combine potatoes, onions, celery, pimiento, and hard-cooked eggs.

2. Blend evaporated milk, vinegar, sugar, salt, and mustard with salad dressing. Stir into salad ingredients gently, to avoid loss of ingredient shape.

MACARONI SALAD

YIELD: 1-3/4 gal., 48 1/2 cup or No. 8 scoop servings

INGREDIENTS

ELBOW MACARONI	1-3/4 lb.
SALAD DRESSING	6 cups
CIDER VINEGAR	3/4 cup
INSTANT CHOPPED ONIONS,	2 tbsp
or FRENCH ONIONS, minced	1/2 cup
SALT	5 tsp.
EGGS, hard-cooked, chopped	1 doz.
CELERY, chopped	1 lb.
GREEN PEPPER, chopped	5 oz.
PIMIENTO, chopped	4 oz.

PROCEDURE

1. Cook macaroni in boiling, salted water until tender; drain.
2. Blend salad dressing with next three ingredients.
3. Toss dressing with macaroni, eggs, and remaining ingredients. Chill.

Note

1-3/4 lb. uncooked elbow macaroni equals approx. 1 to 1-1/4 gal. cooked macaroni.

SHRIMP MACARONI SALAD

YIELD: 30 servings

INGREDIENTS

MACARONI, cooked	1-1/2 lb. AP
SALT	1-1/2 tbsp.
PAPRIKA	1 tsp.
FRENCH DRESSING	1 cup
CELERY, chopped	1 qt.
GREEN PEPPER, chopped	1 cup
PIMIENTO, chopped	1 cup
ONION, ground or grated	1 cup
SHRIMP, cooked, shelled	1-1/2 lb.
MAYONNAISE	1 qt.

PROCEDURE

1. Marinate the cooked macaroni with the french dressing, salt, and paprika while the macaroni is still warm.

2. When cold combine with all other ingredients.

3. Serve in lettuce cups and garnish with parsley and hard-cooked egg.

BREADS

POPOVERS
Excellent to serve from baskets passed around during meals

YIELD: 24 popovers

INGREDIENTS

FLOUR	2 cups
SALT	1-1/2 tsp.
OIL	2 tbsp.
EGGS	5
MILK	2 cups

PROCEDURE

1. Grease medium-sized custard cups (or foil cups) and place on baking sheets. Preheat oven to 375°F.

2. Into a mixing bowl, sieve the flour and salt. Add oil and stir until the mixture resembles corn meal.

3. In another bowl beat eggs slightly and add milk. Add the flour mixture and beat until smooth.

4. Fill cups 1/3 full and bake for 50 min.

5. Remove from oven and quickly cut a slit in side of popover to let out steam; return to oven for 10 min. Remove from cups and serve at once.

BANANA TEA BREAD

YIELD: 1 loaf

INGREDIENTS

FLOUR, sifted	1-3/4 cups
BAKING POWDER	2 tsp.
BAKING SODA	1/4 tsp.
SALT	1/2 tsp.
SHORTENING	1/3 cup
SUGAR	2/3 cup
EGGS, well beaten	2
BANANAS, FULLY RIPE, mashed	3

PROCEDURE

1. Sift together flour, baking powder, baking soda, and salt.

2. Whip shortening until creamy. Add sugar gradually and continue beating until light and fluffy.

3. Add eggs and beat well.

4. Add flour mixture alternately with bananas, a small amount at a time, beating after each addition until smooth.

5. Turn into well-greased bread pan (8-1/2-in. by 4-1/2-in. by 3-in.) and bake in oven at 350°F. for about 1 hr. 10 min. until done.

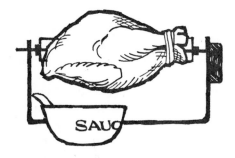

BARBECUES AND GRILLS

RECIPES FOR BARBECUES AND GRILLS

SIRLOIN or PINBONE SIRLOIN (from loin end just above hips): Good for larger groups for open pit grilling. Should be no less than 1-1/2 in. thick. Sear both sides over white-hot coals to retain juices. Move to slightly cooler side of grill and continue cooking. Turn with tongs until proper degree of doneness has been reached. Slice in thin diagonal slices. Sauteed onions or mushrooms will greatly enhance presentation.

SALT CRUST STEAK: Spread liberally one side of steak with english or dijon mustard. Cover thickly with quarter inch of coarse or kosher salt. Dampen the salt and cover with piece of heavy brown paper. Roll firmly back and forth with rolling pin until salt is crusted. Turn steak over and repeat process. Place in wire grill and broil over fairly hot heat from 10 to 12 min. each side. Remove salt crust and drizzle butter mixed with steak sauce over surface. Slice diagonally.

STEAK MARINADE: Simple yet effective flavor-improver. Place steaks in shallow container and cover generously with olive oil, lemon juice, and a clove or so of finely minced garlic and a few sprinkles of oregano. Allow to remain in marinade, turning occasionally, for at least 24 hr.

STEAK AU POIVRE: Crack peppercorns coarsely with rolling pin or mallet. Use sirloin, porterhouse, or flank steak. Sprinkle both sides of steak generously with cracked peppercorns and press into meat using flat dish. Let rest for 1/2 hr.; broil.

WHOLE FILLET: 5 to 8 lb. Trim well. If grilled on flat surface fold thin ends under and tie securely. If open fire is used, do not tie, but cut off thin ends and save for another purpose. Rub well with butter or oil and allow to rest for 15 to 20 min. Broil over medium fire about 25 min.; turn frequently to keep color even.

BROILED HAMBURGER STEAKS: 4 lb. ground beef seasoned with salt and pepper and 1 tsp. monosodium glutamate. Add 2 eggs, a sprinkle or two of worcestershire, 1/4 cup catsup, and enough bread crumbs to absorb moisture. Form into oval cakes 1-1/2 in. thick; broil over fairly high heat, turning to cook evenly.

TURKISH STEAKS WITH GARLIC: 5 to 6 lb. rump steak, 12 cloves of garlic, 3/4 lb. butter, 3 lb. sliced potatoes, and a No. 2-1/2 can of crushed tomatoes. Cut steak into long pieces about 3/4 in. thick. With point of paring knife make a hole near each end of slices. Insert half a clove of garlic. Place slices on top of each other to original shape and tie securely. Place meat in heavy stew pan with 3/4 lb. of butter. Cover and place over moderate charcoal fire for about 3 hr., turning occasionally. Partially fry the potatoes in butter, then add to beef together with crushed tomatoes. Salt and pepper to taste. Replace cover and continue to simmer until meat and potatoes are well done. A few bay leaves added during the last hour will add more flavor. Serves 10.

GARLICKED LAMB CHOPS*: Cut chops about 1 in. thick. Mince 4 cloves garlic and 1 tbsp. chopped parsley. Soak this in 1/2 cup oil and 1 tsp. coarse salt and 1 tsp. ground pepper. Rub this mixture well into chops and allow to marinate from 3 to 4 hr., turning once or twice. Broil slowly and, when ready, char quickly on hottest area of grill. (Lamb center should show pink!)
*Lamb Steaks cut from shoulder or leg may be treated as above but red wine should be added to marinade.

PORK: A rather hazardous dish for summer service. **MUST ALWAYS BE COOKED WELL DONE** and must be kept refrigerated until time to cook. Broil thick chops slowly and apply glaze several times during cooking. Glaze: Prepare 2/3 cup honey, 1/3 cup of undiluted orange juice, and 1/3 cup brandy.

PORK SPARERIBS: 1 lb. per person. Parboil or roast ribs about 3/4 hr. until just tender. Combine 1 cup honey, 1/2 tsp. lemon juice, and 1 tbsp. curry powder; brush each side of spareribs with this mixture and broil over medium-hot fire until highly browned and glazed.

POULTRY: Split 2-1/2 lb. chicken; remove backbone and breast cartilage. Turn wings back to lock. Wipe chicken with towels moistened with lemon juice. For 12 servings, combine 3/4 cup peanut oil, 3/4 cup melted butter, 3 tsp. salt, 1-1/2 tsp. ground pepper, and 2 tsp. paprika. Brush with mixture and allow to rest for 15 min. Brush again and place bone-side down over white coals. Cook for additional 12 to 14 min. Turn and finish. *Variations:* Chopped parsley, garlic, rosemary, oregano, shallots, or scallions may be added to "paint."

GRILLED CHICKEN: Split 2 chickens of 3 lb. eviscerated weight, and remove all bones. Cut each into 4 parts and lay on flat surface. Cover with waxed paper or foil and flatten with mallet or cleaver or rolling pin. Sprinkle with salt, pepper, and ground cinnamon; allow to rest for at least 1 hr. Broil over medium coals until nicely browned. Place in stew pan and add 3/4 lb. of prunes and 3 sliced raw carrots. Add chicken broth to depth of 1/2 in. over contents. (A little brown sugar or honey may be added if desired.) Cover pan and cook over moderate charcoal fire until tender.

FISH: More difficult to produce and requires, in many cases, more attention. It quite often requires "locking" each fish in a wire grill or wrapping in foil to retain form, shape, and flavor. Lobster tails, crab legs, can be surface-grilled, using cooking techniques and recipes available.

SAUSAGES, salami, canadian bacon, kolbassi, pepperoni, knockwurst, and frankfurters are all excellent candidates for grilling. Cured slabs of pastrami also may be grilled. Creamed horseradish mixed with prepared mustard spread over the pastrami about 10 min. before removing from grill will add "beautiful flavor." **COOKED** slabs of corned beef can be spread with a mixture of pineapple juice, honey, prepared mustard, and a little ground cinnamon, ginger, and cloves, which impart a most delicious flavor and surface to the corned beef. Slice thinly but "pile high" for service on pumpernickel or seeded rye. Foil-roasted potatoes are a good accompaniment.

Bear in mind that sauces and glazes can be individually compounded by combining complementary relishes such as mustards, soy sauces, liquefied jams, jellies, steak sauce, herbed butter, sliced or shredded cheeses, mayonnaise, and sour cream.

BURGOO

YIELD: 1200 gal.

INGREDIENTS

SOUP MEAT, LEAN, no fat or bones	600 lb.
FAT HENS	200 lb.
POTATOES, peeled, diced	2000 lb.
CABBAGE, chopped	5 bushels
ONION	200 lb.
TOMATOES	60 No. 10 cans
PUREE of TOMATOES	24 No. 10 cans
PUREE of CARROTS	24 No. 10 cans
CORN	18 No. 10 cans
RED PEPPER	to taste
SALT	to taste
WORCESTERSHIRE, LIQUID HOT PEPPER SAUCE or STEAK SAUCE	to season

PROCEDURE

Mix the ingredients a little at a time and cook outdoors in huge iron kettles over wood fires from 15 to 20 hr. Use squirrels in season—one dozen squirrels to each 100 gal. burgoo.

BARBECUE SAUCE FOR BASTING

YIELD: 1-1/2 gal.

INGREDIENTS

SUGAR	2 cups
SALT	2 tbsp.
PAPRIKA	1 tbsp.
PEPPER	2 tsp.
GARLIC, minced	1 tbsp.
CIDER VINEGAR	3 qt.
TOMATO CATSUP	2 qt.
WORCESTERSHIRE SAUCE	1 5-1/4 oz. bottle
PREPARED MUSTARD	1/2 cup

PROCEDURE

1. Combine ingredients in a saucepan. Simmer 20 min., stirring occasionally.

2. Brush sauce over chicken, spareribs, or chops to be barbecued. Baste frequently. One pt. sauce should be used for every 5 lb. of meat. (If desired, meat may be salted during cooking.)

SWEET AND SOUR SAUCE

YIELD: 16 gal.

INGREDIENTS

TOMATO SAUCE	6 No. 10 cans
TOMATO CATSUP	6 No. 10 cans
VINEGAR	2 gal.
WORCESTERSHIRE SAUCE	2 cups
SOY SAUCE	2 cups
DRY MUSTARD	1 cup
GINGER, grated	1/2 cup
PINEAPPLE, CRUSHED	1 No. 10 can
SUGAR	32 cups
BROWN SUGAR	32 cups
SALT	2 cups
CORNSTARCH	3 cups

PROCEDURE

1. Combine all ingredients in suitable pot except sugar, brown sugar, salt, and cornstarch. When ingredients begin to simmer add sugar, brown sugar, and salt.

2. Mix cornstarch with water and add slowly.

3. Let sauce simmer for 1 to 2 hr. Stir from bottom often with paddle.

HOT BEEF BARBECUES

YIELD: 48 sandwiches, 1 gal. 2 cups sauce

INGREDIENTS

INSTANT CHOPPED ONION	3 oz.
WATER	1 cup
CELERY, finely chopped	2 lb. AP
SHORTENING	4 oz.
TOMATO CATSUP	2 qt.
WATER	1 qt.
BROWN SUGAR, firmly packed	9 oz.
CIDER VINEGAR	1 cup
PREPARED MUSTARD	1 cup
WORCESTERSHIRE SAUCE	1/2 cup
LIQUID HOT PEPPER SAUCE	1/4 cup
CRUSHED RED PEPPER	2 tbsp.
WHITE PEPPER	1 tbsp.
GARLIC POWDER	1 tbsp.
TOP ROUND of BEEF, CHOICE, roasted, thinly sliced	10 lb. 5 oz. EP
SANDWICH BUNS, toasted	48

PROCEDURE

1. Cover onion with water. Let stand 20 min.

2. Saute onion and celery in shortening until tender.

3. Add catsup and remaining ingredients; bring to a boil. Reduce heat; simmer 5 min.

4. Add sliced beef, simmer 10 min.

5. For each sandwich, serve 2-1/2 to 3 oz. meat with 2 tbsp. sauce on toasted sandwich bun, preferably hard-crusted french style.

DESSERTS

APPLE STRUDEL

YIELD: 24 servings

INGREDIENTS
  STRUDEL

FLOUR, sifted	1 lb.
SALT	1/2 tsp.
SHORTENING	2 oz.
EGG	1
WATER, lukewarm	1 cup

  FILLING

STRAWBERRY JAM	1-1/2 cups
APPLES, FRESH, sliced	6 to 7 cups
CINNAMON	2 tsp.
SUGAR	1-1/2 cups
RAISINS	1 cup
BREAD CRUMBS, toasted	1 cup

PROCEDURE

1. Sift flour and salt. Cut in the shortening. Add egg and water to form a soft dough. Let dough rest in oiled bowl 30 min. Roll dough very thin.

2. Spread with strawberry jam. Add sliced fresh apples, raisins, and toasted bread crumbs. Combine cinnamon and sugar, and sprinkle over all. Roll up in long strips like jelly roll. Place in bake pan; bake in oven at 400°F. for 25 to 30 min.

PINEAPPLE CHIFFON PIE

YIELD: 4 10-in. pies

INGREDIENTS

KOSHER GELATINE	3 oz.
PINEAPPLE JUICE	1 qt.
EGG WHITES	1 pt. (16)
SUGAR	3 cups
PINEAPPLE, CRUSHED	1-1/2 qt.
PINEAPPLE JUICE	1 qt.

PROCEDURE

1. Hydrate gelatine. Dissolve in hot pineapple juice. Cool.
2. Beat egg whites until frothy. Gradually add the sugar and beat until stiff enough to mound.
3. Combine gelatine mixture, pineapple juice, and crushed pineapple. Fold in egg white. Pour into baked pie shells. Chill until filling is set.

QUANTITY BAKED BLINTZES

YIELD: 60 blintzes

INGREDIENTS

BLINTZES, FILLED	5 doz.
CINNAMON-SUGAR	
EGGS	20
SOUR CREAM	2 qt.
ORANGE JUICE, FROZEN, undiluted	1/2 cup

PROCEDURE

1. Arrange blintzes on a greased sheet pan allowing 1/2 in. between each blintz. Sprinkle blintzes with cinnamon-sugar.
2. Beat eggs until fluffy. Add sour cream and undiluted orange juice and blend well. Pour over blintzes.
3. Bake in oven at 350°F. for 45 min.

This is an excellent tea, luncheon, or Sunday brunch presentation.

TRADITIONAL CREPES SUZETTES

YIELD: 18 crepes

INGREDIENTS

SUGAR	3 tbsp.
ORANGE RIND, grated	1/2 tsp.
SWEET BUTTER, room temperature	5 tbsp.
LEMON JUICE, from	1 lemon
ORANGE JUICE	1/2 cup
COINTREAU, CURACAO, or GRAND MARNIER	1/2 tsp.
COGNAC or BRANDY (for flaming)	1/4 cup

PROCEDURE

For French service or Exhibition cooking, the crepes should be made tableside in a chafing dish.

1. Place sugar in small bowl. Mix in grated orange rind and 2 tbsp. of the butter. Set aside.

2. Combine remaining butter with the lemon juice, orange juice, and liqueur. Stir over medium flame until butter melts. When it comes to a boil, stir in sugar mixture.

3. Add 4 crepes to sauce, stir. Turn crepes over and fold top one in half—spoon over liquid—fold half in quarter. Repeat until all are used.

4. Pour brandy over surface and ignite. Serve flaming.

Note

Crepes may be used as a main course at luncheon (serving 2 or more with contrasting flavor and vegetable color) or a single crepe may be served as a mini-entree before the main course.

TRADITIONAL CHEESE FILLING

INGREDIENTS

FARMER'S CHEESE (COMPRESSED COTTAGE CHEESE)	2-1/2 lb.
CREAM CHEESE, softened	10 oz.
BUTTER, soft	5 tbsp.
SUGAR	2/3 cup plus 1 tbsp.

PROCEDURE

Mix ingredients until smooth and creamy. Chill.

CREPES SUZETTES OR BLINTZES
(Basic dessert crepes)

YIELD: 20 crepes

INGREDIENTS

FLOUR	3/4 cup
SALT	pinch
SUGAR	1 tbsp.
EGGS, WHOLE	3
EGG YOLK	1
MILK	1-3/4 cups
BUTTER, melted, cooled	2 tbsp.
COGNAC or BRANDY	2 tbsp.
MELTED BUTTER for cooking crepes	

PROCEDURE

1. Sift flour with salt and sugar in mixing bowl.

2. Beat whole eggs with egg yolk and add to milk. Blend in with flour and salt and whisk to a smooth batter.

3. Stir in melted butter and cognac. Cover and set aside at room temperature for at least 1-1/2 hr. before making crepes.

4. Heat 6-in. teflon fry pan or crepe pan. Use a pastry brush to grease pan lightly with butter.

5. Pour in about 2 tbsp. of batter and quickly rotate pan so that batter covers the bottom evenly. Cook until underside is lightly browned. Turn and cook second side for a moment or two. Remove from pan and set aside. Repeat until all batter has been used.

Note

Crepes may be made ahead and kept warm or reheated briefly in oven at 300°F. They should never be stacked while warm.

DESSERT FILLING

INGREDIENTS

WHITE RAISINS	1/3 cup
COGNAC	3 tbsp.
CREAM CHEESE, softened	1-1/2 lb.
SUGAR	1/2 cup
LEMON RIND, grated, from	2 lemons
FLOUR	3 tbsp.
EGG YOLKS	4
SOUR CREAM	3 tbsp.
BUTTER, melted	3 tsp.
VANILLA	3/4 tsp.

PROCEDURE

1. Marinate raisins in cognac 6 hr.
2. Mix cream cheese, sugar, and flour until fluffy.
3. Add remaining ingredients except raisins, and mix well.
4. Add raisins, mix and chill for 2 hr.
5. Fill crepes as indicated. Saute slowly in margarine or butter and when lightly browned, turn and fry second side. Serve hot "as is," or spoon a heavy dollop of sour cream or unsweetened whipped cream over top.

Note

Method used to "season" a black iron french crepe pan:
Scrub a No. 18 black iron crepe pan with a soapy fine steel wool pad. Dry well. Pour 1 in. of salad oil into it and place in oven at 300°F. Turn oven off after 2 hr. and keep pan in oven for about 12 hr. longer. Pour off oil and discard it. Wipe pan thoroughly with paper towels until no trace of the oil remains. This process "seasons" pan so that crepes will not stick. NEVER wash the pan after use, but wipe with paper towels until it is grease-free. Use pan only for crepes.

MACAROON FRUIT SLICE

INGREDIENTS
SWEET DOUGH

BUTTER	8 oz.
SUGAR	4 oz.
EGGS, beaten	3
ORANGE, rind and juice	1
LEMON, rind and juice	1
SALT	pinch
CAKE FLOUR, sifted	1 lb.

MACAROON MIX

ALMOND PASTE	8 oz.
CONFECTIONERS' SUGAR	8 oz.
EGG WHITES	4

PROCEDURE

1. Cream butter and sugar; add beaten eggs, fruit juices, and rinds. Stir in the flour and salt.

2. Mix to a smooth dough. Turn out on lightly floured board. Roll out in two strips 5 in. wide and as long as the baking pan.

3. Place in baking pan and bake in oven at 350°F. until only half cooked.

4. In meantime, combine ingredients for macaroon mix and mix to a smooth paste.

5. Remove pan from oven. Place a strip of macaroon mix along the edge of each sweet dough strip. Return to oven to finish cooking.

6. When cool, fill center with Fresh Stewed Strawberries or any other colorful fruit.

LUKSHEN KUGEL

YIELD: 8 to 12 portions

INGREDIENTS

BROAD EGG NOODLES	1 lb.
COTTAGE CHEESE	1 lb.
EGGS, lightly beaten	5
GOLDEN RAISINS	1-1/2 cups
SOUR CREAM	1 cup
BUTTER or MARGARINE, melted	1/4 cup
SUGAR	1/4 cup
CINNAMON, GROUND	4-1/2 tsp.
LEMON PEEL, grated	2 tsp.
SALT	1-3/4 tsp.
NUTMEG, GROUND	1/4 tsp.

TOPPING

CORN FLAKE CRUMBS	3/4 cup
BUTTER or MARGARINE, melted	1/4 cup

PROCEDURE

1. Cook noodles as directed. Drain, rinse, and place in large bowl.

2. Combine remaining ingredients except topping. Pour over noodles, mix gently but thoroughly. Spoon mixture into a buttered 13-1/2-in. by 9-in. by 2-in. pan.

3. Combine corn flake crumbs and melted butter or margarine; sprinkle over noodle mixture.

4. Bake in a preheated oven at 375°F. for 30 min. Remove from oven and let stand 10 min. before cutting.

POIRE A L'IMPERIALE
(Pears and Rice)
(Excellent buffet presentation)

YIELD: 25 portions

INGREDIENTS

RICE	12 oz.
MILK, warm	2 qt.
SUGAR	1-1/4 lb.
GELATINE, UNFLAVORED	2 oz.
HEAVY CREAM	1-1/2 pt.
PEAR HALVES, CANNED	24
COINTREAU	3 oz.
APRICOT JAM	as needed
RED CHERRIES	for garnish

PROCEDURE

1. Put rice in warm milk and cook for 20 min.; add sugar.

2. Dissolve gelatine in a little water, add to rice. Place in bowl and stir over ice until thick.

3. Whip cream until stiff and add to rice mixture, reserving some cream for decoration.

4. Add the Cointreau; put into display bowl and chill.

5. Decorate surface with pears and glaze with warmed jam. Pipe whipped cream between pears; coat with a little apricot jam; sprinkle with Cointreau. Red cherries may be used as a garnish.

SPICED WINE PASSOVER CAKE

YIELD: 8 to 10 servings

INGREDIENTS

MATZO CAKE MEAL	1-1/4 cups
SALT	1/2 tsp.
CINNAMON, GROUND	1 tsp.
ALMONDS, finely ground	6 tbsp.
EGGS, LARGE, separated	8
SUGAR	1-1/2 cups
SWEET RED WINE	1/3 cup
ORANGE JUICE, FRESH	1/3 cup
LEMON PEEL, grated	1 tsp.
CONFECTIONERS' SUGAR	

PROCEDURE

1. Mix first 4 ingredients together. Set aside.

2. Beat egg yolks until thick and lemon colored. Gradually beat in sugar and continue beating until thick and light.

3. Add wine, orange juice, orange and lemon peels and beat with an electric mixer set at medium speed for 4 min.

4. Fold in dry ingredients. Beat egg whites until they stand in soft, stiff peaks, and fold into the batter.

5. Turn into a 14-in. by 4-in. spring-form pan or into a 10-in. by 4-in. round tube cake pan. Bake in a preheated oven at 325°F. for 1-1/2 hr. or until done.

6. Invert cake on a wire rack to cool. Remove from pan when cold.

7. Dust confectioners' sugar over the top.

RICE PUDDING

YIELD: 35 portions

INGREDIENTS

RICE	12 oz.
MILK	2-1/2 qt.
SALT	1/2 tsp.
MARGARINE	10 oz.
SUGAR	1-1/4 lb.
EGGS, separated	15
LEMON, grated peel from	1 lemon
or VANILLA	1-1/2 tsp.

PROCEDURE

1. Simmer rice in milk with salt until soft.

2. Cream margarine, sugar, grated lemon peel, and egg yolks, and mix with cooled rice.

3. Fold in stiffly beaten egg whites; put into 6-qt. hotel pan and bake in water bath for about 1 hr. in oven at 325°F.

Note

Drained canned fruit or raisins may be added.

PASSOVER SPONGE CAKE

YIELD: 12 servings

INGREDIENTS

EGGS, LARGE, separated	6
EGG, WHOLE, LARGE	1
SUGAR	1-1/2 cups
LEMON JUICE, FRESH	1-1/2 tbsp.
LEMON PEEL, grated	1 tsp.
POTATO STARCH, sifted	3/4 cup
SALT	1/4 tsp.
GINGER, GROUND	1/2 tsp.
CONFECTIONERS' SUGAR	

PROCEDURE

1. Beat 6 egg yolks and 1 whole egg together until frothy. Gradually beat in sugar, lemon juice, and peel.

2. Sift potato starch with salt and ginger and add gradually, blending thoroughly.

3. Beat egg whites until stiff, but not dry. Gently fold into egg yolk mixture.

4. Turn batter into a 10-in. by 4-in. tube pan. Bake in a preheated oven at 350°F. for 50 to 60 min. or until cake is firm in the center. Cool in pan. Turn out on wire rack, having the top side up. Sift confectioners' sugar over the top.

ALMOND TART SHELLS WITH RUM CHIFFON FILLING

YIELD: 32 individual tarts

INGREDIENTS

ALMOND TART SHELLS*	32
GELATINE, UNFLAVORED	1 oz.
WATER, cold	1 cup
EGG YOLKS	1-1/2 cups (approx. 12)
SUGAR	1 lb.
MILK	1 qt.
RUM	3/4 cup
EGG WHITES	1-1/2 cups (approx. 12)
SALT	1 tsp.
CREAM, whipped	1-1/2 cups
CONFECTIONERS' SUGAR	1/2 cup
SWEET CHOCOLATE, grated	1/2 cup

PROCEDURE

1. Soak the gelatine in cold water.

2. Beat the egg yolks and sugar; add the milk and cook over hot water, until thick. Remove from the fire and stir in the soaked gelatine, stirring until it is completely dissolved.

3. Add rum and allow the mixture to cool until it begins to congeal.

4. Fold in the egg whites which have been beaten with the salt.

5. Fill the baked tart shells and chill until the filling is firm.

6. Top with sweetened whipped cream and sprinkle the grated sweet chocolate over this.

Note

*To make the almond tart shells, add 1/2 cup finely chopped, lightly toasted almonds for each pound of flour used in making the pastry. Add them after the fat has been cut into the flour but before the water is added. Bake as any tart shells.

BLACK CHERRY TOPPING

YIELD: 7 lb.; for low cost variation 10 lb.

INGREDIENTS
REGULAR RECIPE

DARK SWEET CHERRIES*, PITTED	1 No. 10 can
CHERRY SYRUP, drained from No. 10 can	approx 2 lb.
	14 oz.
CORNSTARCH	2 oz.
WATER (for softening cornstarch)	2 oz.
KIRSCHWASSER	1-1/2 oz.

LOW COST VARIATION

DARK SWEET CHERRIES*, PITTED	1 No. 10 can,
	heavy syrup
CHERRY SYRUP, drained from No. 10 can	approx. 2 lb.
	14 oz.
WATER	1 qt.
CORNSTARCH	4 oz.
WATER (for softening cornstarch)	4 oz.
KIRSCHWASSER	3 oz.

*If extra heavy syrup pack is used, no sugar is added. For heavy syrup pack, add 1/2 lb. sugar; for light syrup pack, 1 lb. sugar.

PROCEDURE

1. Bring drained syrup to boil (with water added in low cost variation). Add sugar as indicated.

2. Stir cornstarch into cold water, then into boiling syrup. Cook for 5 min. or until thickened syrup is clear.

3. When syrup is clear, add cherries, blending lightly with spoon or rolling motion to avoid crushing or damaging cherries.

4. Cook 5 min. longer. Remove sauce from heat.

5. Pour mixture into earthenware container. As it cools add kirschwasser, taking care in blending not to crush cherries.

APRICOT BARS

YIELD: 1 12-in. by 18-in. sheet pan, approx. 32 servings

INGREDIENTS

MARGARINE	6 oz.
SUGAR	8 oz.
LIGHT CORN SYRUP	1 cup
EGGS	2
FLOUR	1 lb.
BAKING POWDER	1/2 oz.
SALT	1 tsp.
MILK	1 cup
PECANS or WALNUTS, chopped	6 oz.
DRIED APRICOTS, coarsely ground	1-1/4 lb.

PROCEDURE

1. Cream margarine and sugar. Add the corn syrup and eggs. Beat thoroughly.

2. Sprinkle 1 cup of the flour on the apricots and nuts. Sift the remaining flour, baking powder, and salt together.

3. Add this alternately with the milk to the creamed mixture. Add the nuts and apricots last.

4. Spread in well-oiled sheet pan. Bake in oven at 350°F. for 30 min.

5. Cool, cut in bars, and sprinkle with confectioners' sugar.

APPLE SOUR CREAM PIE

YIELD: 8 9-in. pies, 48 servings, 6 per pie

INGREDIENTS

PIE SHELLS, lightly browned	8
FILLING	
APPLE SLICES, CANNED, drained	10 lb.
RAISINS, SEEDLESS	1 lb.
EGGS	1 lb. 12 oz.
SUGAR	2 lb.
FLOUR	5 oz.
SALT	2 tsp.
SOUR CREAM	4 lb.
LEMON RIND, grated	1 oz.
ORANGE RIND, grated	1 oz.
LEMON JUICE	10 oz.
TOPPING	
FLOUR	11 oz.
BROWN SUGAR, firmly packed	1 lb.
NUTMEG	2 tsp.
BUTTER	1 lb.

PROCEDURE

1. Arrange apple slices in pastry shells, sprinkle with raisins.

2. Beat eggs; add sugar, flour, salt, sour cream, grated rinds, and lemon juice. Pour over fruit. Bake in oven at 400°F. for 10 min.

3. To make topping, combine flour, sugar, and nutmeg. Cut in butter with blender until mixture is crumbly. Sprinkle mixture on top of the pies and continue baking 20 to 30 min., or until brown and filling is set. Chill before serving.

SPICE SQUARES

YIELD: 192 squares from four 22-in. by 13-in. by 2-in. sheet pans cut 6 by 8 per sheet.

INGREDIENTS

SHORTENING	2-1/2 lb.
SUGAR	4-1/4 lb.
VANILLA	2 oz.
EGGS	2-1/2 lb. (22)
SALT	2-1/2 tsp.
MACE	2-1/2 tsp.
CLOVES, GROUND	2 tsp.
NUTMEG	2-1/2 tsp.
CINNAMON	1 oz.
CAKE FLOUR	4 lb.
COCOA	1 oz.
BAKING POWDER	1/4 lb.
NONFAT DRY MILK	1/2 lb.
or INSTANT	3 cups
WATER	1-1/2 qt.

PROCEDURE

1. Use flat paddle attachment of mixer. Blend shortening, sugar, and vanilla at 2nd speed for 10 min. Scrape down.

2. Add eggs to above mixture, continuing to beat on 2nd speed. Scrape down.

3. Blend spices, cake flour, cocoa, baking powder, and nonfat dry milk with french whip until completely mixed. (May sift together to mix.) Add alternately with water to first mixture, starting and ending with dry ingredients.

4. Pour into two greased and floured pans. Bake for 30 min. in oven at 375°F.

5. Squares may be iced with butter cream frosting or served warm with whipped cream.

EGGNOG PUDDING

YIELD: 30 servings

INGREDIENTS

GRAHAM CRACKER or ZWEIBACK CRUMBS	1 qt.
NUTMEG	1 tsp.
BUTTER, melted	1 lb.
GELATINE, UNFLAVORED	3/4 oz.
WATER, cold	3/4 cup
EGG YOLKS (about 8)	3/4 cup
MILK or LIGHT CREAM	1-1/2 qt.
SALT	1 tsp.
SUGAR	4 oz.
RUM FLAVORING	2 tbsp.
EGG WHITES (about 8)	1 cup
SUGAR	12 oz.
HEAVY CREAM, whipped	1 pt.

PROCEDURE

1. Combine crumbs, nutmeg, and melted butter. Pat this in the bottom of a 12-in. by 18-in. sheet pan.

2. Soak the gelatine in cold water for at least 5 min.

3. Beat egg yolks slightly. Add milk, salt, and 4 oz. of sugar. Cook over hot water until mixture begins to thicken. Remove from fire.

4. Add softened gelatine and stir until it is completely dissolved. Add flavoring. Chill in refrigerator until mixture begins to congeal.

5. Beat the egg whites until they are stiff. Beat in 12 oz. of sugar gradually. Fold this into the chilled, cooked mixture and pile lightly into the crumb mixture in the sheet pan. Chill until firm.

6. When ready to serve, cut and garnish with whipped cream.

CHOCOLATE CREAM PUFFS

YIELD: 30 large cream puffs

INGREDIENTS

SHORTENING	1/2 lb.
WATER	1 pt.
BREAD FLOUR)	9 oz.
COCOA) sifted together	1-1/2 oz.
SALT)	1/2 tsp.
EGGS	1 pt.

PROCEDURE

1. Combine the shortening and water in kettle and place over medium heat. When boiling, add the dry ingredients all at once. Stir briskly until well combined and until the mixture comes away from the edge of the kettle.

2. Remove the mixture to the mixer bowl. Using the batter beater, beat at medium speed, adding the eggs gradually. Beat until well mixed and not stringy.

3. Drop with a pastry tube on lightly oiled sheet pans. A mound 2 in. in diameter makes a large puff.

4. Bake in oven at 375°F. for 40 to 45 min.

5. Fill with a regular cream filling, a chocolate cream filling, or ice cream. If filled with a cream filling, be sure to keep cream puffs refrigerated until serving time.

BASIC BUTTER CAKE*

YIELD: 24 2-in. by 2-in. squares

INGREDIENTS

BUTTER	1/4 lb.
SUGAR	1 cup
EGG YOLKS, beaten	3
VANILLA	1 tsp.
CAKE FLOUR	1-1/2 cups
BAKING POWDER, double action	3 tsp.
MILK	1/2 cup
EGG WHITES, stiffly beaten	3

PROCEDURE

1. Cream butter. Add sugar; cream with butter. Beat egg yolks and add; then beat mixture again. Add vanilla and beat.

2. Sift cake flour with baking powder. Add milk and flour mixtures alternately, folding in gently.

3. Gently fold in stiffly beaten egg whites. Put batter into buttered 8-in. by 12-in. by 2-in. pan. Bake in oven at 350°F. for 35 min.

Note

You can use this basic for any cupcake or layer cake or you can bake it in sheets to ice or top it with a wonderful coffee cake streusel.

The Complete Book of Entertaining by Nata Lee, Nata Lee, Inc., Hawthorn Books, New York City.

INDEX